**WHERE COUNTRIES
COME TO PLAY**

ANDREW PODNIEKS

WHERE COUNTRIES COME TO PLAY

IIHF
INTERNATIONAL ICE HOCKEY FEDERATION

Celebrating the World of Olympic Hockey and the Triple Gold Club

FENN

M&S

Library and Archives Canada Cataloguing in Publication

Podnieks, Andrew
Where countries come to play : celebrating the world of
Olympic hockey and the Triple Gold Club / Andrew Podnieks.

Includes bibliographical references and index.
ISBN 978-0-7710-7113-3

1. Hockey–History. 2. Hockey–History–Pictorial works.
3. Hockey teams–History. 4. Winter Olympics–History. I. Title.

GV847.7.P6238 2013   796.96209   C2013-900691-5

Published simultaneously in the United States of America by
McClelland & Stewart, a division of Random House of Canada Limited, a Penguin Random House Company
P.O. Box 1030, Plattsburgh, New York 12901

Library of Congress Control Number: 2013931567

Typeset in Electra and Q Type by M&S, Toronto
Printed and bound in Canada

Fenn/McClelland & Stewart,
a division of Random House of Canada Limited,
a Penguin Random House Company
One Toronto Street, Suite 300
Toronto, Ontario
M5C 2V6
www.randomhouse.ca

1   2   3   4   5   17   16   15   14   13

CONTENTS

INTRODUCTION

There is no team sport quite so international as hockey, and no team sport in which league players and international players serve double duty to the extent of hockey players. That is a 21st-century fact that is mirror opposite to how the sport functioned until the late 1970s.

In hockey's longest and earlier incarnation, amateur athletes played at international tournaments such as the Olympics and World Championships. Professional athletes aspired to the National Hockey League (NHL), and those who didn't make it to the highest level played in lower pro leagues such as the American Hockey League (AHL) or International Hockey League (IHL).

Things started to change after the 1972 Summit Series. That touchstone in hockey history pitted pros (Canadian players in the NHL) against amateurs (Soviet players who played internationally), and its success led to a series of developments: the Canada Cup in 1976, the first true best-on-best tournament featuring several countries; the return of Canada to international hockey (using pros) in 1977; the drafting of European players into the NHL with increasing frequency in the 1980s and 1990s; and, eventually, the participation of NHL players at the Olympics, beginning in Nagano in 1998.

During these years, the line between amateur and pro first blurred and then evaporated to the point that the best players who play in the NHL come from all over the world, and the best players who appear in the Olympics and World Championships are, by and large, those same NHLers. Once separated by contracts and continents, there is no such distinction anymore.

The creation of the Triple Gold Club (TGC) comes out of this modern hockey world and can be pinpointed to a specific date. On November 8, 2001, Szymon Szemberg, then media relations manager of the International Ice Hockey Federation (IIHF), drew up plans for a "Grand Slam Club," which he parenthetically called the "Triple Gold Club," to honour players who have won the three greatest prizes hockey has to offer: Olympic gold, the Stanley Cup, and World Championship gold.

"This is an idea to promote general interest for our game by officially highlighting the prestige of winning the three biggest team championships in the hockey world today," he wrote. "This would be our equivalent of Golf's Major Winners or Tennis's Major Winners. In general, I believe it would be a great publicity boost for our sport and the IIHF . . . it would increase interest in North America for the IIHF World Championship as a legitimate part of the Grand Slam."

The Triple Gold Club is almost by definition a modern club. Indeed, the first TGC members

After scoring the golden goal in 2010, Sidney Crosby needs only a World Championship gold to become a member of the Triple Gold Club.

were three Swedes in 1994 – Tomas Jonsson, Mats Naslund, and Hakan Loob – whose Olympic victory earned them their TGC membership. The distinction of the first TGC member who won one of the honours earliest goes to Slava Fetisov, who won World Championship gold in 1978 and, unbeknownst to him at the time, put him on the road to TGC success.

Nevertheless, it remains incredible that only 25 players of the thousands who have played the game at the highest level have won all three titles. More than 7,000 players have appeared in the NHL, and many more who competed for the Cup between its creation, in 1893, and the formation of the NHL, in 1917. More than 12,000 players have played at either the Olympics or World Championships, hoping to reach the top of the podium.

Perhaps more amazingly, of the current 25 players who have earned TGC status, not one is a goalie. In fact, only five have come particularly close to winning all three honours: Martin Brodeur, Dominik Hasek, Roberto Luongo, Ilya Bryzgalov, and J-S Giguere.

Brodeur has won the Stanley Cup three times with New Jersey as well as the Olympic gold in 2002 and 2010 with Canada. He has also had two close calls at the World Championships, most recently in 2005 at the end of the lockout season when Canada lost 3–0 to the Czech Republic in the gold-medal game. Brodeur also won silver at the World Championship in 1996.

Hasek led his nation to an historic gold medal at the 1998 Olympics in Nagano and won his Stanley Cup with Detroit. The closest the Dominator came to World Championship gold was a silver medal, in 1983. Hasek also won three bronze medals – in 1987, 1989, and 1990.

Luongo also came within a game of making TGC history. Having won Olympic gold (in 2010) and World Championship gold twice (in 2003 and 2004), he took the Vancouver Canucks to game seven of the Cup finals in 2011, only to lose to Boston.

Bryzgalov was the backup goalie to Giguere for the 2007 Mighty Ducks' Stanley Cup victory and was also the winning goalie for Russia at the 2009 World Championship in Switzerland, but he hasn't come particularly close to winning Olympic gold.

The 36-year-old Giguere was also part of that 2007 Cup victory with Anaheim and was the winning goalie for Canada at the 2004 World Championship in Prague. That leaves Olympic gold on his to-do list for TGC honours, but chances are slim to none that he'll be on Canada's team for Sochi 2014.

The first 22 members of the TGC were honoured during the Vancouver Olympics. In a special ceremony on February 22, 2010, at Hockey House, TSN broadcast a show in which all 22 players were in attendance. The IIHF presented each player with several gifts: a Nike sweater of his national federation, with his name and number on the back and a patch on the front featuring the dates of his Triple Gold Club championships; a special timepiece, on the back of which is engraved the player's name and the order of his Triple Gold Club achievement within the official TGC logo; and a specially designed gold lapel pin, also with his TGC number.

Nike also produced ten special Triple Gold Club sweaters with the TGC logo on the front and the names of all inductees on the back. Since 2010, there have been three new members and the first coach, and the coming years are likely to see only a trickle of new members rather than a stream. The TGC is an achievement as difficult to achieve today as it was when the first players succeeded in joining it.

If Russia can win Olympic gold on home ice in Sochi, Yevgeni Malkin will join the Triple Gold Club.

TOMAS
JONSSON

BIRTH PLACE: **Falun, Sweden**
BIRTH DATE: **April 12, 1960**
POSITION: **Defence—shoots Left**
HEIGHT: **5'10" (1.78m)**
WEIGHT: **185 lbs. (83.9 kg)**

TRIPLE GOLD CLUB HONOURS

STANLEY CUP 1982, 1983 (New York Islanders)
WORLD CHAMPIONSHIP 1991 (Sweden)
OLYMPICS 1994 (Sweden)

TGC AGE
33 YEARS, 321 DAYS

TGC MEMBER AS OF
FEBRUARY 27, 1994
OLYMPIC FINAL WIN VS. CANADA

NHL		Regular Season					Playoffs				
Season	Team	GP	G	A	P	PIM	GP	G	A	P	PIM
1981–82	NYI	70	9	25	34	51	10	0	2	2	21
1982–83	NYI	72	13	35	48	50	20	2	10	12	18
1983–84	NYI	72	11	36	47	54	21	3	5	8	22
1984–85	NYI	69	16	34	50	58	7	1	2	3	10
1985–86	NYI	77	14	30	44	62	3	0	1	1	4
1986–87	NYI	47	6	25	31	36	10	1	4	5	6
1987–88	NYI	72	6	41	47	115	5	2	2	4	10
1988–89	NYI/EDM	73	10	33	43	56	4	2	0	2	6
NHL Totals		552	85	259	344	482	80	11	26	37	97

Olympics						
Year	Team	GP	G	A	P	PIM	Finish
1980	SWE	7	2	2	4	6	B
1994	SWE	8	1	3	4	10	G
Totals		15	3	5	8	16	G,B

World Championship						
Year	Team	GP	G	A	P	PIM	Finish
1979	SWE	8	1	3	4	8	B
1981	SWE	2	0	0	0	2	S
1986	SWE	8	0	5	5	10	S
1990	SWE	8	0	1	1	8	S
1991	SWE	10	0	4	4	8	G
1995	SWE	8	0	2	2	12	S
Totals		44	1	15	16	48	G,4S,B

I n many ways it's fitting that the first member of the Triple Gold Club was Tomas Jonsson. He was equal parts NHL and European player; in a career split evenly between Europe and North America, Jonsson was one of the first Europeans to have his name stamped on the Cup and a star player in the Elitserien (known in English as the Swedish Elite League).

Jonsson was drafted 25th overall by the ascending New York Islanders in 1979 on the eve of their run of four consecutive Stanley Cup championships. He continued to play in Sweden for two seasons thereafter with Modo, the team he started his professional career with in 1977 as a 17-year-old. He did not play in the NHL until the fall of 1981, at the age of 21. In the meantime, Jonsson decided to focus on gaining international experience at the highest levels.

He represented Sweden three times at the World Junior (U20) Championship (in 1978, '79, and '80) and was named to the All-Star Team in the last of these. He won a silver medal in 1978 as well as a bronze in both 1979 and 1980 under coach Bengt Ohlson. The silver medal in his first U20 came on the final day when he helped his team beat Canada 6–5, giving Sweden second place and pushing Canada to third.

Jonsson's skills were so impressive that even as he was playing top-level junior hockey he was already being groomed at the senior level as well. He played in the World Championship in 1979 and again in 1981, winning a bronze medal in the former and a silver two years later.

However, it was the years immediately after he was drafted that he matured into a world-class player. Jonsson played for Tre Kronor at the 1980 Olympics in Lake Placid, winning a bronze medal behind the Miracle on Ice team from the United States and the second-place Soviets. It was their first medal since 1964 and only their fourth in Olympic history.

A year and a half later, at the 1981 Canada Cup, Jonsson was again playing for Tre Kronor, but the

Jonsson tries to check Wayne Gretzky as number 99 comes out from behind the goal.

team finished a disappointing fifth. Immediately after the event, which finished in Montreal, he attended the Islanders' training camp, where his skill from the blue line ensured he was a member of the team almost from the day he arrived. He may have been only 21 years old, but he had been playing world-class hockey for the better part of four years.

At the end of his rookie NHL season, Jonsson was celebrating the team's third successive Cup, and in the process he made history of his own. He became only the third European-trained player to have his name on the Stanley Cup after countrymen Stefan Persson and Anders Kallur the previous two seasons with the Islanders, who were clearly scouting Swedes with greater success than any other NHL team at this time. A year later, Jonsson helped the Islanders win for a fourth successive time, to this date the only expansion team to do so.

What separated Jonsson from so many defencemen was his combination of skills. He was a great skater and passer and played with poise under pressure, never throwing the puck away carelessly or making mental mistakes that ended up costing his team a goal. Reliable in his own end and capable of contributing to the attack, he was less heralded than teammate Denis Potvin but not so far removed talent-wise.

Jonsson played in the NHL for eight years, all with the Islanders except the final 20 games of the 1988–89 season after he was traded to the Edmonton Oilers. Still only 29 years old, he elected to return to Sweden at this point and continued playing with Leksands in Elitserien, close to his hometown of Falun, where he starred for the next nine years. In fact, he was Sweden's player of the year in 1994–95, several years past his NHL days, to be sure, but at 34 years old still very much in his prime.

During the second half of his career – the European half, as it were – Jonsson played at four more tournaments for Tre Kronor – three World Championships and the 1994 Olympics. He won his World Championship gold in 1991, a tournament

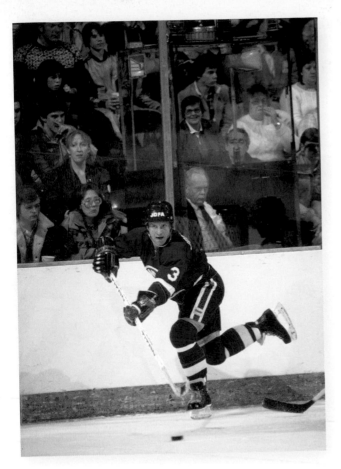

Jonsson added his first Stanley Cup with the New York Islanders in 1982 to his international achievements with Sweden.

more minutes of sudden-death overtime, the teams went to a shootout, the first ever to decide Olympic gold. Sweden won thanks to the one-handed backdoor move by Peter Forsberg at one end of the ice and Tommy Salo's fine save off Paul Kariya at the other end. Jonsson had now won all three of the greatest prizes in hockey – the Stanley Cup, World Championship gold, and Olympic gold.

There were two other players on this '94 Olympic team who joined Jonsson as the first Triple Gold Club members – Mats Naslund and Hakan Loob – both of whom had also been part of the 1991 World Championship team. All three won their first part of the triple – the Stanley Cup – with different teams. Jonsson is ranked first, however, among all TGC members because he was the first to win the Stanley Cup, four years before Naslund (with Montreal) and seven years prior to Loob (with Calgary).

Jonsson was inducted into the IIHF Hall of Fame in 2000.

made famous by Mats Sundin's spectacular third-period goal that gave Sweden a 2–1 win over the Soviet Union for the gold medal. Jonsson was on the ice for both goals in that deciding game.

Jonsson was again part of history in 1994 when he captained Sweden to its first Olympic gold. After beating Germany and Russia in the early playoff rounds, Tre Kronor faced Canada for the gold on the afternoon of February 27, 1994. Jonsson opened the scoring for Sweden early in the game, but Canada took a 2–1 lead midway through the third period to take control. Late in the game, though, with Brad Werenka in the penalty box, Jonsson set up Magnus Svensson for the tying goal.

Tied after 60 minutes of regulation time and ten

Jonsson was among the first players to win TGC honours thanks to Olympic gold in 1994.

2

MATS
NASLUND

BIRTH PLACE: **Timra, Sweden**
BIRTH DATE: **October 31, 1959**
POSITION: **Forward—shoots left**
HEIGHT: **5'7" (1.70 m)**
WEIGHT: **160 lbs. (72.6 kg)**

TRIPLE GOLD CLUB HONOURS

STANLEY CUP 1986 (Montreal Canadiens)
WORLD CHAMPIONSHIP 1991 (Sweden)
OLYMPICS 1994 (Sweden)

TGC AGE
34 YEARS, 119 DAYS

TGC MEMBER AS OF
FEBRUARY 27, 1994
OLYMPIC FINAL WIN VS. CANADA

NHL		Regular Season					Playoffs				
Season	Team	GP	G	A	P	PIM	GP	G	A	P	PIM
1982–83	MON	74	26	45	71	10	3	1	0	1	0
1983–84	MON	77	29	35	64	4	15	6	8	14	4
1984–85	MON	80	42	37	79	14	12	7	4	11	6
1985–86	MON	80	43	67	110	16	20	8	11	19	4
1986–87	MON	79	25	55	80	16	17	7	15	22	11
1987–88	MON	78	24	59	83	14	6	0	7	7	2
1988–89	MON	77	33	51	84	14	21	4	11	15	6
1989–90	MON	72	21	20	41	19	3	1	1	2	0
NHL Totals		651	251	383	634	111	102	35	57	92	33

• Lady Byng Trophy (1987–88)

Olympics							
Year	Team	GP	G	A	P	PIM	Finish
1980	SWE	7	3	7	10	6	B
1992	SWE	8	1	5	6	27	5th
1994	SWE	8	0	7	7	0	G
Totals		23	4	19	23	33	G,B

World Championship							
Year	Team	GP	G	A	P	PIM	Finish
1979	SWE	8	5	2	7	8	B
1981	SWE	8	0	3	3	6	S
1982	SWE	10	2	4	6	6	4th
1983	SWE	10	3	4	7	2	4th
1991	SWE	10	3	5	8	0	G
Totals		46	13	18	31	22	G,S,B

Mats Naslund receives his TGC honours at
the inaugural ceremony in Vancouver.

n 1979 it was still uncommon for an NHL team to draft a European, so when the Montreal Canadiens used their second pick (37th overall) to select a small, 19-year-old from Timra of Elitserien, it caused more than a ripple of conversation. That ripple died over time, however, as Naslund stayed in Sweden for three more years to play with Brynas, where he developed his skills, built his strength, and matured in all ways, far removed from the pressure not only of the NHL but of the intimidating shadow cast by the great Montreal Forum.

Like his Triple Gold Club teammate Tomas Jonsson, Naslund gained enormous experience and confidence playing at three successive U20 tournaments (1977–79), winning a silver and a bronze medal while staring down opponents including Wayne Gretzky and Slava Fetisov. As well, he played at the senior level for the first time in 1979, winning a bronze medal.

One year later, Naslund was part of the Tre Kronor team that went to Lake Placid for the 1980 Olympics. He led the team with seven assists and tied for the team lead with ten points in seven games, and, despite being only 20 years old, it was clear he was one of the stars of the team. Sweden won a bronze medal, and a year later Naslund won silver at the 1981 World Championship.

By 1982, Naslund was 22 years old and a veteran of international and European hockey. He was ready to move to North America, and although he was one of the smallest players of his era, he impressed the Montreal coaching staff at training camp and made the team, becoming the first European player in the venerable history of the Canadiens. He had 26 goals and 71 points as a rookie and established himself as a speedy left winger with a great scoring touch. Finesse, not physicality, was his trademark.

Naslund scored 29 goals in his second year and exploded for 42 in his third and 43 in his fourth. "Le Petit Viking," as Montrealers called him, also had 67 assists in 1985–86, an NHL record for left wingers

Naslund celebrates Stanley Cup victory in 1986 with the Montreal Canadiens.

Calgary. However, he never quite replicated the magic of '85–'86. His point totals dropped, at first slightly and later dramatically, and he found it difficult to endure the wear and tear of the 80-game schedule and cross-continental travel.

Needing a fresh start, Naslund signed with Lugano in Switzerland for the 1990–91 season. The short season and little travel ensured he had plenty of energy late in the year, after which he played for Tre Kronor at the World Championship, helping the team to a gold medal in that first year in Switzerland. It turned out to be his final World Championship appearance, but not his last with Tre Kronor.

Naslund played in Sweden for three years thereafter, winning two national titles with Malmo. He played well with Sweden during the team's victory at the 1994 Olympics, winning gold and completing his Triple Gold Club honours. Incredibly, this was only his second Olympics, coming some 14 years after his debut at Lake Placid.

The start of the 1994–95 NHL season was delayed by months as a result of a lockout. Wayne Gretzky's Ninety-Nine All-Stars toured Europe, and Naslund was invited to play in one game. His play at the Olympics and

that stood for six years. His 110 points marked the first time a Canadiens player reached the century mark since Guy Lafleur in 1979–80, and it still remains – some 27 years later – the last time a Habs player has reached 100 points in a season.

At the start of the 1984–85 season players from around the world participated in the Canada Cup, and it was here, playing best on best, that Naslund again shone bright. While Canada was the favourite and the Soviets were considered their logical opponents for the championship, it was Sweden that advanced to the best-of-three finals in Alberta to face the hosts. Although Canada won in two straight, Naslund was impressive in creating this surprise finals appearance.

Although goalie Patrick Roy is rightly given the lion's share of the glory for taking the Canadiens to the Stanley Cup in the 1985–86 season, Naslund's offence was certainly a huge factor in the surprise victory as well. In the playoffs, his 19 points was tops on the Habs as he played on the number-one line with Bobby Smith and Ryan Walter. Naslund became the first European to win the Cup with the Canadiens, a team that was winning the glorious silverware for the 23rd time in its illustrious history.

Naslund remained with the team for four more years—having another productive post-season en route to the 1989 Stanley Cup final loss versus

Few Swedish players have the reputation Naslund has for his combination of skill, success, and sportsmanship.

Naslund's 110 points in 1985–86 represent the last time a Canadiens player surpassed the century mark for points.

in this exhibition attracted the notice of the Boston Bruins. Feeling good about his skills and conditioning, he signed with the Bruins soon after and played the lockout-shortened season before retiring from the game for good.

In a nationwide poll conducted in 1987, Naslund was named to the Tre Kronor all-time all-star team on left wing as selected by Swedish hockey fans. Known for his gentlemanly play, he was also awarded the Lady Byng Trophy in the NHL in 1987–88.

Naslund was inducted into the IIHF Hall of Fame in 2005.

HAKAN
LOOB

3

BIRTH PLACE: Visby, Sweden
BIRTH DATE: July 3, 1960
POSITION: Forward—shoots right
HEIGHT: 5'9" (1.75 m)
WEIGHT: 170 lbs. (77.1 kg)

TRIPLE GOLD CLUB HONOURS

WORLD CHAMPIONSHIP 1987, 1991 (Sweden)
STANLEY CUP 1989 (Calgary Flames)
OLYMPICS 1994 (Sweden)

TGC AGE
33 YEARS, 239 DAYS

TGC MEMBER AS OF
FEBRUARY 27, 1994
OLYMPIC FINAL WIN VS. CANADA

NHL			Regular Season					Playoffs			
Season	Team	GP	G	A	P	PIM	GP	G	A	P	PIM
1983–84	CAL	77	30	25	55	22	11	2	3	5	2
1984–85	CAL	78	37	35	72	14	4	3	3	6	0
1985–86	CAL	68	31	36	67	36	22	4	10	14	6
1986–87	CAL	68	18	26	44	26	5	1	2	3	0
1987–88	CAL	80	50	56	106	47	9	8	1	9	4
1988–89	CAL	79	27	58	85	44	22	8	9	17	4
NHL Totals		450	193	236	429	189	73	26	28	54	16

Olympics							
Year	Team	GP	G	A	P	PIM	Finish
1992	SWE	8	4	4	8	0	5th
1994	SWE	8	4	5	9	2	G
Totals		16	8	9	17	2	G

World Championship							
Year	Team	GP	G	A	P	PIM	Finish
1982	SWE	8	3	1	4	6	4th
1987	SWE	8	5	4	9	4	G
1990	SWE	10	4	7	11	10	S
1991	SWE	10	2	7	9	6	G
Totals		36	14	19	33	26	2G,S

(Left to right) Hakan Loob, Mats Naslund, and Tomas Jonsson celebrate Olympic gold in 1994, making this trio the first members of the Triple Gold Club.

The third player inaugurated into the Triple Gold Club as a result of winning gold at the 1994 Olympics in Lillehammer was Hakan Loob, whose career bears a striking resemblance to compatriots Tomas Jonsson and Mats Naslund.

He, too, started a fine international career at the U20, playing alongside Naslund in 1979 and 1980 and winning two bronze medals. The Calgary Flames drafted him in the summer of 1980, but the 181st selection did not augur well for the Swede, who was small and compact. But like Jonsson and Naslund, he didn't come over to the NHL right away. By the time he made his NHL debut with the Flames in 1983, he was an established superstar in Elitserien and a veteran for the national team as well.

About the same size as Mats Naslund, Loob was perhaps more a pure scorer to Naslund's play-maker, but both made significant contributions to their team's success in the middle part of the 1980s. Also like Naslund and Tomas Jonsson, Loob had two distinct parts to his career. While hockey fans in North America know him for his years with the Flames, fans back in Sweden know him as possibly the greatest player in Farjestads BK history. Indeed, after he retired, the club retired his number 5.

Loob started his professional career with Farjestads in 1979 and was an immediate success. He led the team to a national championship in his second season, and in his fourth and final year before leaving for the NHL he was named the Elitserien's top player thanks to setting records for goals (42) and points (76). By the summer of 1983, it was clear Loob was ready for new challenges, and so he accepted an offer from Calgary general manager Cliff Fletcher to join the Flames.

In Calgary, Loob was an instant success, scoring 30 goals in his rookie season. Prior to his second season, he played for Tre Kronor at the 1984 Canada Cup, played mainly in Calgary and Edmonton, and was a vital contributor to the team's stunning play.

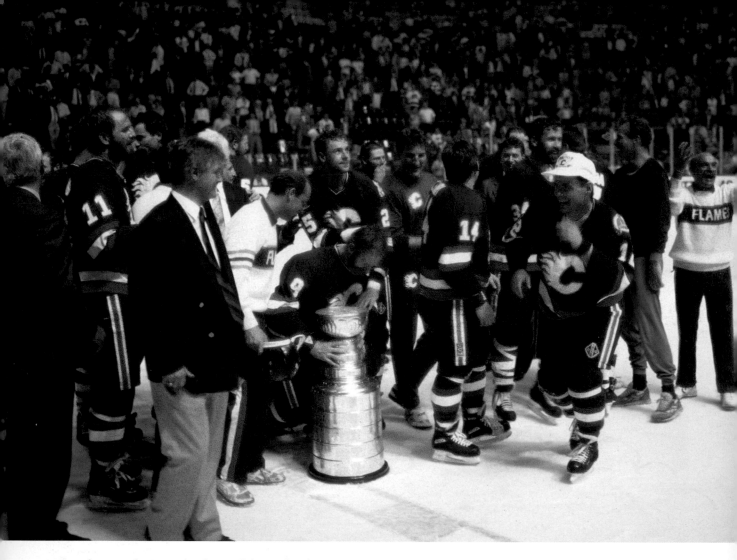

Sweden made it to the best-of-three finals against Canada, losing in two straight.

Loob improved to 37 goals the next season and helped the team to the Stanley Cup finals in 1986, a year made memorable when Steve Smith of Edmonton inadvertently banked the puck off goaltender Grant Fuhr in the third period to eliminate the Oilers and advance the Flames. Calgary, however, was bested by Montreal in the finals and had to wait three years to exact revenge.

Loob reached 50 goals in 1987–88, a year in which he also finished with 106 total points. He remains the only Swede to score 50 goals in a single season. However, his great season did not produce team success in the playoffs, as the Flames were pushed aside by the mighty Edmonton Oilers in six games.

In 1987, Loob was instrumental in Sweden's historic World Championship win, Tre Kronor's

Loob's NHL success was highlighted by Stanley Cup victory in 1989 with the Calgary Flames.

first gold in 25 years. The win was made possible by Loob's amazing behind-the-back pass to a wide-open Tomas Sandstrom, who had snuck in behind Soviet defenceman Alexei Kasatonov and goalie Yevgeni Belosheikan to the back side of the play. The goal, at 18:39 of the third period, gave Sweden a 2–2 tie with the Soviets, ensuring Sweden the gold medal and CCCP the silver. This gave the diminutive Loob his first TGC honour.

It was in 1988–89 NHL season that all the pieces fell into place for Loob and the Flames. The team went all the way to the finals, facing Montreal in a rematch of 1986. This time, however, Calgary came out on top, defeating Montreal in six games. The decisive game came at the Forum, the first and only

Loob was one of the top producers in the 1989 playoffs, recording 17 points in 22 playoff games.

time Montreal ever lost the Stanley Cup on home ice. Loob had a hand in Lanny McDonald's go-ahead goal in the final game. This gave Loob the second notch in his Triple Gold Club belt.

Loob had long decided that he wanted to raise his children in Sweden, and after six years with the Flames, capped by the Stanley Cup, the time was perfect for him to return to Farjestad and resume his career in the Elitserien. So, as did his countrymen Jonsson and Naslund, Loob returned to his place of supremacy in the Swedish league.

Loob, Jonsson, and Naslund then completed their Triple Gold Club honours together, winning gold at the 1994 Olympics in Lillehammer. At the time, there was no such thing as the Triple Gold Club, but the threesome are subjects of an historic photo on ice after the Olympic gold, savouring the win together along the boards, the five Olympic rings on the boards in behind. They were the pioneers, the first players to combine international and European success with North American success.

Loob was inducted into the IIHF Hall of Fame in 1998.

A right winger, Loob was known for his speed and skill more than for size and strength.

VALERI
KAMENSKI

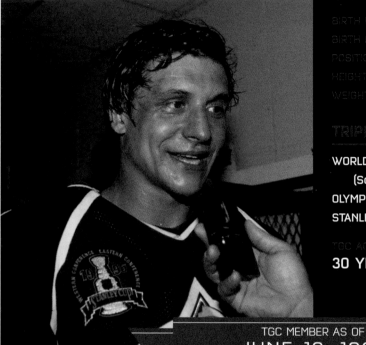

BIRTH PLACE: Voskresensk, Soviet Union (Russia)
BIRTH DATE: April 18, 1966
POSITION: Left wing—shoots right
HEIGHT: 6'2" (1.88 m)
WEIGHT: 198 lbs. (89.8 kg)

TRIPLE GOLD CLUB HONOURS

WORLD CHAMPIONSHIP 1986, 1989, 1990
    (Soviet Union)
OLYMPICS 1988 (Soviet Union)
STANLEY CUP 1996 (Colorado Avalanche)

TGC AGE
30 YEARS, 53 DAYS

TGC MEMBER AS OF
JUNE 10, 1996
STANLEY CUP WIN VS. FLORIDA

NHL		Regular Season					Playoffs				
Season	Team	GP	G	A	P	PIM	GP	G	A	P	PIM
1991–92	QUE	23	7	14	21	14			DNQ		
1992–93	QUE	32	15	22	37	14	6	0	1	1	6
1993–94	QUE	76	28	37	65	42			DNQ		
1994–95	QUE	40	10	20	30	22	2	1	0	1	0
1995–96	COL	81	38	47	85	85	22	10	12	22	28
1996–97	COL	68	28	38	66	38	17	8	14	22	16
1997–98	COL	75	26	40	66	60	7	2	3	5	18
1998–99	COL	65	14	30	44	28	10	4	5	9	4
1999–2000	NYR	58	13	19	32	24			DNQ		
2000–01	NYR	65	14	20	34	36			DNQ		
2001–02	DAL/NJ	54	7	14	21	20	2	0	0	0	0
NHL Totals		637	200	301	501	383	66	25	35	60	72

Olympics							
Year	Team	GP	G	A	P	PIM	Finish
1988	URS	8	4	2	6	4	G
1998	RUS	6	1	2	3	0	S
Totals		14	5	4	9	4	G,S

World Championship							
Year	Team	GP	G	A	P	PIM	Finish
1986	URS	9	2	0	2	8	G
1987	URS	10	5	3	8	6	S
1989	URS	10	4	4	8	8	G
1990	URS	10	7	2	9	20	G
1991	URS	10	6	5	11	10	B
1994	RUS	6	5	5	10	12	5th
2000	RUS	6	0	0	0	10	9th
Totals		61	29	19	48	74	3G,S,B

● IIHF Directorate World Championship
  Best Forward (1991), World Championship
  All-Star Team/Forward (1991)

B y the time Valeri Kamenski made his NHL
debut with the Quebec Nordiques late in the
1991–92 season, his place in international
hockey had long been established. He played in two
World Junior (U20) Championships, winning a silver
medal in 1985 and a gold one year later. He also
won gold at the World Championship three times,
starting in 1986 just four days after his 20th birthday.
In all, he played five straight World Championships,
winning a silver in 1987, a gold again in 1989 and
1990, and a bronze in 1991.

Surprisingly, he won his biggest individual
honour in an event in which the Soviet Union didn't
win gold. He was named Best Forward by the IIHF
Directorate and selected to the All-Star Team at the
1991 World Championship in Finland, the year his
team was upset by Sweden 2–1 in the final game with
gold on the line.

As well, he claimed Olympic gold in 1988 in
Calgary, the last time the old Soviet Union competed at
the quadrennial event. Kamenski scored four goals and
added two assists in eight games at the Calgary Games.

He was drafted 129th overall by the Quebec
Nordiques in 1988, even though the team knew full
well one of the country's top young talents was not
going to be allowed to up and leave the communist
Soviet Union. Indeed, Kamenski was forced to remain
at home and play for CSKA Moscow, the nation's best
team and place where the best players trained for the
most important international tournaments.

To fans of the NHL, Kamenski first burst onto
the scene during, appropriately, Rendez-vous '87 in
Quebec City, the best-of-two mini-series between
the top players from the NHL and the top players
from the Soviet Union, which replaced the All-Star
Game this year. He scored twice and added an assist
in the second of the two-game series, a 5–3 win,
giving the Soviets a split in the exciting series. While
Wayne Gretzky was named MVP for Team Canada,
Kamenski was named the top Soviet player. He
was 20 years old.

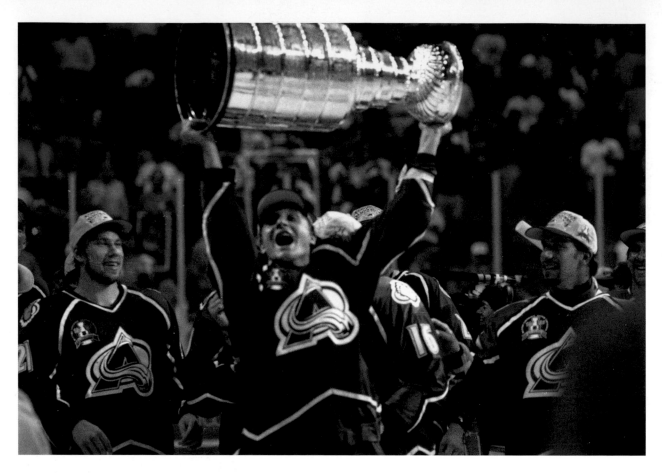

Kamenski joined the Triple Gold Club after winning the Stanley Cup with Colorado in 1996.

Just a few months later he was again front and centre, this time at the Canada Cup. When Canada and the Soviets played the best-of-three finals in Hamilton and Montreal, all scores were 6–5 and most hockey experts called it the best three games ever played. It was his goal with just 64 seconds left in the third period of game two that sent the game into overtime to temporarily silence the local fans.

Kamenski broke his leg during the 1991 Canada Cup in September, and the Nordiques negotiated successfully to get him into the NHL before the end of the year. Bad luck dogged him, though, and he broke his thumb and then his ankle early the next year. In all, he played just 55 games and scored 22 goals in his first two, short seasons with the Nordiques, but he was nowhere near showing fans in Quebec what he was capable of doing with the puck.

It wasn't until 1993–94 that patient Nordiques fans had a true chance to see what Kamenski was made of. That year he scored 28 goals and showed many flashes of genius with the puck, for which he was famous. The next year, however, the owners' lockout

forced the delay of the season, and again Kamenski was unable to build momentum in his NHL career.

That shortened '94–'95 season also proved to be the end of hockey in Quebec City. The team moved to Colorado for the start of the '95–'96 season. Settled, experienced in NHL play, and healthy for the full season, Kamenski scored 38 goals and 85 points. He played all but one game in the season, and in the playoffs he was dominant, the team's best player after goalie Patrick Roy and captain and Conn Smythe Trophy winner Joe Sakic.

The Avalanche swept aside the Florida Panthers in four games to win the franchise's first Cup, and with the win Kamenski became the fourth member of the Triple Gold Club.

In 1997, Kamenski scored a goal that still leaves one in awe. Playing for Colorado against Florida, he curled to the net as Alexei Gusarov brought the puck in over the blue line. Gusarov waited until Kamenski

Kamenski was named the Best Forward at the 1991 World Championship.

was right in front of the goal and made a perfect pass. Kamenski got the puck off balance, and as he spun in the air he backhanded the puck along the ice between the goalie's pads. No greater goal has been captured on film.

He played three more years in Colorado and then took his game on the road, first with three more teams in the NHL and finally two seasons with Khimik Voskresensk in Russia before retiring in 2005.

A longtime star in his homeland, Kamenski played for both the Soviet Union and Russia during his international career.

ALEXEI
GUSAROV

5

BIRTH PLACE: Leningrad (St. Petersburg), Soviet Union (Russia)
BIRTH DATE: July 8, 1964
POSITION: Defence—shoots left
HEIGHT: 6'3" (1.91 m)
WEIGHT: 185 lbs. (83.9 kg)

TRIPLE GOLD CLUB HONOURS

WORLD CHAMPIONSHIP 1986, 1989, 1990 (Soviet Union)
OLYMPICS 1988 (Soviet Union)
STANLEY CUP 1996 (Colorado Avalanche)

TGC AGE
31 YEARS, 338 DAYS

TGC MEMBER AS OF
JUNE 10, 1996
STANLEY CUP WIN VS. FLORIDA

NHL		Regular Season					Playoffs				
Season	Team	GP	G	A	P	PIM	GP	G	A	P	PIM
1990–91	QUE	36	3	9	12	12			DNQ		
1991–92	QUE	68	5	18	23	22			DNQ		
1992–93	QUE	79	8	22	30	57	5	0	1	1	0
1993–94	QUE	76	5	20	25	38			DNQ		
1994–95	QUE	14	1	2	3	6			DNP		
1995–96	COL	65	5	15	20	56	21	0	9	9	12
1996–97	COL	58	2	12	14	28	17	0	3	3	14
1997–98	COL	72	4	10	14	42	7	0	1	1	6
1998–99	COL	54	3	10	13	24	5	0	0	0	2
1999–2000	COL	34	2	2	4	10			DNP		
2000–01	COL/NYR/STL	51	1	8	9	18	13	0	0	0	4
NHL Totals		607	39	128	167	313	68	0	14	14	38

Olympic						
Year	Team	GP	G	A	P	PIM	Finish
1988	URS	8	1	3	4	6	G
1998	RUS	6	0	1	1	8	S
Totals		14	1	4	5	14	G,S

World Championship						
Year	Team	GP	G	A	P	PIM	Finish
1985	URS	10	2	1	3	6	B
1986	URS	9	1	2	3	8	G
1987	URS	10	1	2	3	8	S
1989	URS	9	2	1	3	2	G
1990	URS	10	1	3	4	6	G
1991	URS	10	1	4	5	2	B
Totals		58	8	13	21	32	3G,S,2B

Alexie Gusarov receives his TGC honours at the inaugural ceremony in Vancouver.

The Triple Gold Club careers of Valeri Kamenski and Alexei Gusarov are nearly identical. The only real difference is that while Kamenski started his career in his hometown of Voskresensk, Gusarov first gained his footing in the hockey world in Leningrad (later renamed St. Petersburg), much farther from the Moscow capital.

Nonetheless, Gusarov, two years older than Kamenski, left Leningrad to join the famed CSKA Moscow club team in 1984 (in North America more commonly known as Central Red Army), a year before Kamenski. This was where nearly all top national team players skated during the season. When Kamenski left the Soviet Union in 1991 to join the Quebec Nordiques, he did so because Gusarov had left a year earlier to join the same team. Both had been drafted by Quebec in 1988, but Soviet authorities, as they had done with Tretiak, Kamenski, and all other key players, refused to permit their young stars to leave for the NHL.

By this time Gusarov had won three World Championship gold medals as well as Olympic gold from Calgary in 1988. His first taste of international experience came in 1984 when he played a central role in the team's winning gold at the U20. He was named the tournament's Best Defenceman by the IIHF Directorate and was voted to the media All-Star Team.

Despite being only 20 years old, his performance at the U20 tournament earned him a spot on the Soviet Union team for the 1984 Canada Cup. From there he joined CSKA Moscow, where he remained one of the team's top defencemen for the next seven years. Of course, he also played at the 1987 Canada Cup, considered by many to be the finest finals ever contested. During his time in the Soviet Union he played in every major tournament from 1984 to 1991, including six straight World Championships. Gusarov won medals each time, including three gold, one silver, and two bronze.

It wasn't until the summer of 1990, when he was 26, that he was allowed to leave to play in the NHL.

In addition to his TGC honours, Gusarov also won gold at the U20 in 1984 with the Soviet Union.

Gusarov ended his career after the 2000–01 season, one that saw him go from Colorado to the Rangers to St. Louis. He immediately settled in Wheat Ridge, Colorado, and went into business. Such was his reputation during his career with the Avs that in October 2009 he was honoured with one of ten alumni nights held by the team, his contributions not forgotten.

When he was given a chance to return home, though, he took it, and today he is the assistant general manager of SKA St. Petersburg, working alongside another legend, Alexei Kasatonov.

The defenceman stayed 11 years, first with Quebec and then Colorado, becoming part of the great Colorado team that won the Stanley Cup in 1995–96, the first year after the team's relocation from Quebec. That win, combined with his earlier international successes with CCCP, earned him a place in the Triple Gold Club.

A mainstay on the blue line, "Goose" was a large and physical defenceman, one of the key members of the team's multinational blue line corps that included Adam Foote (Canada), Uwe Krupp (Germany), and Sandis Ozolinsh (Latvia).

His last hurrah internationally came at the Nagano Olympics, where the Russians were one goal away from gold, losing 1–0 to the Czechs for the top of the podium. Nevertheless, Gusarov took a silver medal home to take its place beside his gold from 1988.

Gusarov was the first defenceman to join the TGC, although a year later Slava Fetisov joined him in this group.

Like compatriot Valeri Kamenski, Gusarov won his Stanley Cup with the Colorado Avalanche in 1996.

PETER FORSBERG

6

BIRTH PLACE: **Ornskoldsvik, Sweden**
BIRTH DATE: **July 20, 1973**
POSITION: **Centre—shoots left**
HEIGHT: **6' (1.83 m)**
WEIGHT: **205 lbs. (93.0 kg)**

TRIPLE GOLD CLUB HONOURS

WORLD CHAMPIONSHIP 1992, 1998 (Sweden)
OLYMPICS 1994, 2006 (Sweden)
STANLEY CUP 1996, 2001 (Colorado Avalanche)

TGC AGE
22 YEARS, 326 DAYS

TGC MEMBER AS OF
JUNE 10, 1996
STANLEY CUP WIN VS. FLORIDA

NHL		Regular Season					Playoffs				
Season	Team	GP	G	A	P	PIM	GP	G	A	P	PIM
1994–95	QUE	47	15	35	50	16	6	2	4	6	4
1995–96	COL	82	30	86	116	47	22	10	11	21	18
1996–97	COL	65	28	58	86	73	14	5	12	17	10
1997–98	COL	72	25	66	91	94	7	6	5	11	12
1998–99	COL	78	30	67	97	108	19	8	16	24	31
1999–2000	COL	49	14	37	51	52	16	7	8	15	12
2000–01	COL	73	27	62	89	54	11	4	10	14	6
2001–02	COL			DNP			20	9	18	27	20
2002–03	COL	75	29	77	106	70	7	2	6	8	6
2003–04	COL	39	18	37	55	30	11	4	7	11	12
2005–06	PHI	60	19	56	75	46	6	4	4	8	6
2006–07	PHI/NAS	57	13	42	55	88	5	2	2	4	12
2007–08	COL	9	1	13	14	8	7	1	4	5	14
2010–11	COL	2	0	0	0	4			DNP—RETIRED		
NHL Totals		708	249	636	885	690	151	64	107	171	163

- Calder Trophy (1994–95)
- Hart Trophy (2002–03)
- Art Ross Trophy (2002–03)

Olympics						
Year	Team	GP	G	A	P	PIM	Finish
1994	SWE	8	2	6	8	6	G
1998	SWE	4	1	4	5	6	5th
2006	SWE	6	0	6	6	0	G
2010	SWE	4	0	1	1	2	5th
Totals		22	3	17	20	14	2G

World Championship						
Year	Team	GP	G	A	P	PIM	Finish
1992	SWE	8	4	2	6	6	G
1993	SWE	8	1	1	2	12	S
1998	SWE	7	6	5	11	0	G
2003	SWE	8	4	5	9	6	S
2004	SWE	2	0	1	1	2	S
Totals		33	15	14	29	26	2G,3S

- IIHF Directorate World Championship
  Best Forward (1998)
- World Championship All-Star Team/
  Forward (1998, 2003)

A contemplative Peter Forsberg has a quiet moment during the hectic TGC inaugural ceremonies in Vancouver.

The career of Peter Forsberg has been exceptional, and his Triple Gold Club credentials are, without question, unique. Forsberg achieved his triple in the fewest tournaments of any of the 25 current members (four, tied with Jonathan Toews), and once he had become a member he then went back and achieved all three again, becoming the only player to achieve "double TGC" credentials in this way. He also completed his first Triple Gold Club at age 22, the second youngest of all members to date (after Toews).

Forsberg's father, Kent, was a successful coach at the national and international level for Sweden, and given young Peter's rise to stardom the two often were part of the same team, son as player, father as coach. The Forsberg name and the Modo hockey club of their hometown of Ornskoldsvik are intertwined.

Peter's first important career moment came in 1992. He was part of the team that defeated all comers to win gold at the World Championship in Prague. It was his first World Championship and came just weeks after he played at the U20. He

scored the opening goal during the gold-medal game, a 5–2 win over Finland, and just a few weeks later he was drafted sixth overall by the Philadelphia Flyers in the NHL Entry Draft. Although he would have some great years with the Flyers later in his career, Forsberg made his NHL debut with the Quebec Nordiques after the two teams were part of a large deal that sent the disgruntled first-overall draft choice, Eric Lindros, to Philadelphia and Forsberg (and a large package of players and cash) to the Nordiques.

But Forsberg didn't start his NHL career right away, instead returning to Sweden to play with Modo in Elitserien for three more years. During that time, he played at the U20 on two occasions, 1992 and 1993, winning silver both years, but it was the second of those that indicated that his rise to stardom was not a question of if but when. Playing on a line with childhood friend Markus Naslund and Niklas Sundstrom, Forsberg set records that almost certainly will never

Forsberg took the Stanley Cup home to Ornskoldsvik, Sweden, after winning in 1996 with the Colorado Avalanche.

Olympic gold, and his daring was rewarded with the greatest of victories.

The next, lockout-shortened season, 1994–95, Forsberg finally moved to Canada and joined the Nordiques. His NHL debut was January 21, 1995, against the Flyers, in which he earned one assist. By season's end, his scoring average was more than a point a game, good enough to win him the Calder Trophy as rookie of the year. Despite his individual success, the team lost in the first round of the playoffs.

The next season the Nordiques moved to Colorado, and the team won the Stanley Cup in only Forsberg's second NHL season. His performance all season long was explosive. Although captain Joe Sakic was the face of the team and goalie Patrick Roy its saving grace in the crease, Forsberg dominated the league, scoring 116 points in the regular season and helping the Avs sweep Florida in a four-game finals. In game two, Forsberg scored three goals in a period, only the sixth NHLer to turn the hat trick in a Cup finals game.

By this time, Forsberg was 22 years old he had already completed his Triple Gold Club honours. Two years later, Forsberg began his quest for a second TGC run by leading Sweden to a gold medal at the World Championship in Switzerland (Zurich and Basel) after the Olympics in Nagano.

Forsberg continued to be a dominant presence with the Avalanche, helping the team to a second Stanley Cup in 2001 and giving him the second prize of a second Triple Gold Club. Although he had 89 points in the regular season, his playoffs were cut short because of a spleen injury, and he was unable to play in the Cup-clinching game.

Indeed, his declining health forced him to miss the entire regular season of 2001–02, but he came back for the playoffs and had one of the most incredible returns ever, leading the post-season in scoring with 27 points despite not playing in the Stanley Cup finals, one of only two players to achieve this feat since the NHL began in 1917.

Forsberg was in fine form in 2002–03 when he led the league in scoring for the first and only time in his career, and he was also named winner of the Hart Trophy for his outstanding season. Indeed,

be beat. He had 24 assists and 31 total points in just seven games, including the only ten-point night in U20 history during a 20–1 drubbing of Japan. He was named Best Forward of the tournament by the IIHF Directorate and was the top vote-getter for the media All-Star Team.

The final European season for "Foppa" culminated with the 1994 Olympics in Lillehammer. Forsberg scored one of the most famous – and bravest – goals in Olympic and shootout history when he one-handed the puck to the far side past a sliding Corey Hirsch of Canada to score the winning goal in the gold-medal game. Forsberg had been stopped by Hirsch in the first round of the shootout – five shots each – but after that was tied 2–2, sudden-death shots were required. He was the seventh shooter during the heart-stopping series for as the league tried to cope with the retirement of Wayne Gretzky in 1999, it now seemed that "Foppa" might well deserve the title of "best hockey player in the world."

Alas, injuries were taking their toll. They not only kept him out of the lineup, but they also made recovery more and more difficult and made him seemingly susceptible to even more problems. He dislocated his wrist, had a bursa sac removed from his ankle, broke his foot, endured surgeries to correct an abnormal arch, and experienced unendurable pain in his feet.

Despite being in and out of active duty the last several years or his career, Forsberg rallied and was healthy enough to dress for the 2006 Tre Kronor team that won Olympic gold in Turin, giving him his second complete set of Triple Gold Club honours. He assisted on Niklas

Forsberg's shootout goal was so famous that Swedish Post turned his Olympic heroics into a stamp.

Lidstrom's gold-medal-winning goal early in the third period against Finland. He later played in the Vancouver Olympics, his international swansong, but played a diminished role in light of his failing health. Despite missing most of the last five years with injury, he attempted a comeback with the Avs in February 2011, but after two ineffectual games, he retired for good.

Forsberg had his number 21 retired by Colorado early the following season and was inducted into the IIHF Hall of Fame in 2013.

Forsberg was not big, but he was exceptionally difficult to knock off the puck and had great vision, especially in the offensive end.

VYACHESLAV
FETISOV

7

BIRTH PLACE: Moscow, Soviet Union (Russia)
BIRTH DATE: April 20, 1958
POSITION: Defence—shoots left
HEIGHT: 6'1" (1.85 m)
WEIGHT: 215 lbs. (97.5 kg)

TRIPLE GOLD CLUB HONOURS

WORLD CHAMPIONSHIP 1978, 1981, 1982, 1983, 1986, 1989, 1990 (Soviet Union)
OLYMPICS 1984, 1988 (Soviet Union)
STANLEY CUP 1997, 1998 (Detroit Red Wings)

TGC AGE
39 YEARS, 48 DAYS

TGC MEMBER AS OF
JUNE 7, 1997
STANLEY CUP WIN VS. PHILADELPHIA

NHL			Regular Season				Playoffs				
Season	Team	GP	G	A	P	PIM	GP	G	A	P	PIM
1989–90	NJ	72	8	34	42	52	6	0	2	2	10
1990–91	NJ	67	3	16	19	62	7	0	0	0	15
1991–92	NJ	70	3	23	26	108	6	0	3	3	8
1992–93	NJ	76	4	23	27	158	5	0	2	2	4
1993–94	NJ	52	1	14	15	30	14	1	0	1	8
1994–95	NJ/DET	18	3	12	15	2	18	0	8	8	14
1995–96	DET	69	7	35	42	96	19	1	4	5	34
1996–97	DET	64	5	23	28	76	20	0	4	4	42
1997–98	DET	58	2	12	14	72	21	0	3	3	10
NHL Totals		546	36	192	228	656	116	2	26	28	145

Olympics							
Year	Team	GP	G	A	P	PIM	Finish
1980	URS	7	5	4	9	10	B
1984	URS	7	3	8	11	8	G
1988	URS	8	4	9	13	6	G
Totals		22	12	21	33	24	2G,B

World Championship							
Year	Team	GP	G	A	P	PIM	Finish
1977	URS	10	3	3	6	2	B
1978	URS	10	4	6	10	11	G
1981	URS	8	1	4	5	6	G
1982	URS	10	4	3	7	6	G
1983	URS	10	3	7	10	8	G
1985	URS	10	6	7	13	15	B
1986	URS	10	6	8	14	10	G
1987	URS	10	2	8	10	2	S
1989	URS	10	2	4	6	17	G
1990	URS	8	2	8	10	8	G
1991	URS	10	3	1	4	4	B
Totals		106	36	59	95	89	7G,S,3B

- IIHF Directorate World Championship Best Defenceman (1978, 1982, 1985, 1986, 1989)
- World Championship All-Star Team/Defence (1978, 1982, 1983, 1985, 1986, 1987, 1989, 1990, 1991)

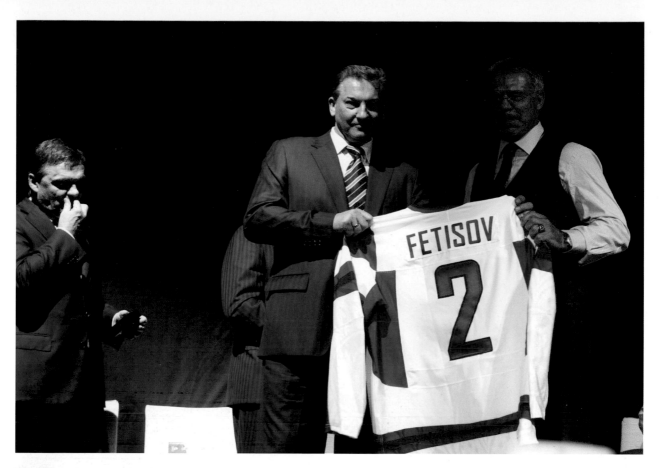

No one could possibly dispute the fact that the greatest Russian goalie of all time was Vladislav Tretiak or that the greatest forward was Valeri Kharlamov. In that same vein, there is one defenceman who towers above all others – Vyacheslav Fetisov. Often called the Bobby Orr of international hockey, he had a career that lasted 20 years, cut through a regime change in the Soviet Union – which he himself helped institute – and became a champion wherever he played.

As Gordie Howe is to Canada or Borje Salming is to Sweden, the very name *Fetisov* elicits gasps to the next generation of Russian stars who see him as not just a hockey player but an iconic figure in the nation's sporting and cultural history. He may have been the oldest player to attain membership in the Triple Gold Club, but that he did so at all is testament to a changing political climate that had prevented Tretiak and Kharlamov from doing the same.

When the IIHF asked 60 hockey experts from around the world to vote for its Centennial All-Star Team in 2008, Fetisov received 54 votes, more than any other player named to the all-century team. Additionally, he was named World Championship Best Defenceman by the IIHF Directorate five times and was selected to the World Championship All-Star Team on nine occasions – a record.

Fetisov first emerged from behind the Iron Curtain to play in the 1977 and 1978 U20 championships. He led the team to back-to-back gold medals and was named Best Defenceman by the IIHF Directorate both years, the only U20 to receive a Directorate Award twice at the World Juniors. He averaged better than a point a game and proved physically superior to any other player in the tournament.

During these two years he also played for the senior CCCP team at the World Championship, winning a bronze medal in 1977 and a gold a year later. It was at age 20 that Fetisov started with the senior CSKA Moscow team, one he played for for 11 years and six World Championship gold medals

Fetisov was the first Russian to take the Stanley Cup to Red Square in Moscow, which he did in 1997 after winning with the Detroit Red Wings.

In the 11 events he played at the World Championship, 1977–91, Fetisov won a medal every year, but for all his success with the national team he was lobbying for his release so he could test himself against the best of the NHL.

Finally, a group of players, led by Fetisov and Larionov, threatened never to play for the Soviet Union again unless they were allowed to play in North America. Soviet authorities eventually relented, and in 1989, at the age of 31, Fetisov made his NHL debut with the New Jersey Devils. By this time he wasn't the force he was a decade ago, but his was still an imposing presence, and as more and more Russians came to the NHL they looked at him with an awe reserved only for the greatest of the greats. His word was gospel to the Russians around the league; his every word and action to be admired and revered.

Fetisov played nine years in the NHL, and his team made the playoffs each time. Early in the 1994–95 season he was traded to Detroit, but it was New Jersey that went on to win the Stanley Cup, defeating

Big, strong, and powerful, Fetisov was also gifted offensively, making him a star at both ends of the ice.

despite a back injury early on that nearly ended his career before it had blossomed.

Like Tretiak, Fetisov was drafted by the Montreal Canadiens in 1978, but of course Fetisov was not allowed to leave. After Montreal was unable to sign him, he was selected again in 1983, this time by New Jersey. Again he was denied. As the 1980s progressed, however, he and longtime teammate Igor Larionov became more defiant of the Soviet regime to which they had been so subservient. They continued to provide their country with international glory – but they received no personal reward in return.

That glory was ever-present in the 1980s. Although the Soviets settled for a crushing silver medal at the Lake Placid Olympics, they won gold in 1984 and 1988, and in what many feel was their greatest achievement of the decade, they pummelled Canada 8–1 at the finals of the 1981 Canada Cup.

the up-and-coming Red Wings in a one-sided, four-game sweep.

But Fetisov was playing on a Detroit team coached by Scotty Bowman, and the coach's plan included recreating a "Russian five" unit similar to what Fetisov had played with his entire Soviet career. Whereas the NHL had forward lines of three that played together and separate defensive pairings of two, the Soviets kept all five players together as a unit for enhanced unity and cohesion. Bowman liked that approach and decided to make it the core of his coaching strategy with the Wings.

The coach acquired four former Soviets – Fetisov, Larionov, Vyacheslav Kozlov, and Vladimir Konstantinov – and he already had Sergei Fedorov on the roster. Using these five together in many key situations, Bowman was able to take Detroit to consecutive Stanley Cup victories in 1997 and 1998 (Dmitri Mironov replaced Konstantinov for 1998 after the latter was seriously injured in the summer).

No more remarkable moment occurred than in 1997 when the Russians took the Stanley Cup to Red Square in Moscow. A city and its hockey players once cut off from the Western world were now celebrating in joyous unison the winning of hockey's greatest, and most democratic, trophy.

Fetisov holds a special and amazing record in that he is the Triple Gold Club member with the most TGC honours – 11 in all. This includes two Stanley Cup wins with the Red Wings, two Olympic gold medals, and seven World Championship gold medals.

Although he won his first World Championship in 1978, he had to wait 19 years to complete his triple, the longest time of all TGC members. Fetisov became a member of the Triple Gold Club at age 39 in Detroit, his career reaching its zenith in a place he could never have imagined finishing his career when he first played for CCCP in 1977 as an 18-year-old in the communist Soviet Union.

The defenceman many called the Bobby Orr of Soviet hockey won seven World Championship gold medals during his illustrious career.

IGOR
LARIONOV

8

BIRTH PLACE: **Voskresensk, Soviet Union (Russia)**
BIRTH DATE: **December 3, 1960**
POSITION: **Centre—shoots left**
HEIGHT: **5'9" (1.75 m)**
WEIGHT: **170 lbs. (77.1 kg)**

TRIPLE GOLD CLUB HONOURS

WORLD CHAMPIONSHIP 1982, 1983, 1986, 1989
   (Soviet Union)
OLYMPICS 1984, 1988 (Soviet Union)
STANLEY CUP 1997, 1998, 2002 (Detroit Red Wings)

TGC AGE
36 YEARS, 186 DAYS

TGC MEMBER AS OF
JUNE 7, 1997
STANLEY CUP WIN VS. PHILADELPHIA

NHL			Regular Season					Playoffs			
Season	Team	GP	G	A	P	PIM	GP	G	A	P	PIM
1989–90	VAN	74	17	27	44	20			DNQ		
1990–91	VAN	64	13	21	34	14	6	1	0	1	6
1991–92	VAN	72	21	44	65	54	13	3	7	10	4
1993–94	SJ	60	18	38	56	40	14	5	13	18	10
1994–95	SJ	33	4	20	24	14	11	1	8	9	2
1995–96	SJ/DET	73	22	51	73	34	19	6	7	13	6
1996–97	DET	64	12	42	54	26	20	4	8	12	8
1997–98	DET	69	8	39	47	28	22	3	10	13	12
1998–99	DET	75	14	49	63	48	7	0	2	2	0
1999–2000	DET	79	9	38	47	28	9	1	2	3	6
2000–01	FLO/DET	65	9	31	40	38	6	1	3	4	2
2001–02	DET	70	11	32	43	50	18	5	6	11	4
2002–03	DET	74	10	33	43	48	4	0	1	1	0
2003–04	NJ	49	1	10	11	20	1	0	0	0	0
NHL Totals		921	169	475	644	474	150	30	67	97	60

Olympics							
Year	Team	GP	G	A	P	PIM	Finish
1984	URS	7	1	4	5	6	G
1988	URS	8	4	9	13	4	G
2002	RUS	6	0	3	3	4	B
Totals		21	5	16	21	14	2G,B

World Championship							
Year	Team	GP	G	A	P	PIM	Finish
1982	URS	10	4	6	10	2	G
1983	URS	9	5	7	12	4	G
1985	URS	10	2	4	6	8	B
1986	URS	10	7	1	8	4	G
1987	URS	10	4	8	12	2	S
1989	URS	8	3	0	3	11	G
Totals		57	25	26	51	31	4G,S,B

• World Championship All-Star Team/
  Forward (1983, 1986)

Just as Valeri Kamenski and Alexci Gusarov achieved their Triple Gold Club honours at the same time, so, too, did defenceman Vyacheslav Fetisov and forward Igor Larionov. And, despite playing in the Soviet Union for 12 years, Larionov still managed a 15-year, 921-game career in the NHL that took him to the Hockey Hall of Fame and the IIHF Hall of Fame after his playing days. The result was enough championships in all corners of the world to give him honours aplenty for two Triple Gold Club memberships.

Two years younger than Fetisov, Larionov started his career at the U20 in 1979 alongside teammates Vladimir Krutov and Alexei Kasatonov. Like Fetisov, Larionov led his team to consecutive gold medals, and the two first played together at the historic Canada Cup in 1981 in which the team was so dominant.

Rare are the times when the careers of two players are as connected as Larionov's and Fetisov's. Not only did they play for the Soviet Union together for so long, but they also played on the famed Green Unit of five players, every shift, every game. (They were called the Green Unit because as the team's top line, they wore green sweaters during practice.) Many thousands of times did Fetisov pass the puck to Larionov, the centreman of the great KLM line, which also included Vladimir Krutov and Sergei Makarov (Alexei Kasatonov was Fetisov's partner on defence).

Larionov played on two Olympic champion teams – 1984 in Sarajevo and 1988 in Calgary (where he finished second in scoring) – as well as four World Championship gold-medal teams. He alone took a firm stance against his dictatorial coach, Viktor Tikhonov, by writing a scathing article in a Soviet magazine that openly criticized his coach. Larionov was nearly removed from the national team, but Fetisov and teammates came to his rescue, refusing to play for CCCP unless Larionov were reinstated. Left with little choice, Tikhonov relented.

Larionov was drafted by the Vancouver Canucks a distant 214th overall in 1985, and like several other

Soviet teammates he tried to persuade their coach to allow them to go to the NHL. Tikhonov, with all the power on his side, said *nyet*. But Larionov was persistent, and as times changed and money became more important to the Soviet program, he was finally allowed to leave in 1989 along with all the members of the Green Unit.

Larionov and Krutov headed to Vancouver, the team that had drafted them years earlier. Nicknamed "Professor" in part because of his intelligent play with the puck on-ice and his use of horn-rimmed glasses off-ice, which gave him an intellectual look, Larionov had trouble adjusting to the more physical game, the smaller ice, and the grinding schedule. After three average years with the Canucks, he was claimed in the Waiver Draft by San Jose, where he joined former linemate Sergei Makarov.

The Sharks, though, were not a good team at this point, and after a little more than two seasons they traded him to Detroit for Ray Sheppard. It was at the Joe Louis Arena that Larionov played for most of the next seven years, winning back-to-back championships with the Red Wings – and Fetisov – in 1997 and '98, and winning again in 2002 as the last of the old Soviet guard to play during this era in Detroit. Not only were their contributions on ice tremendous, they also mentored a younger generation of Russians on the team, notably Sergei Fedorov, Slava Kozlov, and Vladimir Konstantinov.

As with the Soviet team, Larionov was more passer than scorer in the NHL, but he was a complete player in every sense of the word. Strong on the faceoffs, sound defensively, and not known to cough up the puck under pressure, he was simply reliable and consistent the way a world-class player needs to be. Testament to his skills and the healthy change of scenery for him, Larionov was a -6 in his first four games of the 1995–96 season with the Sharks and then recorded a +37 in 69 games with the Red Wings, recording career highs in assists (50) and points (71) along the way.

Larionov played in the three Canada Cups in the 1980s, including 1984 against Dominik Hasek and the Czechoslovaks.

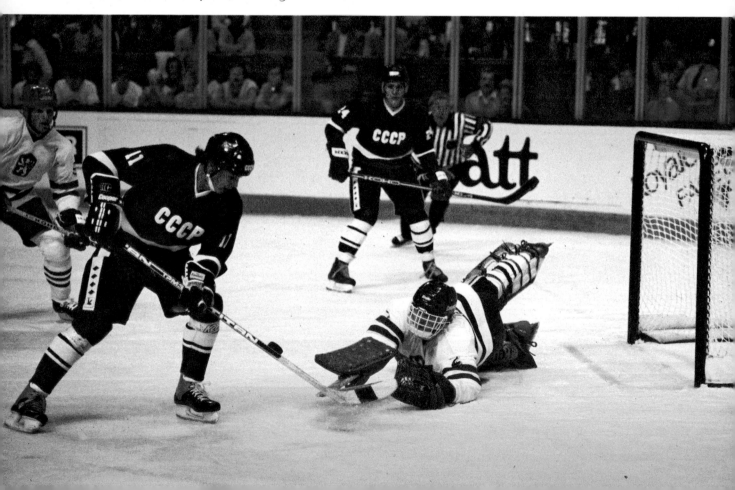

One of the "Russian five" that helped the Detroit Red Wings win the Stanley Cup in 1997, Larionov hoists the trophy high in celebration.

En route to the 2002 Cup win, Larionov, at age 42, scored one of the most memorable Stanley Cup overtime goals, at 54:47 of the third extra period, against Carolina in the finals. He is the only member of the Green Unit to score a Stanley Cup overtime goal. He played a final season in the NHL in 2003–04 with New Jersey, his longtime teammate Fetisov now an assistant coach there, after which he retired from top-level hockey, his place in the game's history and the world's politics well entrenched.

In 2008, Larionov joined Fetisov as an inductee of the Hockey Hall of Fame, an honour acknowledging equally his incredible international career as well as his great success in the NHL. Additionally, both men were already members of the IIHF Hall of Fame, and in 2010 the IIHF announced that Krutov would be inducted into its Hall of Fame as well, thus ensuring all members of the Green Unit had been so honoured.

Only Larionov and Fetisov, however, are members of the Triple Gold Club. These two also join Canadians Joe Sakic and Scott Niedermayer to have won the Canada Cup/World Cup as well as U20 gold to go with their TGC credentials.

Larionov was one of only a few players from Soviet times to play later for Russia.

ALEXANDER
MOGILNY

9

BIRTH PLACE: Khabarovsk, Soviet Union (Russia)
BIRTH DATE: February 18, 1969
POSITION: Right wing—shoots left
HEIGHT: 5'11" (1.80 m)
WEIGHT: 200 lbs. (90.7 kg)

TRIPLE GOLD CLUB HONOURS

OLYMPICS 1988 (Soviet Union)
WORLD CHAMPIONSHIP 1989 (Soviet Union)
STANLEY CUP 2000 (New Jersey Devils)

TGC AGE:
31 YEARS, 113 DAYS

TGC MEMBER AS OF
JUNE 10, 2000
STANLEY CUP WIN VS. DALLAS

NHL		Regular Season					Playoffs				
Season	Team	GP	G	A	P	PIM	GP	G	A	P	PIM
1989–90	BUF	65	15	28	43	16	4	0	1	1	2
1990–91	BUF	62	30	34	64	16	6	0	6	6	2
1991–92	BUF	67	39	45	84	73	2	0	2	2	0
1992–93	BUF	77	76	51	127	40	7	7	3	10	6
1993–94	BUF	66	32	47	79	22	7	4	2	6	6
1994–95	BUF	44	19	28	47	36	5	3	2	5	2
1995–96	VAN	79	55	52	107	16	6	1	8	9	8
1996–97	VAN	76	31	42	73	18		DNQ			
1997–98	VAN	51	18	27	45	36		DNQ			
1998–99	VAN	59	14	31	45	58		DNQ			
1999–2000	VAN/NJ	59	24	20	44	20	23	4	3	7	4
2000–01	NJ	75	43	40	83	43	25	5	11	16	8
2001–02	TOR	66	24	33	57	8	20	8	3	11	8
2002–03	TOR	73	33	46	79	12	6	5	2	7	4
2003–04	TOR	37	8	22	30	12	13	2	4	6	8
2005–06	NJ	34	12	13	25	6		DNP			
	NHL Totals	990	473	559	1,032	432	124	39	47	86	58

Olympics						
Year	Team	GP	G	A	P	PIM	Finish
1988	URS	6	3	2	5	2	G

World Championship						
Year	Team	GP	G	A	P	PIM	Finish
1989	URS	10	0	3	3	2	G

• Lady Byng Trophy (2002–03)

An iconoclast and enigma with a twist of humour, a brilliant skater with a quick release and tremendous shot, Alexander Mogilny was one of the greatest Russian players in NHL history. But unlike his Soviet teammates, he was unwilling to ask politely for permission to play in North America and then wait patiently for an answer. Instead, he used the 1989 World Championship in Stockholm, Sweden, as a means of defecting to the NHL, becoming the first Soviet hockey player to do so.

A man's life came at an early age for Mogilny, who started playing and training with CSKA Moscow at age 14. This meant spending some 300 days of the year in a barracks with teammates most of whom were old enough to be his father. A great player he may have been, but a lonesome and unhappy teen he was as well.

Mogilny later played on a line in CSKA with two other rising stars his own age, Sergei Fedorov and Pavel Bure, but it was only Mogilny who travelled to Calgary and helped his team win gold at the 1988 Olympics, the first of his Triple Gold Club honours.

At age 19, he scored five points (two goals, three assists) in six games at the Calgary Olympics.

This Olympic appearance was sandwiched around three memorable U20 tournaments for the teen sensation. His first World Juniors came in 1987 but was marred by the bench-clearing brawl with Canada in Piestany, Czechoslovakia, which saw both teams disqualified from the competition. The next two years, though, Mogilny was dominant playing alongside Fedorov and Bure, averaging almost a goal a game (19 goals in 20 games) and at a rate of a point and a half in his junior career (35 points in 20 games). He won silver in 1988 and gold in 1989 in Anchorage, Alaska, as his skill allowed him to play the three top international events within a year.

Just a few months later, Mogilny and Fedorov won World Championship gold in Sweden. It was his first and only career appearance at the World

Championship, but it gave him the second honour toward Triple Gold Club membership. The reward for victory was two days to shop and see the sights, and it was during this time that Mogilny defected with the help of the Buffalo Sabres, the NHL team that had selected him 89th overall at the 1988 Entry Draft.

Mogilny joined the Buffalo Sabres for the 1989–90 season. He wore number 89 to remember both his draft position and the year he defected. He didn't turn the league on its head right away, but over the first four years he increased his goal production from a modest 15 to 30 to 39 to a whopping 76 in 1992–93 in 77 games, tied for the league lead with Teemu Selanne.

As well, his 127 points were a career best, but the Sabres lost in the first round of the playoffs, as they

Although he had his best offensive years with the Buffalo Sabres, Mogilny won his lone Stanley Cup with the New Jersey Devils in 2000.

did in each of the six seasons Mogilny was with the team. It was in '92–'93 that he also split the duties of captain with Pat LaFontaine, becoming the first Soviet/Russian in NHL history to wear the "C."

In an effort to shake up a talented but under-achieving team in the playoffs, the Sabres sent shock-waves through their dressing room in 1995 by trading Mogilny to Vancouver with a fifth-round draft choice (Todd Norman) for Michael Peca, Mike Wilson, and a first-round draft choice (who turned out to be Jay McPhee).

But after a sensational first year in which he

By the time he retired, Mogilny had amassed 1,032 points, only the second Russian to reach the 1,000-point milestone after Fedorov (who got there only days earlier in the 2005–06 season, thanks to injuries to Mogilny).

The politics of communism, the fallout of perestroika, and the enmity of defection cast a pall over Russian hockey for some 15 years, and it is only a shame in retrospect that Mogilny, Fedorov, and Bure played internationally just three times together at the senior level. Those games came at the 1996 World Cup, but a loss in the semifinals to the United States ended any dream for the troika. Incredibly, Mogilny played only the one Olympics and World Championship, as a teenager, making his mark more as an NHLer than as a Russian.

Mogilny was known for his blazing speed and ability to stickhandle with wizard-like ability.

scored 55 goals and recorded 107 points, Mogilny failed to deliver the Canucks to the Stanley Cup, and Vancouver, in turn, traded him to New Jersey at the deadline in 2000. A few weeks later, he was celebrating the Stanley Cup, his days of 76 goals behind him, but his moment as champion and Triple Gold Club member at hand.

The next year was also impressive for Mogilny as he had 43 goals and 83 points and the Devils returned to the Cup finals, only to lose to Colorado. He moved on to Toronto and back to New Jersey to close out his career, retiring in 2006.

Mogilny usually wore number 89 to mark the year he defected (1989).

10 VLADIMIR MALAKHOV

BIRTH PLACE: Ekaterinburg, Soviet Union (Russia)
BIRTH DATE: August 30, 1968
POSITION: Defence—shoots left
HEIGHT: 6'4" (1.93 m)
WEIGHT: 225 lbs. (102.1 kg)

TRIPLE GOLD CLUB HONOURS

WORLD CHAMPIONSHIP 1990 (Soviet Union)
OLYMPICS 1992 (Russia)
STANLEY CUP 2000 (New Jersey Devils)

TGC AGE
31 YEARS, 285 DAYS

TGC MEMBER AS OF
JUNE 10, 2000
STANLEY CUP WIN VS. DALLAS

NHL		Regular Season					Playoffs				
Season	Team	GP	G	A	P	PIM	GP	G	A	P	PIM
1992–93	NYI	64	14	38	52	59	17	3	6	9	12
1993–94	NYI	76	10	47	57	80	4	0	0	0	6
1994–95	NYI/MON	40	4	17	21	46	DNQ				
1995–96	MON	61	5	23	28	79	DNP				
1996–97	MON	65	10	20	30	43	5	0	0	0	6
1997–98	MON	74	13	31	44	70	9	3	4	7	10
1998–99	MON	62	13	21	34	77	DNQ				
1999–2000	MON/NJ	24	1	4	5	23	23	1	4	5	18
2000–01	NYR	3	0	2	2	4	DNP				
2001–02	NYR	81	6	22	28	83	DNQ				
2002–03	NYR	71	3	14	17	52	DNQ				
2003–04	NYR/PHI	62	3	16	19	55	17	1	5	6	12
2005–06	NJ	29	4	5	9	26	DNP				
NHL Totals		712	86	260	346	697	75	8	19	27	64

Olympics							
Year	Team	GP	G	A	P	PIM	Finish
1992	RUS	8	3	0	3	4	G
2002	RUS	6	1	3	4	4	B
	Totals	14	4	3	7	8	G,B

World Championship							
Year	Team	GP	G	A	P	PIM	Finish
1990	URS	10	0	1	1	10	G
1991	URS	10	0	0	0	4	B
1992	RUS	6	2	1	3	4	5th
	Totals	26	2	2	4	18	G,B

Vladimir Malakhov was perhaps the only NHLer who was as skilled at bandy as he was at ice hockey because his father coached the outdoor soccer version of the game throughout Vladimir's childhood. And, unlike the Fetisov–Larionov era of players who forced Soviet authorities to let them play in the NHL, or Alexander Mogilny, who defected, Malakhov patiently waited for official permission to play in the NHL. Drafted by the New York Islanders only 191st overall in 1989, he didn't play in North America until 1992, well after perestroika had allowed him to move to the NHL freely.

But like his countrymen, he was an experienced international player by the time he dressed for his first NHL game. He played at the ill-fated 1987 World Junior Championship in Czechoslovakia, when his country and Canada were disqualified after a brawl, and he played at the senior World Championship in 1990, helping the dominating Soviets to a gold medal, his first Triple Gold Club honour. Malakhov was also on the 1991 Canada Cup team and,

more important, was part of history in 1992 at the Albertville Olympics.

That year was a time of unprecedented change in Soviet politics, and the fragmentation of the country led to the players in Albertville covering up the CCCP on their sweaters and refusing to listen to the old national anthem after victories. Instead, the Olympic anthem was played. Although the team was coached by Viktor Tikhonov, the very emblem of Soviet authority, the IOC called the team the Commonwealth of the Independent States (CIS). It was, in essence, the start of a new Russia, and after the tournament every player signed a declaration stating they would play only for Russia in the future.

After beating Finland 6–1 in the quarter-finals and the United States 5–2 in the semis, Malakhov and the Russians faced Canada for the gold medal. This was the most important meeting between the great rivals since the 1987 Canada Cup finals, but in the end the game wasn't as dramatic. The Russians built a 2–0 lead on third-period goals from Vyacheslav Butsayev and Igor Boldin, but Chris Lindberg cut the lead to one goal with 2:40 left in regulation time. Undaunted, the Russians added a third goal to make it a 3–1 final and win their first (and still only) Olympic gold as a new country.

The 24-year-old Malakhov joined the Islanders that fall and made an immediate impact, the team shocking two-time Cup champions Pittsburgh in the playoffs and advancing to the semi-finals before losing to Montreal. The rookie had an impressive season, though, scoring 14 goals from the blue line and recording 52 points.

After only two and a half seasons he was traded to Montreal in a blockbuster deal that saw Pierre Turgeon join him with the Canadiens and the Islanders acquiring Kirk Muller, Craig Darby, and Mathieu Schneider. Malakhov played the better part of five years with the Habs (1995–2000), but the team never made particularly impressive inroads in the playoffs and he was sent to New Jersey at the trade deadline in 2000. A serious knee injury prior to the deadline didn't help his stock.

He arrived at the Meadowlands exactly two weeks before countryman Alexander Mogilny. The pair had an immediate impact, helping the Devils win the Stanley Cup in six games over Dallas. The deciding game went into double overtime and was won by

Like teammate Alexander Mogilny, Malakhov won his Stanley Cup with the New Jersey Devils in 2000.

A big, tough defenceman, Malakhov won World gold in 1990 and Olympics gold in 1992 and then waited eight years to complete his TGC honours.

Jason Arnott, and Malakhov had more ice time than all but two teammates – hall-of-famers Scott Stevens and Scott Niedermayer. This Cup victory completed the Triple Gold Club requirements for both Malakhov and Mogilny.

Malakhov cashed in on his playoff success and signed a long-term deal with the New York Rangers in the summer of 2000, but after only three games he suffered another serious knee injury and missed the season. Less than four years later – and with no playoff appearances – he was traded to Philadelphia. He played just one more partial season, with the Devils in 2005–06, before retiring.

Malakov's only World Championship appearances were in the three-year burst of 1990–92, but he did play for Russia at the 1996 World Cup and again at the 2002 Olympics, winning a bronze medal in Salt Lake.

Malakhov retired in 2006 at age 37 after 14 NHL seasons.

11

ROB
BLAKE

BIRTH PLACE: Simcoe, Ontario, Canada
BIRTH DATE: December 10, 1969
POSITION: Defence—shoots right
HEIGHT: 6'4" (1.93 m)
WEIGHT: 220 lbs. (99.8 kg)

TRIPLE GOLD CLUB HONOURS

WORLD CHAMPIONSHIP 1994, 1997 (Canada)
STANLEY CUP 2001 (Colorado Avalanche)
OLYMPICS 2002 (Canada)

TGC AGE

32 YEARS, 76 DAYS

TGC MEMBER AS OF
FEBRUARY 24, 2002
OLYMPIC FINAL WIN VS. UNITED STATES

NHL			Regular Season						Playoffs		
Season	Team	GP	G	A	P	PIM	GP	G	A	P	PIM
1989–90	LA	4	0	0	0	4	8	1	3	4	4
1990–91	LA	75	12	34	46	125	12	1	4	5	26
1991–92	LA	57	7	13	20	102	6	2	1	3	12
1992–93	LA	76	16	43	59	152	23	4	6	10	46
1993–94	LA	84	20	48	68	137			DNQ		
1994–95	LA	24	4	7	11	38			DNQ		
1995–96	LA	6	1	2	3	8			DNQ		
1996–97	LA	62	8	23	31	82			DNQ		
1997–98	LA	81	23	27	50	94	4	0	0	0	6
1998–99	LA	62	12	23	35	128			DNQ		
1999–00	LA	77	18	39	57	112	4	0	2	2	4
2000–01	LA/COL	67	19	40	59	77	23	6	13	19	16
2001–02	COL	75	16	40	56	58	20	6	6	12	16
2002–03	COL	79	17	28	45	57	7	1	2	3	8
2003–04	COL	74	13	33	46	61	9	0	5	5	6
2005–06	COL	81	14	37	51	94	9	3	1	4	8
2006–07	LA	72	14	20	34	82			DNQ		
2007–08	LA	71	9	22	31	98			DNQ		
2008–09	SJ	73	10	35	45	110	6	1	3	4	4
2009–10	SJ	70	7	23	30	60	15	1	1	2	10
NHL Totals		1,270	240	537	777	1,679	146	26	47	73	166

- James Norris Trophy (1997–98)

Olympics							
Year	Team	GP	G	A	P	PIM	Finish
1998	CAN	6	1	1	2	2	4th
2002	CAN	6	1	2	3	2	G
2006	CAN	6	0	1	1	2	7th
Totals		18	2	4	6	6	G

World Championship							
Year	Team	GP	G	A	P	PIM	Finish
1991	CAN	2	0	2	2	0	S
1994	CAN	8	0	2	2	6	G
1996	CAN	4	0	1	1	0	S
1997	CAN	11	2	2	4	22	G
1998	CAN	5	1	0	1	6	6th
1999	CAN	10	2	5	7	12	4th
Totals		36	5	11	16	46	2G, 2S

- IIHF Directorate Olympics Best Defenceman (1998)
- IIHF Directorate World Championship
  Best Defenceman (1997)
- World Championship All-Star Team/Defence (1997)

One of the longest-serving defencemen in NHL history, Rob Blake was one of three Canadians to complete his Triple Gold Club requirements by winning gold at the 2002 Olympics in Salt Lake City (along with Joe Sakic and Brendan Shanahan). It was a fitting honour, given his frequent participation for Canada internationally (six World Championships, three Olympics, one World Cup) and his incredible success at every level of hockey he played.

Blake is the only member of the Triple Gold Club to choose the U.S. college route over junior hockey in Canada as his means to get to the NHL (via Bowling Green Falcons in the CCHA). Drafted 70th overall in 1988 by Los Angeles, he remained with the Falcons for two more seasons, joining the Kings full-time in 1990 at age 20.

A late bloomer, he never played for Canada at the World Junior Championship, but his maturation during his three-year NCAA career was impressive and constant. By the time he got to the NHL, he was ready for a pro career, fully aware of how to use his size and strength – and nastiness in front of his own goal – to be an effective defenceman inside his own blue line and on offence as well.

Blake never played a game in the minors, but when he got to the NHL the small-town boy was awed by big-city and big-league life. He roomed with veteran Dave Taylor on road trips to help with the adjustment, the boy becoming a man off-ice (although Blake was already a man on-ice). As well, Blake had the thrill of a lifetime looking up the ice every night to see teammate Wayne Gretzky available for a pass.

Despite playing a full season with the Los Angeles Kings in 1990–91 and another 12 games in the play-offs, Blake hopped on a plane, played the final two games of the World Championship, which always ran concurrently, and helped Canada win a silver medal, his first international experience.

He spent the first 11 years of his career with the Kings (1990–2001), but the pinnacle of his time

Blake (far right) celebrates Canada's first Olympic gold in half a century in 2002 with Al MacInnis (left) and Eric Lindros.

there came early on. In 1992–93, he and Gretzky led the team to its first trip to the Stanley Cup finals, losing to Montreal in six games. By this point he was considered one of the best young defencemen in the game, and a year later he had another chance to represent his country.

Blake was part of Canada's historic 1994 World Championship gold medal team, the first victory since the Trail Smoke Eaters in 1961. He played alongside stars Luc Robitaille, Joe Sakic, Brendan Shanahan, and Paul Kariya, and the gold was decided against Finland in a shootout. Blake, meanwhile, continued to excel. When the Kings traded Gretzky to St. Louis, they named Blake team captain, a responsibility he kept for the next five years.

Blake played for Canada again at the 1996 World Cup of Hockey, when the team lost to the United States in a best-of-three finals, and he won a second World Championship gold medal with Canada in 1997. He was named Best Defenceman by the IIHF Directorate at that tournament.

Through all these years he provided Los Angeles and Team Canada with a special type of defence few could provide. Blake was big and strong, making it an unpleasant task for any opponent to try to station himself in front of Blake's goalie. He was physical, to be sure, but he also skated well, moved quickly, and got the puck out of his own end as well as anyone. He also had excellent offensive skills. At the same time, his physical play took its toll on his body. He missed small numbers of games throughout his career for various injuries, from back and ankle problems to a broken leg and groin, jaw, and foot injuries.

In 1997–98, he won the Norris Trophy as the league's best blueliner, his first and only individual award. During that season, he played for Canada at the first-ever Olympics with full NHL participation, but Canada fell just short in the semi-finals and had to settle for fourth place.

Blake was one of only two players from the Olympic team to accept the invitation to play at the 1998 World Championship after the season (with Keith Primeau), and he played at his sixth Worlds a year later. In the NHL, though, he was set to become a free agent, and with no new contract pending the Kings traded him to Colorado at the deadline in early 2001. The deal included Steve Reinprecht, while the Kings acquired Adam Deadmarsh, Aaron Miller, a first-round draft choice in 2001, a player to be named later, and future considerations. This proved to be a masterful acquisition for the Avs as Blake took the team to the Stanley Cup, the second criteria for Triple Gold Club candidacy.

Blake spent his day with the Stanley Cup at home in Simcoe, Ontario.

Blake was back with Team Canada for the 2002 Olympics midway through the following season, a team that featured captain Mario Lemieux, goalie Martin Brodeur, and veteran star Steve Yzerman. Blake was now more experienced and surrounded by a more formidable lineup, and this edition of Team Canada won gold with a 5–2 win over the United States in the final game, giving Blake all he needed to become a member of the Triple Gold Club.

He participated in his third Olympics in Turin in 2006, a disappointing seventh-place finish for Canada, and in the summer of 2006 Blake resigned with Los Angeles for two years. He finished his career with San Jose, retiring in 2010 at age 40 with some 1,270 NHL regular-season games to his credit (and another 146 in the playoffs).

Few defencemen of the modern era combined Blake's toughness with his leadership and offensive talent.

JOE
SAKIC

12

BIRTH PLACE: Burnaby, British Columbia, Canada
BIRTH DATE: July 7, 1969
POSITION: Centre—shoots left
HEIGHT: 5'11" (1.80 m)
WEIGHT: 195 lbs. (88.5 kg)

TRIPLE GOLD CLUB HONOURS

WORLD CHAMPIONSHIP 1994 (Canada)
STANLEY CUP 1996, 2001 (Colorado Avalanche)
OLYMPICS 2002 (Canada)

TGC AGE
32 YEARS, 232 DAYS

TGC MEMBER AS OF
FEBRUARY 24, 2002
OLYMPIC FINAL WIN VS. UNITED STATES

NHL		Regular Season					Playoffs				
Season	Team	GP	G	A	P	PIM	GP	G	A	P	PIM
1988–89	QUE	70	23	39	62	24			DNQ		
1989–90	QUE	80	39	63	102	27			DNQ		
1990–91	QUE	80	48	61	109	24			DNQ		
1991–92	QUE	69	29	65	94	20			DNQ		
1992–93	QUE	78	48	57	105	40	6	3	3	6	2
1993–94	QUE	84	28	64	92	18			DNQ		
1994–95	QUE	47	19	43	62	30	6	4	1	5	0
1995–96	COL	82	51	69	120	44	22	18	16	34	14
1996–97	COL	65	22	52	74	34	17	8	17	25	14
1997–98	COL	64	27	36	63	50	6	2	3	5	6
1998–99	COL	73	41	55	96	29	19	6	13	19	8
1999–2000	COL	60	28	53	81	28	17	2	7	9	8
2000–01	COL	82	54	64	118	30	21	13	13	26	6
2001–02	COL	82	26	53	79	18	21	9	10	19	4
2002–03	COL	58	26	32	58	24	7	6	3	9	2
2003–04	COL	81	33	54	87	42	11	7	5	12	8
2005–06	COL	82	32	55	87	60	9	4	5	9	6
2006–07	COL	82	36	64	100	46			DNQ		
2007–08	COL	44	13	27	40	20	10	2	8	10	0
2008–09	COL	15	2	10	12	6			DNP		
NHL Totals		1,378	625	1,016	1,641	614	172	84	104	188	78

Olympics						
Year	Team	GP	G	A	P	PIM	Finish
1998	CAN	4	1	2	3	4	4th
2002	CAN	6	4	3	7	0	G
2006	CAN	6	1	2	3	0	7th
Totals		16	6	7	13	4	G

World Championship						
Year	Team	GP	G	A	P	PIM	Finish
1991	CAN	10	6	5	11	0	S
1994	CAN	8	4	3	7	0	G
Totals		18	10	8	18	0	G,S

• Conn Smythe Trophy (1996), Lester B. Pearson Award (2000–01),
Hart Trophy (2000–01), Lady Byng Trophy (2000–01)

Captain of Canada's 2006 Olympic team, Joe Sakic receives his TGC honours at the inaugural ceremony in Vancouver.

Q uite simply one of the greatest hockey players in the game's history, Joe Sakic is as likely a member of the Triple Gold Club as any player. He was a winner at every level he played, and his consistency was undiminished by time. Indeed, he won IIHF events in three decades, starting with gold at the 1988 World Junior Championship, before embarking on a professional and senior career that carried him to Triple Gold Club glory early in the 21st century.

In fact, to pare down the list of Triple Gold Club winners, he is the only player to have won the TGC and been named winner of the Conn Smythe Trophy (as playoff MVP) and tournament MVP at the Olympics.

While Sakic's junior career with Swift Current in the WHL was exceptional, his life was changed forever on December 30, 1986, when the team bus crashed on the way to a game in Regina. Four team-mates were killed, and Sakic was lucky to survive. The incident was never far from his thoughts, though he had a sensational season on-ice and was selected

15th overall by the Quebec Nordiques at the 1987 Entry Draft. Sakic opted to stay in the WHL for another season and had another stellar year in junior while also leading Canada to gold at the U20 championship in Moscow. In the fall of 1988 the 19-year-old was ready for the NHL. Only an ankle injury slowed him down in an otherwise strong rookie season. And in his second year he had 102 points, portents of even greater things to come.

These early years were opportune for Sakic because the Nordiques were a terrible team. He could develop out of the spotlight, and the team was able to draft first overall three years in a row, selecting Mats Sundin (1989), Owen Nolan (1990), and Eric Lindros (1991). Lindros refused to report to the Nordiques, and the team traded him to Philadelphia in a large deal that saw Peter Forsberg come to Quebec. Everything was starting to fall into place for a young team to develop as one. In four of his first six full NHL seasons

Sakic played his entire career with the Quebec Nordiques/Colorado Avalanche franchise and captained the team for 17 of his 21 NHL seasons.

Sakic eclipsed 100 points, and when the team moved to Colorado in the summer of 1995, it was ready to take on the best the league could offer.

On the international front, Sakic played at the 1991 World Championship, winning a silver medal, and three years later he won his first TGC event by helping Canada win gold at the Worlds, the nation's first since 1961.

By no means the biggest or toughest player, Sakic learned to thrive in the NHL by using his lightning-quick wrist shot to great effect and becoming one of the best playmakers in the game. He was often called "Gentleman Joe" for his demeanour on ice and off (averaging only 30 penalty minutes a season), a class act and ambassador for the sport who was virtually unmatched.

The Avalanche acquired goalie Patrick Roy during the 1995–96 season and went on to win the Stanley Cup in its first year in Denver, and Sakic, in his fourth year as team captain, hoisted the silverware

above his head to clinch TGC criteria number two. He scored a record eight game-winning goals in the playoffs (two in overtime) and was named Conn Smythe Trophy winner for his outstanding performance during hockey's gruelling "second season." As always, he was a winner in large measure because of his own performance, not relying on others to win the glory for him.

His career reached its pinnacle early in the 21st century. In 2000–01, he led the Avs to a second Cup victory. He had a career-high 54 goals in the regular season, and after the season he was named winner of the Hart Trophy, Lester B. Pearson Award, and Lady Byng Trophy. It marked the first time a player had been named the most gentlemanly in the same season he was named MVP by both reporters and players.

Known for his amazing wrist shot, "gentleman Joe" was also known for being one of the most gentlemanly and sporting players in the game's history.

By the time he retired in the summer of 2009, Sakic and the term *all-time* could be spoken together in many ways. His games-played, goals, assists, and points totals put him among the all-time leaders in those categories in NHL play (1,378; 625; 1,016; and 1,641, respectively). In all, he surpassed the 100-point mark in a season six times, most recently in 2006–07 at age 37, and twice he reached 50 goals in a year. His 20 seasons with one organization also puts him in elite company, and his 16-year tenure as captain of Quebec/Colorado is also one of the longest all-time in any team sport.

Motivation was never a problem for Gentleman Joe, and he played with the same intensity game in, game out, year after year. He was named to Canada's Olympic team for 1998, a disappointing fourth-place finish, but in 2002 everything fell into place. While goalie Martin Brodeur proved to be rock-solid in net, and Mario Lemieux the great leader, Sakic quietly put in a career performance. Canada won gold, and Sakic became a new member of the Triple Gold Club, along with Rob Blake and Brendan Shanahan. Sakic was a dominant presence on ice, scoring four goals in six games, and being named the team's MVP after the medals were presented.

Sakic passed all the great milestones a player dreams about as a kid, scoring his 500th goal, 1,000th point, and playing in his 1,000th game. He also played for Canada again at the 2004 World Cup, another victory, and in 2006, when Mario Lemieux retired, he was named captain of Canada's Olympic team for Turin.

Sakic was inducted into the Hockey Hall of Fame in 2012, and it's only a matter of time before the IIHF accords him a similar honour for his outstanding international career. The Avs, of course, retired his number 19, and while hockey continues to be played throughout the world, it is a lesser place without Joe Sakic in the lineup.

In addition to his TGC credentials, Sakic also won the World Cup and World Juniors with Canada.

13 BRENDAN SHANAHAN

BIRTH PLACE: Mimico, Ontario, Canada
BIRTH DATE: January 23, 1969
POSITION: Left wing—shoots right
HEIGHT: 6'3" (1.91 m)
WEIGHT: 220 lbs. (97.8 kg)

TRIPLE GOLD CLUB HONOURS

WORLD CHAMPIONSHIP 1994 (Canada)
STANLEY CUP 1997, 1998, 2002 (Detroit Red Wings)
OLYMPICS 2002 (Canada)

TGC AGE
33 YEARS, 32 DAYS

TGC MEMBER AS OF
FEBRUARY 24, 2002
OLYMPIC FINAL WIN VS. UNITED STATES

NHL		Regular Season					Playoffs				
Season	Team	GP	G	A	P	PIM	GP	G	A	P	PIM
1987–88	NJ	65	7	19	26	131	12	2	1	3	44
1988–89	NJ	68	22	28	50	115			DNQ		
1989–90	NJ	73	30	42	72	137	6	3	3	6	20
1990–91	NJ	75	29	37	66	141	7	3	5	8	12
1991–92	STL	80	33	36	69	171	6	2	3	5	14
1992–93	STL	71	51	43	94	174	11	4	3	7	18
1993–94	STL	81	52	50	102	211	4	2	5	7	4
1994–95	STL	45	20	21	41	136	5	4	5	9	14
1995–96	HAR	74	44	34	78	125			DNQ		
1996–97	HAR/DET	81	47	41	88	131	20	9	8	17	43
1997–98	DET	75	28	29	57	154	20	5	4	9	22
1998–99	DET	81	31	27	58	123	10	3	7	10	6
1999–2000	DET	78	41	37	78	105	9	3	2	5	10
2000–01	DET	81	31	45	76	81	2	2	2	4	0
2001–02	DET	80	37	38	75	118	23	8	11	19	20
2002–03	DET	78	30	38	68	103	4	1	1	2	4
2003–04	DET	82	25	28	53	117	12	1	5	6	20
2005–06	DET	82	40	41	81	105	6	1	1	2	6
2006–07	NYR	67	29	33	62	47	10	5	2	7	12
2007–08	NYR	73	23	23	46	35	10	1	4	5	8
2008–09	NJ	34	6	8	14	29	7	1	2	3	2
NHL Totals		1,524	656	698	1,354	2,489	184	60	74	134	279

Olympics							
Year	Team	GP	G	A	P	PIM	Finish
1998	CAN	6	2	0	2	0	4th
2002	CAN	6	0	1	1	0	G
Totals		12	2	1	3	0	G

World Championship							
Year	Team	GP	G	A	P	PIM	Finish
1994	CAN	6	4	3	7	6	G
2006	CAN	8	3	1	4	10	4th
Totals		14	7	4	11	16	G

- King Clancy Trophy (2002–03)

Absolutely unique among not only Triple Gold Club members but all world-class players, Brendan Shanahan was both a fierce competitor in the NHL as a premier power forward and also a scoring star in international play. He could drop the gloves to stand up for a teammate or make a statement to opponents (NHL), or he could leave them on and score as well as any forward in any tournament (Team Canada). He is without doubt the only power forward in the TGC and is the only player in NHL history to have scored 600 goals and accrued more than 2,000 penalty minutes.

Shanahan was born to play hockey. During his short but brilliant career in junior hockey, with the London Knights of the OHL (1985–87), he quickly earned a reputation as scorer and physical player both. He also played for Canada's ill-fated World Junior team in 1987, one that was on its way to a medal when the Soviets, out of the medals, partook in a fight that was the famous Piestany brawl and disqualification.

Shanahan wasn't able to earn retribution a year later, though. He was NHL-bound after being drafted second overall by New Jersey in the summer of 1987. While the team wasn't very good, he developed quickly, going from 7 to 22 to 30 goals in his first three seasons.

But it was four years into his career, when he signed with St. Louis, that he blossomed into a premier player in the league. The signing, however, was one of the most contentious in league history. The year was 1991, and teams that lost a player to free agency were awarded equal compensation. So, when the Devils lost Shanahan, they petitioned the league for Scott Stevens, one of the premier young defencemen in the game. The Blues countered by offering a package that included Curtis Joseph and Rod Brind'Amour, but the ruling went in favour of the Devils. So the Blues got the best young power forward in the game, and the Devils got what turned out to be a franchise player around whom a Cup-quality team could be developed.

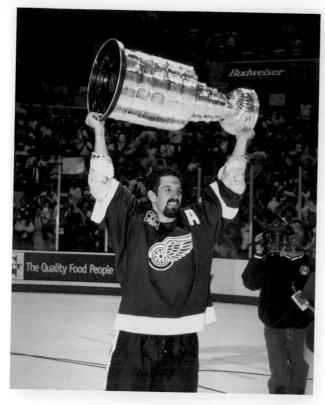

"Shanny" won the Stanley Cup three times with Detroit – in 1997, 1998, and 2002.

attention to defence and team play. "Shanny" was still a consistent 30-goal scorer, but the team racked up wins with almost unparalleled consistency. He was among the team's top forwards, but he also paid greater attention to the puck in his own end, and the results in the playoffs were impressive.

The Red Wings won the Cup in each of his first two years, and in February 1998 he also played for Canada at the Olympics, finishing fourth. As it turned out, 2002 was a career year for Shanahan. He became one of a small group of players to win the Stanley Cup and Olympic gold in the same year. In his case, the Olympic victory came in Salt Lake in February 2002, where he and teammate Steve Yzerman helped Canada win gold for the first time in half a century. Just a few months later, the pair won the Cup with Detroit again, establishing the Wings as the finest team of this generation.

Shanahan had seasons of 51 and 52 goals in '92–'93 and '93–'94, and his 102 points in the latter season with the Blues proved to be a career best for him. The team never went far in the playoffs, though, and in 1994 he accepted an invitation to play in the World Championship. Shanahan helped Canada win gold, his first Triple Gold Club notch.

After four years with the Blues, he was traded in another blockbuster deal. This time he went to Hartford while St. Louis acquired Chris Pronger, the next great defenceman in the game after Stevens. After only a little more than a year with the Whalers, Shanahan requested a trade and was sent to Detroit early in the 1997–98 season. It was here that he spent nine seasons and captured three Stanley Cups with the Red Wings, in 1997, 1998, and 2002.

Although his goalscoring dropped with the Red Wings, it wasn't because of a loss of speed or skill. Instead, it was because the coaching philosophy of Scotty Bowman demanded greater

Shanahan is the only player to have scored 600 goals and accrued 2,000 penalty minutes during his NHL career, indicators of both his skill around the net and toughness all over the ice.

Shanahan's last appearance with Canada was Sidney Crosby's first at the senior level – the 2006 World Championship.

telling being his 656 goals and 2,489 penalty minutes. His 1,524 games played and 1,354 total points also rank him among the greats of the game, and when he is eligible he will surely be inducted into the Hockey Hall of Fame and IIHF Hall of Fame.

As much as he was respected and commanded respect on-ice, Shanahan was a sportsman and ambassador for the game off-ice. During the lockout of 2004–05, he organized a "summit" of sorts to try to deal with pertinent issues pertaining to improving the game, and he was forever promoting the game to those who mattered the most—the fans.

His career may show he is a member of the Triple Gold Club, but his reputation shows something just as valuable—he was one of hockey's finest men.

They were the first to win this incredible double since Ken Morrow in 1980 with Team USA and the New York Islanders. The Olympic gold gave Shanahan membership to the Triple Gold. Yzerman never won World Championship gold and as such never quite made it to TGC membership.

During Shanahan's 21 NHL seasons, his teams failed to qualify for the playoffs only twice. His streak of 19 consecutive seasons of 20 goals or more is second only to Mike Gartner all-time. Shanahan's only other international appearance came at the World Championship in 2006, at age 37, the same year 18-year-old Sidney Crosby made his World Championship debut (Crosby was only two months old when Shanahan made his NHL debut in October 1987).

Shanahan retired in 2009 with astounding statistics, most

Shanahan is one of the few players in hockey history to win Olympic gold and the Stanley Cup in the same season (2001–02).

14 SCOTT NIEDERMAYER

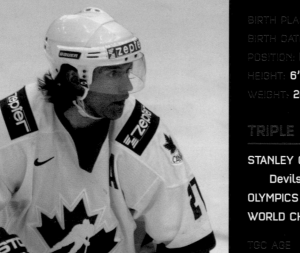

BIRTH PLACE: Edmonton, Alberta, Canada
BIRTH DATE: August 31, 1973
POSITION: Defence—shoots left
HEIGHT: 6' (1.83 m)
WEIGHT: 200 lbs. (90.7 kg)

TRIPLE GOLD CLUB HONOURS

STANLEY CUP 1995, 2000, 2003 (New Jersey
      Devils), 2007 (Anaheim Ducks)
OLYMPICS 2002 (Canada)
WORLD CHAMPIONSHIP 2004 (Canada)

TGC AGE
30 YEARS, 252 DAYS

TGC MEMBER AS OF
MAY 9, 2004
WORLD CHAMPIONSHIP FINAL WIN VS. SWEDEN

NHL		Regular Season					Playoffs				
Season	Team	GP	G	A	P	PIM	GP	G	A	P	PIM
1991–92	NJ	4	0	1	1	2	DNP				
1992–93	NJ	80	11	29	40	47	5	0	3	3	2
1993–94	NJ	81	10	36	46	42	20	2	2	4	8
1994–95	NJ	48	4	15	19	18	20	4	7	11	10
1995–96	NJ	79	8	25	33	46	DNQ				
1996–97	NJ	81	5	30	35	64	10	2	4	6	6
1997–98	NJ	81	14	43	57	27	6	0	2	2	4
1998–99	NJ	72	11	35	46	26	7	1	3	4	18
1999–2000	NJ	71	7	31	38	48	22	5	2	7	10
2000–01	NJ	57	6	29	35	22	21	0	6	6	14
2001–02	NJ	76	11	22	33	30	6	0	2	2	6
2002–03	NJ	81	11	28	39	62	24	2	16	18	16
2003–04	NJ	81	14	40	54	44	5	1	0	1	6
2005–06	ANA	82	13	50	63	96	16	2	9	11	14
2006–07	ANA	79	15	54	69	86	21	3	8	11	26
2007–08	ANA	48	8	17	25	16	6	0	2	2	4
2008–09	ANA	82	14	45	59	70	13	3	7	10	11
2009–10	ANA	80	10	38	48	38	DNQ				
NHL Totals		1,263	172	568	740	784	202	25	73	98	155

Olympics							
Year	Team	GP	G	A	P	PIM	Finish
2002	CAN	6	1	1	2	4	G
2010	CAN	7	1	2	3	4	G
Totals		13	2	3	5	8	2G

World Championship							
Year	Team	GP	G	A	P	PIM	Finish
2004	CAN	9	3	2	5	12	G

- James Norris Trophy (2003–04), Conn Smythe Trophy (2007)

Of all Triple Gold Club members, there is perhaps none who has won at more levels than Scott Niedermayer. In addition to the three honours of the TGC, he also won the Memorial Cup, with the Kamloops Blazers in 1992, at which he was also named MVP of the finals. He won the 1991 World Junior Championship and the 2004 World Cup of Hockey. That's six major championships in virtually every league and level possible. Wherever he played, he won.

Niedermayer comes from the line of defencemen that began with Bobby Orr in the 1970s and carried through to Paul Coffey in the 1980s. A gifted and powerful skater, as fluid as a dancer, he had outstanding offensive abilities to go with his exceptional play in his own end. That he played from the blue line allowed him to control play and move the puck up the ice like a general leading his army.

Drafted third overall in 1991, Niedermayer might well have started his career in Toronto, but the Leafs traded the third pick that year to New Jersey. He played the better part of three years with the Blazers

(1989–92), appearing in four games with the Devils in his final year. His junior career culminated with the Memorial Cup win. A year earlier he had played for Canada at the World Juniors, alongside Eric Lindros and Kris Draper, winning his first international medal.

By the end of his second full NHL season, 1993–94, Niedermayer had taken the Devils to the semi-finals of the playoffs, where they lost to the eventual champion New York Rangers. This was the year of Rangers captain Mark Messier's "guaranteed win," in which he promised victory in game six of a series the team was losing 3–2 and on the verge of being eliminated from, and while Niedermayer was on the losing end, he learned from the experience and became a better player as a result. One year later, he was hoisting the Cup himself, the Devils having swept an emerging Detroit team in four straight games in a season shortened to 48 games because of a lockout.

Scott (right) and brother Rob celebrate World Championship gold in 2004, the event that made Scott the 14th member of the Triple Gold Club.

Always able to skate the puck out of his own end, or make a perfect pass to clear the zone, he ensured the team played most of the game in the other team's end of the ice.

After the lost lockout season of 2004–05, Niedermayer was a free agent and opted to sign with Anaheim. The contract was worth $27 million over four years and made him one of the highest paid players in the game, but more important he signed for two more personal reasons.

First, the California coast was due south of his home in British Columbia; second, he wanted to play alongside his brother, Rob, who had been with the Ducks in 2002–03 when the Devils beat Anaheim to win their third Cup in eight seasons. Before the season started, he was named captain of the Ducks.

Part of Scott's decision to join Rob on the West Coast was the result of a memorable World Championship in 2004 in Prague, Czech Republic. Both brothers played for Canada that year, leading the team to an impressive gold medal. Indeed, Canada trailed Sweden 3–1 in the gold-medal game until Scott made a sensational pass to Dany Heatley, who scored, starting Canada's come-from-behind victory of 5–3. The Niedermayers' parents made the trip overseas to watch their sons play, and this familial experience proved to Scott that there was more to life than hockey.

The end of the 2003–04 season also saw Scott win the Norris Trophy, the first of two individual awards of his tremendous career. Later that fall, he played for Canada at the World Cup, adding another championship to his unique and unparalleled success.

The brothers thrived in Anaheim together and led the Ducks to the first California Cup, in 2006–07, defeating the Ottawa Senators in five games. Scott was named winner of the Conn Smythe Trophy for his exceptional playoffs, his combination of offence, defence, and leadership a key reason for the team's historic victory. The Niedermayers became the first brothers to win the Cup together since Duane and Brent Sutter in 1983. That Rob and Scott won the World Championship and Stanley Cup together marks the closest any brother combination has come to achieving Triple Gold Club status.

Although the circumstances might have afforded the Devils an easy chance to win the Cup, the team had a core of great players assembled by general manager Lou Lamoriello, starting with Martin Brodeur in goal and continuing with Niedermayer and Scott Stevens on defence. The Devils went to the Cup finals three more times, winning twice.

In 2000, they beat Dallas, winners the previous year, and in 2001 they lost to Colorado. Niedermayer's career reached new heights in February 2002 when he played for Canada at the Olympics in Salt Lake City. His calm and reliable presence under pressure played a major role in the team winning gold for the first time in half a century and gave him the second honour in his quest for Triple Gold Club membership.

While the team had plenty of offensive firepower, his leadership from the blue line was essential.

Niedermayer is one of the few players to have won gold with Canada at both the 2002 and 2010 Olympics.

Niedermayer had to withdraw from the 2006 Olympics because of a knee injury, and in the fall of 2007 he went into a sort of unofficial retirement. The season started, and he wasn't there, but finally in early December he returned to the club, invigorated and ready to play. When the Vancouver Olympics were at hand, Niedermayer was one of the first players named to the team – and he was made captain as well. That year saw Canada win gold on home ice, in his home province, and at season's end he retired from the game as, in some ways, the most successful player of all time.

Cut from the same cloth as Bobby Orr and Paul Coffey, Niedermayer was a brilliant skater from the blue line and a sensational offensive talent.

15

JAROMIR JAGR

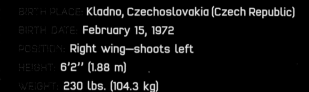

BIRTH PLACE: **Kladno, Czechoslovakia (Czech Republic)**
BIRTH DATE: **February 15, 1972**
POSITION: **Right wing—shoots left**
HEIGHT: **6'2" (1.88 m)**
WEIGHT: **230 lbs. (104.3 kg)**

TRIPLE GOLD CLUB HONOURS

STANLEY CUP 1991, 1992 (Pittsburgh Penguins)
OLYMPICS 1998 (Czech Republic)
WORLD CHAMPIONSHIP 2005 (Czech Republic)

TGC AGE
33 YEARS, 89 DAYS

TGC MEMBER AS OF
MAY 15, 2005
WORLD CHAMPIONSHIP FINAL WIN VS. CANADA

NHL		Regular Season					Playoffs				
Season	Team	GP	G	A	P	PIM	GP	G	A	P	PIM
1990-91	PIT	80	27	30	57	42	24	3	10	13	6
1991-92	PIT	70	32	37	69	34	21	11	13	24	6
1992-93	PIT	81	34	60	94	61	12	5	4	9	23
1993-94	PIT	80	32	67	99	61	6	2	4	6	16
1994-95	PIT	48	32	38	70	37	12	10	5	15	6
1995-96	PIT	82	62	87	149	96	18	11	12	23	18
1996-97	PIT	63	47	48	95	40	5	4	4	8	4
1997-98	PIT	77	35	67	102	64	6	4	5	9	2
1998-99	PIT	81	44	83	127	66	9	5	7	12	16
1999-2000	PIT	63	42	54	96	50	11	8	8	16	6
2000-01	PIT	81	52	69	121	42	16	2	10	12	18
2001-02	WAS	69	31	48	79	30			DNQ		
2002-03	WAS	75	36	41	77	38	6	2	5	7	2
2003-04	WAS/NYR	77	31	43	74	38			DNQ		
2005-06	NYR	82	54	69	123	72	3	0	1	1	2
2006-07	NYR	82	30	66	96	78	10	5	6	11	12
2007-08	NYR	82	25	46	71	58	10	5	10	15	12
2011-12	PHI	73	19	35	54	30	11	1	7	8	2
2012-13	DAL/BOS	45	16	19	35	22	22	0	10	10	8
NHL Totals		**1391**	**681**	**1007**	**1688**	**956**	**202**	**78**	**121**	**199**	**159**

- Art Ross Trophy (1994-95, 1997-98, 1998-99, 1999-2000, 2000-01)
- Lester B. Pearson Award (1998-99, 1999-2000, 2005-06)
- Hart Trophy (1998-99)

Olympics							
Year	Team	GP	G	A	P	PIM	Finish
1998	CZE	6	1	4	5	2	G
2002	CZE	4	2	3	5	4	7th
2006	CZE	8	2	5	7	6	B
2010	CZE	5	2	1	3	6	7th
	Totals	23	7	13	20	18	G,B

World Championship							
Year	Team	GP	G	A	P	PIM	Finish
1990	TCH	10	3	2	5	2	B
1994	CZE	3	0	2	2	2	7th
2002	CZE	7	4	4	8	2	5th
2004	CZE	7	5	4	9	6	5th
2005	CZE	6	2	7	9	2	G
2009	CZE	7	3	6	9	6	6th
2010	CZE	9	3	4	7	12	G
2011	CZE	9	5	4	9	4	B
	Totals	60	25	33	58	36	2G,2B

- IIHF Directorate World Championship Best Forward (2011)
- World Championship All-Star Team/ Forward (2004, 2005, 2011)

Jaromir Jagr receives his TGC honours at
the inaugural ceremony in Vancouver.

The ageless wonder that is Jaromir Jagr continues to play – and score and win. From a remarkable entrance into the NHL at age 18 to a career than now spans three decades, as many leagues, and more than 20 years of pro hockey, Jagr's has been a constant presence in hockey for what seems an eternity, thanks to a combination of skill and a focus on conditioning.

Few players could challenge Jaromir Jagr for title of best European player in NHL history. Drafted by Pittsburgh fifth overall in 1990, he was the first Czech player to join the NHL without having to defect. He had already played at the World Championship earlier that year, the last time Czech Republic competed before separating into two countries (Czech Republic and Slovakia), and he fit in perfectly on a Penguins team that featured Mario Lemieux.

By the end of his rookie season, Jagr had scored 27 goals, and by the end of the playoffs he was holding the Stanley Cup. He remains one of only two Triple Gold Club players who won the Stanley Cup in their first try (Tomas Jonsson is the other).

Despite being only 18 years old when he played his first NHL game, Jagr was mature beyond his years. He wore the number 68, a number he has used for every single game he has ever played since. It refers to 1968, the year Soviet tanks rolled through Wenceslas Square in downtown Prague to quash the Prague Spring, a brief period of freedom for the people of Czechoslovakia during the communist era. How remarkable the political change over the course of one man's career that he later sported that same number while playing for Avangard Omsk in Russia's top league in the 21st century (the Kontinental Hockey League).

Jagr was part of a second Stanley Cup team the next year, 1990–91, and although he went on to have a great career in the NHL, these have proved to be his only championships to date. He won the Art Ross Trophy for the first of five times in 1994–95, edging out Eric Lindros because of a superior goals total when both had 70 points in a lockout-shortened season.

While Jagr was always the second best player on the team when Lemieux dressed, life changed when Mario retired in the summer of 1997. Jagr was now 25 years old and in the prime of his career, and he was now the centerpiece of the team. On-ice he thrived; off-ice he felt uncomfortable because of his lack of English skills.

Nevertheless, Jagr averaged 105 points over the next four years and won the Art Ross Trophy in each season. He had set personal best totals in 1995–96 in goals (62), assists (87), and points (149), and three more times he managed to reach the 100-point mark.

Jagr's style of play was unique. Big and strong, he was adept at carrying the puck with one arm and fending off defenders with the other. He was immovable along the boards and guarded the puck with his body, literally barging into the slot and getting a good shot on goal despite being closely checked. As well, he was a brilliant stickhandler, leaving the puck in front of him and pulling it in tight when a checker thought he was vulnerable. His ability to pass or shoot with equal effectiveness made him difficult to check—and impossible to stop altogether.

It was in 1998 that Jagr was part of the Czech Republic's gold medal victory at the Olympics, the first time the nation had won. Two days later, when the entire team was feted by hundreds of thousands of fans in the same Wenceslas Square that had seen Soviet tanks exactly 30 years earlier, number 68 was front and centre as one of the country's greatest heroes. For years the nation existed under the communist thuggery of the Soviet Union, but now, just five years after its own independence, the new Czech Republic had won an historic gold.

The final game of the 1998–99 season was historic for two reasons. The afternoon of April 18, 1999, was the final game in the career of Wayne Gretzky, then of the New York Rangers. The Penguins were in town to play at Madison Square

A brilliant rookie, Jagr benefited from Pittsburgh Penguin teammate Mario Lemieux's genius as "JJ" won the Stanley Cup in his first two NHL seasons.

No player in Czech hockey history has won more and is more revered than Jagr.

Jagr won his World Championship gold at the end of the lockout season, 2004–05, capping a season that saw him play in his hometown of Kladno while the NHL was shut down. It was a fitting victory for a player who embodied international hockey. A European who thrived and dominated in the NHL, he also represented his country just about every chance he got.

It was clear the change of scenery did him good, though. In his first full season on Broadway, 2005–06, he was once again a star attraction, racking up 54 goals and 123 points and winning the Lester B. Pearson Award for the third time. Nevertheless, the team had little success in the playoffs, and in 2008 he left the NHL to play in the KHL. In 2011, he ended his three-year absence and signed with Philadelphia, and at 39 years of age he still managed 19 goals and 54 points.

Jagr is the very embodiment of the Triple Gold Club. He is the all-time goals and points leader among European NHLers, and his international career with the Czech Republic over more than 20 years places him among the greatest national players of all time for his country.

Garden, and it was Jagr who scored the overtime goal to give the visitors the 2–1 win. Jagr asked for Gretzky's final game-used stick after the win, but the on-ice transition went the other way. Jagr won the Art Ross and Hart Trophies and the Lester B. Pearson Award that year, and he won the scoring title again the next two seasons, the fourth and fifth times in his career. Gretzky was being succeeded by Jagr.

But when Lemieux came out of retirement in 2000, there was an uneasy relationship as the current star had to cede his place to the old guard. As well, Jagr's salary couldn't be supported by the Pens, so they traded him to Washington. It was not a successful move, as he went from 121 points in his last season with the Pens down to 79, 77, and finally 74. Midway through this third season he was sent to the Rangers.

Big and imposing, Jagr was virtually impossible to move off the puck, and he often generated scoring chances by sheer force of will.

16

JIRI
SLEGR

BIRTH PLACE: **Jihlava, Czechoslovakia (Czech Republic)**
BIRTH DATE: **May 30, 1971**
POSITION: **Defence—shoots left**
HEIGHT: **6' (1.83 m)**
WEIGHT: **210 lbs. (95.3 kg)**

TRIPLE GOLD CLUB HONOURS

OLYMPICS 1998 (Czech Republic)
STANLEY CUP 2002 (Detroit Red Wings)
WORLD CHAMPIONSHIP 2005 (Czech Republic)

TGC AGE
33 YEARS, 350 DAYS

TGC MEMBER AS OF
MAY 15, 2005
WORLD CHAMPIONSHIP FINAL WIN VS. CANADA

NHL			Regular Season					Playoffs			
Season	Team	GP	G	A	P	PIM	GP	G	A	P	PIM
1992–93	VAN	41	4	22	26	109	5	0	3	3	4
1993–94	VAN	78	5	33	38	86		DNP			
1994–95	VAN/EDM	31	2	10	12	46		DNQ			
1995–96	EDM	57	4	13	17	74		DNQ			
1997–98	PIT	73	5	12	17	109	6	0	4	4	2
1998–99	PIT	63	3	20	23	86	13	1	3	4	12
1999–2000	PIT	74	11	20	31	82	10	2	3	5	19
2000–01	PIT/ATL	75	8	26	34	96		DNQ			
2001–02	ATL/DET	46	3	6	9	59	1	0	0	0	2
2003–04	VAN/BOS	52	6	20	26	35	7	1	1	2	0
2005–06	BOS	32	5	11	16	56		DNQ			
NHL Totals		622	56	193	249	838	42	4	14	18	39

Olympics							
Year	Team	GP	G	A	P	PIM	Finish
1992	TCH	8	1	1	2	14	B
1998	CZE	6	1	0	1	8	G
Totals		14	2	1	3	22	G,B

World Championship							
Year	Team	GP	G	A	P	PIM	Finish
1997	CZE	8	1	1	2	35	B
1998	CZE	6	0	1	1	20	B
2004	CZE	7	0	2	2	10	5th
2005	CZE	9	0	0	0	6	G
Totals		30	1	4	5	71	G,2B

More than any other member of the Triple
Gold Club, Jiri Slegr was a peripatetic
hockey player for much of his career. He
dressed for six NHL teams over an 11-year career,
returned to Europe six times to play in leagues
across the continent, and still managed to find a way
to win the three titles needed for TGC membership. All of this was in large measure because he
might well be the finest defenceman to come out of
Czechoslovakia.

His success, however, is not surprising, given that
his father is Jiri Bubla, one of the best defencemen in
Czechoslovakian history. Bubla left the family when Jiri
Jr., was a small boy, and when Mrs. Bubla remarried,
she and Jiri took her new husband's name of Slegr.

Drafted by Vancouver 23rd overall in 1990 – the
same team for whom Bubla ended his pro career just
four years earlier – Slegr remained in Czechoslovakia
and played with Litvinov until 1992. In his final
season, he played for the Czechoslovaks at the
Albertville Olympics, winning a bronze medal, after
which he came to North America to play.

He played part of his North American rookie
season in the AHL, part with the Canucks in the NHL,
but he wasn't a member of the team when it reached
the Stanley Cup finals at the end of his second season.
These were difficult times for Slegr and Bubla. The
elder Bubla had fallen on hard times and was arrested
in Vienna in 1987 for trafficking cocaine and ended
up serving four years in an Austrian prison. Upon his
release, he returned to Vancouver and worked as a
janitor at the Pacific Coliseum, the same arena where
his estranged son was now a rising star. Father tried to
make amends with son, but Slegr wasn't interested at
the time, preferring to focus on hockey. After three
years Slegr was traded to Edmonton.

After a brief stint with the Oilers, Slegr ended
up in Pittsburgh, playing with compatriot Jaromir
Jagr. The trade was made in the summer of 1997
and saw the Oilers get a third-round draft choice (the
Oilers selected Brian Gionta 82nd overall with the

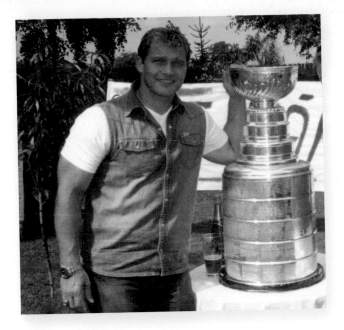
Slegr was one of many Europeans on the Detroit Red Wings' Stanley Cup-winning team in 2001–02.

team had more Europeans on it (nine) than any Cup-winning team in NHL history.

Like Jagr, Slegr returned home for the 2004–05 season when it became clear the NHL lockout would be a long one, returning as always to his Czech club team, Litvinov. He joined the Czech Republic national team after the regular season and, along with Jagr, helped the Czechs defeat Canada 3–0 in the gold-medal game, thus completing his Triple Gold Club membership. It was his fourth and final World Championship. He had won bronze medals in 1997 and 1998, and he played on the fifth-place team at the 2004 Worlds.

Slegr returned home to play after half a season with the Boston Bruins in 2005–06 and remained with Litvinov until he retired in 2010 (a brief stint in Switzerland the only exception).

Slegr's commitment to his hometown has extended beyond the hockey arena and into one far more aggressive – the political arena. Soon after he finished playing he was elected into the Chamber of Deputies as a member of the Social Democrat Party. A year later he left the party to form a new one called National Socialists – 21st Century Left, but he remained in parliament as an unaffiliated MP as well.

pick), but the Pens made the deal because Jagr was suffering from homesickness and having a friend who spoke the same language eased his life in Pittsburgh. For the Oilers, they managed to get something for a player who had returned home to the Czech Republic and played all of 1996–97 in Europe.

Both players were part of the historic 1998 Czech Olympic team that won gold, Slegr's first Triple Gold Club honour and the nation's first Olympic triumph. Slegr had only one goal in the tournament, but it was huge. He scored midway through the third period of the semi-finals game against Canada, putting the pressure on the favoured Canadians, who tied the game later but lost in a shootout. This was also the time in which Slegr played the longest sequence of years in the NHL, 1997–2002.

Trades in both 2000–01 and '01–'02 brought Slegr to Atlanta and then Detroit, and it was with the Red Wings in 2002 that he won the Stanley Cup. In all, he played only nine games with the Red Wings that championship season, but these were enough to get his name on the Cup. At the time, this Detroit

Although Slegr had a difficult relationship with his father, former player Jiri Bubla, the apple didn't fall far from the tree as far as hockey skills go.

Slegr played some 16 years of pro hockey, including stints with six NHL teams.

NICKLAS
LIDSTROM

17

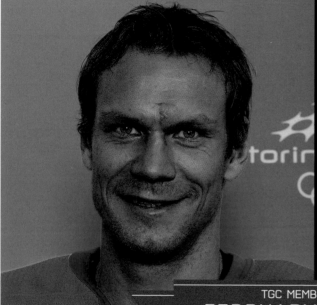

BIRTH PLACE: Vasteras, Sweden
BIRTH DATE: April 28, 1970
POSITION: Defence—shoots left
HEIGHT: 6'1'' (1.85 m)
WEIGHT: 190 lbs. (86.2 kg)

TRIPLE GOLD CLUB HONOURS

WORLD CHAMPIONSHIP 1991 (Sweden)
STANLEY CUP 1997, 1998, 2002 (Detroit Red Wings)
OLYMPICS 2006 (Sweden)

TGC AGE
35 YEARS, 304 DAYS

TGC MEMBER AS OF
FEBRUARY 26, 2006
OLYMPIC FINAL WIN VS. FINLAND

NHL		Regular Season					Playoffs				
Season	Team	GP	G	A	P	PIM	GP	G	A	P	PIM
1991-92	DET	80	11	49	60	22	11	1	2	3	0
1992-93	DET	84	7	34	41	28	7	1	0	1	0
1993-94	DET	84	10	46	56	26	7	3	2	5	0
1994-95	DET	43	10	16	26	6	18	4	12	16	8
1995-96	DET	81	17	50	67	20	19	5	9	14	10
1996-97	DET	79	15	42	57	30	20	2	6	8	2
1997-98	DET	80	17	42	59	18	22	6	13	19	8
1998-99	DET	81	14	43	57	14	10	2	9	11	4
1999-2000	DET	81	20	53	73	18	9	2	4	6	4
2000-01	DET	82	15	56	71	18	6	1	7	8	0
2001-02	DET	78	9	50	59	20	23	5	11	16	2
2002-03	DET	82	18	44	62	38	4	0	2	2	0
2003-04	DET	81	10	28	38	18	12	2	5	7	4
2005-06	DET	80	16	64	80	50	6	1	1	2	2
2006-07	DET	80	13	49	62	46	18	4	14	18	6
2007-08	DET	76	10	60	70	40	22	3	10	13	14
2008-09	DET	78	16	43	59	30	21	4	12	16	6
2009-10	DET	82	9	40	49	24	12	4	6	10	2
2010-11	DET	82	16	46	62	20	11	4	4	8	4
2011-12	DET	70	11	23	34	28	5	0	0	0	0
NHL Totals		1,564	264	878	1,142	514	263	54	129	183	76

Olympics							
Year	Team	GP	G	A	P	PIM	Finish
1998	SWE	4	1	1	2	2	5th
2002	SWE	4	1	5	6	0	5th
2006	SWE	8	2	4	6	2	G
2010	SWE	4	0	0	0	2	5th
Totals		20	4	10	14	6	G

World Championship							
Year	Team	GP	G	A	P	PIM	Finish
1991	SWE	10	3	3	6	4	G
1994	SWE	4	1	0	1	2	B
2004	SWE	2	0	1	1	0	S
Totals		16	4	4	8	6	G,S,B

- James Norris Trophy (2000-01, 2001-02, 2002-03, 2005-06, 2006-07, 2007-08), Conn Smythe Trophy (2002)

Nicklas Lidstrom receives his TGC honours at the inaugural ceremony in Vancouver.

As any of the 25 members of the Triple Gold Club will admit, you have to be good to be lucky and lucky to be good. In the case of Nicklas Lidstrom, it's both good and lucky that he won his World Championship gold before his NHL career began. The truth is that the Red Wings have been such consistent and successful playoff performers that he had almost no opportunity to play at the Worlds once he came to the NHL (notwithstanding brief appearances in 1994 and 2004 when he managed to win a bronze and silver medal, respectively). Indeed, by the time he retired in 2012 he had played 20 NHL seasons, all with Detroit, and qualified for the playoffs 20 times, a record of consistent excellence shared with only one other player – Larry Robinson.

Seventeen years before joining the Triple Gold Club, Lidstrom won the first honour of the TGC by winning the 1991 IIHF World Championship, a win made possible by Mats Sundin's incredible coast-to-coast goal in Turku, Finland, against the Soviets in the deciding game. It was only the second gold for Sweden at the Worlds in 30 years, but it was achieved with a lineup destined for greatness, including Hakan Loob, Mats Naslund, Bengt-Ake Gustafsson, and Kjell Samuelsson.

Given Lidstrom's extraordinary career, which will see him inducted into the IIHF Hall of Fame and the Hockey Hall of Fame just as soon as he becomes eligible, it is both amazing and not surprising that he was drafted 53rd overall in 1989 by Detroit – and in his second year of draft eligibility at that. Amazing because such a talent was passed over 52 times before his name was called; not surprising he was selected by Detroit because the Red Wings have been far and away the best NHL team at drafting Europeans over the last two decades.

Lidstrom was the very definition of poise. Not flashy, not dramatic, he was simply a defenceman without flaw, fault, or deficiency. He never gave the puck away, never missed his man, never made a bad decision, and never got into a fight despite being a

By the time Lidstrom won Olympic gold in 2006, the Triple Gold Club was well established and the great defenceman was happy to pose for this IIHF photo to commemorate the occasion.

season, but they were easily defeated by New Jersey in four straight games.

Two years later, though, they were back and had learned from their earlier loss, this time handing Philadelphia the broom in a four-game sweep and winning the team's first Stanley Cup in 42 years and giving Lidstrom two-thirds of his Triple Gold Club membership. The Red Wings repeated the next year, but as the decade came to a close it was clear that he was arguably the best defenceman in the game and without question the most underappreciated. All of that changed in the 21st century.

The Red Wings continued to be the best team of the past 20 years by winning their third Cup in 2002, and Lidstrom was named winner of the Conn Smythe Trophy, the first European so honoured. This win also came at a time when he won the Norris Trophy for the second of three straight years, becoming the first player since Bobby Orr to pull off a Norris hat trick, as it were. Further, he was the first European to win the Norris Trophy.

After inheriting the captaincy from the retired Steve Yzerman in 2006, Lidstrom became the first

large and physical presence when the situation called for as much. Of course, *never* in hockey means 99 per cent of the time, so Lidstrom wasn't quite perfect – maybe just the closest thing to perfection the NHL has ever seen.

He was drafted after only one year with Vasteras in Elitserien, where he stayed for two more seasons before joining Detroit in 1991 at age 21. His adjustment was seamless. As a rookie, he had 11 goals and 60 points and finished second in Calder Trophy voting behind Pavel Bure.

Lidstrom's timing was also excellent in that he was playing on a team with a star player and captain, Steve Yzerman, that was soon to get a coach who knew how to use great talent to create a Cup winner (Scotty Bowman). The Red Wings made it to the Cup finals in 1995, at the end of the lockout-shortened

Lidstrom's trademark was his nearly flawless play. He seemed never to make a bad pass or be out of position and displayed physicality and sportsmanship that were unique.

The great Swede became the first European to captain his team to the Stanley Cup when the Detroit Red Wings won in 2008.

European to be presented the Cup when he took the Red Wings to victory in 2008. That team had on it a record 12 European players, proof that a team doesn't have to consist of mostly North Americans with a few players from overseas blended into the mix. This victory came just a year and a half after Lidstrom completed the third and final piece of his Triple Gold Club puzzle – Olympic gold.

Sweden faced Finland in the final game in Turin 2006, and tension mounted when the game was tied 2–2 after two periods. At the faceoff to start the third period, Mats Sundin against Saku Koivu, Koivu broke his stick and raced to the bench to get a new one. At the same time, Sundin controlled the puck, skated in over the Finland blue line, and dropped the puck to Lidstrom. He ripped a shot past goalie Miikka Kiprusoff, and this proved to be the only goal of the third period. The first two goals were also scored by Triple Gold Club members – Henrik Zetterberg and Niklas Kronwall. The win gave Sweden its second Olympic gold in the last four Games.

As the centrepiece to the grand success of the Red Wings, Lidstrom was nominated for the Norris Trophy 12 times in the last 14 years of his career,

winning seven times and putting him in a small class whose names include Bobby Orr and Doug Harvey.

The career summary of Lidstrom reads like a shopping list of great achievements. In addition to his status as a Triple Gold Club member, he is the all-time leader among Europeans in games played (1,564), the oldest Norris Trophy winner (41, in 2011–12, his final season), and one of a rare group of defencemen to reach 1,000 career points. He also holds several team records, but perhaps most amazingly – and strangely – he never won the Lady Byng Trophy despite being one of the most sporting and gentlemanly players of his generation. He never had more than 50 penalty minutes in a season and had 514 over 20 years, an average of only 26 PIMs a year.

No matter. His place in hockey history, both in the NHL and for Tre Kronor, will endure for decades to come.

FREDRIK MODIN

18

BIRTH PLACE: Sundsvall, Sweden
BIRTH DATE: October 8, 1974
POSITION: Left wing—shoots left
HEIGHT: 6'4" (1.93 m)
WEIGHT: 215 lbs. (97.5 kg)

TRIPLE GOLD CLUB HONOURS

WORLD CHAMPIONSHIP 1998 (Sweden)
STANLEY CUP 2004 (Tampa Bay Lightning)
OLYMPICS 2006 (Sweden)

TGC AGE
31 YEARS, 141 DAYS

TGC MEMBER AS OF
FEBRUARY 26, 2006
OLYMPIC FINAL WIN VS. FINLAND

NHL

Season	Team	GP	G	A	P	PIM	GP	G	A	P	PIM
				Regular Season					Playoffs		
1996–97	TOR	76	6	7	13	24			DNQ		
1997–98	TOR	74	16	16	32	32			DNQ		
1998–99	TOR	67	16	15	31	35	8	0	0	0	6
1999–2000	TB	80	22	26	48	18			DNQ		
2000–01	TB	76	32	24	56	48			DNQ		
2001–02	TB	54	14	17	31	27			DNQ		
2002–03	TB	76	17	23	40	43	11	2	0	2	18
2003–04	TB	82	29	28	57	32	23	8	11	19	10
2005–06	TB	77	31	23	54	56	5	0	0	0	6
2006–07	CBJ	79	22	20	42	50			DNQ		
2007–08	CBJ	23	6	6	12	12			DNQ		
2008–09	CBJ	50	9	16	25	28	4	1	0	1	0
2009–10	CBJ/LA	44	5	6	11	26	6	3	1	4	2
2010–11	ATL/CAL	40	7	3	10	14			DNP		
NHL Totals		898	232	230	462	453	57	14	12	26	42

Olympics

Year	Team	GP	G	A	P	PIM	Finish
2006	SWE	8	2	1	3	6	G
2010	SWE	3	0	1	1	0	5th
Totals		11	2	2	4	6	G

World Championship

Year	Team	GP	G	A	P	PIM	Finish
1996	SWE	6	1	1	2	4	6th
1998	SWE	5	3	3	6	2	G
2000	SWE	7	3	1	4	4	7th
2001	SWE	9	3	2	5	10	B
Totals		27	10	7	17	20	G,B

Fredrick Modin receives his TGC honours at the inaugural ceremony in Vancouver.

The Triple Gold Club comprises such a unique trio of events that there is no such thing as a fluke member. Perhaps the easiest third of the membership is the Stanley Cup because an individual doesn't have to be a superstar to make the team. He simply has to do a particular job on a team well, even if that means fighting, checking, penalty killing, or taking faceoffs. But the international events require a player to be among the very best from his nation, and in order to win two-thirds of the TGC membership, the player must also be from a nation that is world class year after year.

For instance, Anze Kopitar of Slovenia is among the finest young stars in the NHL, and his play was a critical factor in the success of the Los Angeles Kings winning the Cup in 2012. But he has zero chance to join the TGC because no matter how great a star he is for his country, his country simply can't come close to competing for Olympic or World Championship gold.

Which brings us to perhaps the most curious and unlikely member of the TGC as it stands today, Fredrik Modin. He might not be the purest scorer, the fastest skater, or the finest passer, but Modin played his best when it counted the most, giving him a rather unexpected membership into the Triple Gold Club.

Drafted by the Toronto Maple Leafs 64th overall in 1994 after three years with Timra in the second division of Swedish pro hockey, the 19-year-old graduated to Brynas of Elitserien, where he played two more years before coming to North America to play in the NHL. Not the most graceful skater, he did, however, possess one of the best wrist shots in the game, a shot that could easily match up well against the slap shot of many players.

Although he wasn't named to Sweden's Olympic team of 1998, he was selected for Tre Kronor at the World Championship in Switzerland at the end of the 1997–98 season, his second with the Leafs. Toronto missed the playoffs, and Modin gladly joined. He scored three goals in five games, playing on a line with Toronto teammate Mats Sundin and Peter Forsberg, and Sweden won gold, giving Modin the first honour of the Triple Gold Club.

But in his three years with the Leafs, Modin lacked the confidence to use his incredible shot with any frequency, and the left winger was traded to Tampa Bay after three seasons of 6, 16, and 16 goals. Toronto got Cory Cross and a seventh-round draft choice in 2001 in a deal that seemed minor at the time.

Modin was fortunate enough to be joining a Lightning team that had enormous talent among its

If Modin is an unlikely member of the TGC, his Stanley Cup win with the unheralded Tampa Bay Lightning in 2004 is perhaps even more so.

young players, notably the great threesome of Vincent Lecavalier, Martin St. Louis, and Brad Richards. Modin flourished during his six years with Tampa Bay, slowly but surely gaining confidence and using that hard shot to better and better effect. He had 22 goals in his first season with the Lightning and a career best 32 the following year, but the team failed to qualify for the playoffs in his first three seasons.

In 2003–04, Modin had 29 goals and a career-best 57 points during the regular season, but in the playoffs he took his game to another level, recording 19 points in 23 games and being a big part of the team's improbable Stanley Cup victory. Coached by the ebullient and emotional John Tortorella, the

Modin's best attribute was his shot, a heavy and thunderous weapon that coaches inveighed him to use as often as possible.

team beat Calgary 2–1 in game seven of a classic finals series, giving Modin his second championship of the Triple Gold Club.

His performance here was the first of three important stages to the third and final criteria. After the Cup win, Modin was selected to play for Tre Kronor at the World Cup of Hockey in September 2004, and once again he rose to the occasion and was among the team's best players. Right after the World Cup the league shut down in a bitter lockout, but Modin returned to Timra to play. He then had an excellent start to the 2005–06 season, thus earning a spot on Sweden's team for the 2006 Olympics in Turin.

Modin wasn't the best player on the team, and he wasn't expected to score the winning goal every game, but he did chip in two goals, one against Switzerland in the preliminary round, the other against the Czechs in the quarter-finals. He also played responsibly at both ends of the ice, a factor that contributed

In 14 NHL seasons with six teams, Modin had 232 goals in 898 career games.

to the team's gold medal. The Olympic victory gave him full membership into the Triple Gold Club.

And so, as Triple Gold Club tradition demands, an IIHF official and a photographer ran down to the Swedish dressing room after the victory to take a photograph of Modin displaying his gold medal. He may have won the Stanley Cup thanks to a bit of luck and good timing, but he earned a spot on his national team and won the IIHF components of TGC membership due to skill and good team play.

At the end of the 2005–06 season he was traded to the lowly Columbus Blue Jackets and later played with Los Angeles, making a final appearance for his country at the 2010 Olympics in Vancouver. Injuries, notably to his back, started to take their toll, and he retired in the summer of 2011 after a 14-year NHL career and two glorious victories for Sweden.

19

CHRIS
PRONGER

BIRTH PLACE: **Dryden, Ontario, Canada**
BIRTH DATE: **October 10, 1974**
POSITION: **Defence—shoots left**
HEIGHT: **6'6" (1.98 m)**
WEIGHT: **210 lbs. (95.3 kg)**

TRIPLE GOLD CLUB HONOURS

WORLD CHAMPIONSHIP 1997 (Canada)
OLYMPICS 2002, 2010 (Canada)
STANLEY CUP 2007 (Anaheim Ducks)

TGC AGE
32 YEARS, 239 DAYS

TGC MEMBER AS OF
JUNE 6, 2007
STANLEY CUP WIN VS. OTTAWA

NHL		Regular Season					Playoffs				
Season	Team	GP	G	A	P	PIM	GP	G	A	P	PIM
1993–94	HAR	81	5	25	30	113			DNQ		
1994–95	HAR	43	5	9	14	54			DNQ		
1995–96	STL	78	7	18	25	110	13	1	5	6	16
1996–97	STL	79	11	24	35	143	6	1	1	2	22
1997–98	STL	81	9	27	36	180	10	1	9	10	26
1998–99	STL	67	13	33	46	113	13	1	4	5	28
1999–2000	STL	79	14	48	62	92	7	3	4	7	32
2000–01	STL	51	8	39	47	75	15	1	7	8	32
2001–02	STL	78	7	40	47	120	9	1	7	8	24
2002–03	STL	5	1	3	4	10	7	1	3	4	14
2003–04	STL	80	14	40	54	88	5	0	1	1	16
2005–06	EDM	80	12	44	56	74	24	5	16	21	26
2006–07	ANA	66	13	46	59	69	19	3	12	15	26
2007–08	ANA	72	12	31	53	128	6	2	3	5	12
2008–09	ANA	82	11	37	48	88	13	2	8	10	12
2009–10	PHI	82	10	45	55	79	23	4	14	18	36
2010–11	PHI	50	4	21	25	44	3	0	1	1	4
2011–12	PHI	13	1	11	12	10			DNP		
NHL Totals		1,167	157	541	698	1,590	173	26	95	121	326

Olympics							
Year	Team	GP	G	A	P	PIM	Finish
1998	CAN	6	0	0	0	4	4th
2002	CAN	6	0	1	1	2	G
2006	CAN	6	1	2	3	16	7th
2010	CAN	7	0	5	5	2	G
Totals		25	1	8	9	24	2G

World Championship							
Year	Team	GP	G	A	P	PIM	Finish
1997	CAN	9	0	2	2	12	G

- James Norris Trophy (1999–2000), Hart Trophy (1999–2000)

Perhaps the most ironic statement in NHL history is this: "I'm glad I got drafted first because no one remembers number two." Those words were uttered by Alexandre Daigle after being the top selection of the 1993 NHL Entry Draft, and while Daigle went on to become one of the biggest busts in draft history, number two, Chris Pronger, went on to a career that will land him in the Hockey Hall of Fame and the IIHF Hall of Fame in due course.

One of the most dominant defencemen of the modern era, Pronger is the only Canadian to have appeared in the first four Olympics featuring NHL players (1998–2010), and his 18-year NHL career is a veritable resumé of success and victory.

Drafted by Hartford after two impressive years with the Peterborough Petes in the OHL, Pronger made the team in the fall of 1993 as an 18-year-old. Although he was talented and ready for the pros, the Whalers did him no favours by being one of the weakest teams in the league. Two years later, though, the team signed free agent Brendan Shanahan from

St. Louis, and the Blues received Pronger as compensation, changing the young man's life forever.

St. Louis was coached by Mike Keenan, who at the time lived up to his reputation as Iron Mike with every practice he coached, every game he stood behind the bench. Pronger was forced to become more disciplined in life and on the blue line and developed into the best defenceman in the game. He was nasty, big, strong, and highly skilled on offence. He could lead the power play, kill penalties, and dominate at both ends of the ice. He often played more than 30 minutes a game.

Pronger made his international debut with Canada at the 1997 World Championship. The Blues had been ousted by Detroit in six games in the first round of the playoffs, so Pronger headed to Helsinki to play on a team laden with talent in the form of Owen Nolan, Mark Recchi, and Jarome Iginla, to name but a few stars.

Given Pronger's annual playoff success, it's difficult to believe that his only Stanley Cup win was in 2007 with the Anaheim Ducks.

million contract upon his arrival in Edmonton in the summer of 2005 amid hoopla and optimism unseen in Edmonton since the Gretzky–Messier days of nearly two decades earlier. He had an immediate impact with a team that had a perfect blend of young and veteran players, and he brought his own influence to the team. At mid-season he played for Canada at the Turin Olympics, and back in the NHL the Oilers went to the Stanley Cup finals before losing to Carolina in game seven.

But what seemed like the start of a new era of success in Edmonton came to an abrupt end. Rumour had it that Pronger's wife didn't like Edmonton, but officially it was suggested only that personal reasons led to Pronger asking for a trade in the summer of 2006. Oilers general manager Kevin Lowe managed to pull off a blockbuster, and Pronger went to Anaheim

Canada beat Sweden 2–1 in the deciding game of a best-of-three finals (the only time the World Championship final has had this format), and Pronger was on his way to Triple Gold Club glory.

In the prime of his career, Pronger won both the Norris and Hart trophies in 1999–2000, the first defenceman to do so since Bobby Orr in 1971–72. He bettered Jaromir Jagr by one point in the Hart Trophy balloting, the closest voting ever to that time.

A year and a half later, he was one of the anchors of Canada's Olympic team, which won gold at Salt Lake City, Canada's first Olympic gold in 50 years. That he did so playing on the larger international ice attested to his tremendous abilities. A purely physical defenceman would have had troubles with the wider ice, but Pronger adjusted without problems.

After the lockout, Pronger was traded to the Oilers in a huge deal, signing a five-year, $31

Pronger was the only Canadian to play in the first four Olympics featuring NHL participation (1998–2010), winning two gold medals.

Pronger was an enormous defenceman who moved the puck up the ice with seeming ease, using his size and skill to advantage.

to join Scott Niedermayer as the best one-two blue-line combination in the NHL. The Oilers sent the defenceman to Anaheim for Joffrey Lupul, Ladislav Smid, a first-round draft choice in 2007, a second-round draft choice in 2008, and a conditional draft choice in 2008 (which turned out to be 22nd overall, with which Edmonton selected Jordan Eberle).

While Edmonton's stock plummeted, Anaheim's soared, and for a second year Pronger led his team to the Cup finals, this time winning. The Ducks beat Ottawa in five games, and with the win Pronger had now achieved all three honours associated with the Triple Gold Club, becoming its 19th member.

On June 27, 2009, the ever-active Philadelphia Flyers acquired Pronger in another huge trade, and to no one's surprise the big defenceman had a big impact. He took the Flyers to the Cup finals in his first season, 2009–10, but the Flyers lost to Chicago in six games.

While his style of play often resulted in injuries, none were particularly worrisome until 2011–12 when he suffered a knee injury and then was involved in a scary incident in which he was poked in the eye by an errant stick. Soon after he returned, he suffered a concussion, and he has yet to return to the lineup. Nearing 40, his career might well be over because of post-concussion syndrome, but his place in hockey's history has long been established.

A veteran of more than 1,000 NHL games, a Triple Gold Club member, and the only Canadian to have played in the first four Olympics involving full NHL participation, Pronger ranks among the greatest defencemen of the modern game. He may have been big and strong and offensively gifted, but even more impressive he was a winner everywhere he went. Never a passenger, he was a leader.

NIKLAS
KRONWALL

20

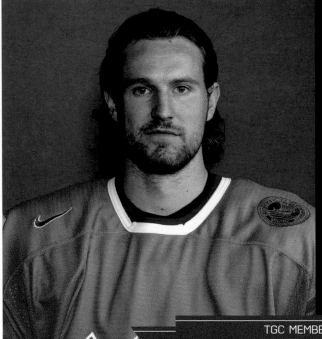

BIRTH PLACE: **Stockholm, Sweden**
BIRTH DATE: **January 12, 1981**
POSITION: **Defence—shoots left**
HEIGHT: **6' (1.83 m)**
WEIGHT: **190 lbs. (86.2 kg)**

TRIPLE GOLD CLUB HONOURS

OLYMPICS 2006 (Sweden)
WORLD CHAMPIONSHIP 2006 (Sweden)
STANLEY CUP 2008 (Detroit Red Wings)

TGC AGE
27 YEARS, 144 DAYS

TGC MEMBER AS OF
JUNE 4, 2008
STANLEY CUP WIN VS. PITTSBURGH

NHL			Regular Season				Playoffs				
Season	Team	GP	G	A	P	PIM	GP	G	A	P	PIM
2003–04	DET	20	1	4	6	16			DNP		
2005–06	DET	27	1	8	9	28	6	0	3	3	2
2006–07	DET	68	1	21	22	54			DNP		
2007–08	DET	65	7	28	35	44	22	0	15	15	18
2008–09	DET	80	6	45	51	50	23	2	7	9	33
2009–10	DET	48	7	15	22	32	12	0	5	5	12
2010–11	DET	77	11	26	37	36	11	2	4	6	4
2011–12	DET	82	15	21	36	38	5	0	2	2	4
2012–13	DET	48	5	24	29	44	14	0	2	2	4
NHL Totals		515	54	192	246	342	94	4	38	42	77

Olympic							
Year	Team	GP	G	A	P	PIM	Finish
2006	SWE	2	1	1	2	8	G
2010	SWE	4	0	0	0	2	5th
Totals		6	1	1	2	10	G

World Championshi							
Year	Team	GP	G	A	P	PIM	Finish
2003	SWE	5	0	0	0	4	S
2005	SWE	9	3	3	6	10	4th
2006	SWE	8	2	8	10	10	G
2012	SWE	8	1	0	1	4	6th
Totals		30	6	11	17	28	G,S

- World Championship MVP (2006)
- IIHF Directorate World Championship Best Defenceman (2006)
- World Championship All-Star Team/ Defence (2005, 2006)

For Niklas Kronwall, TGC membership came like a bolt of lightning. None of the other 25 members has completed the Triple Gold Club honours in as short a time (along with Detroit/Sweden teammates Mikael Samuelsson and Henrik Zetterberg) – two years. Only two – Jonathan Toews and Peter Forsberg – became members at a younger age.

Drafted 29th overall by Detroit in 2000 after just one year with Djurgarden in Elitserien, the 19-year-old Kronwall had made a solid impression at the World Junior Championship earlier that year as well as the 1999 U18 tournament, in which Sweden won a silver medal.

Kronwall opted to remain in Sweden for the next three years, developing at his own pace and in his own country, before feeling ready to take on the NHL challenge. He played again at the 2001 U20, where Sweden finished fourth, and in 2003 he played at the senior World Championship, winning a silver medal after the team went to the gold-medal game, only to lose to Canada 3–2 on an Anson Carter goal in

overtime, the first 4-on-4 OT goal in Worlds history.

At this point Kronwall was 22 years old and had few challenges left outside the biggest one—making the NHL. He made the trip to Detroit for training camp in 2003 and never looked back. He split his first season, 2003–04, between the Red Wings and their AHL farm team, the Grand Rapids Griffins, and the year after he stayed the whole year in Grand Rapids, the lockout giving him a full season of North American professional hockey experience. At the end of that 2004–05 season he played in his second World Championship with Sweden, the team finishing a disappointing fourth.

The 2005–06 season began as disastrously as it ended ecstatically for Kronwall. He suffered a knee injury in an exhibition game in late September and missed the first two and a half months of the season to recover. However, he was named to Sweden's 2006 Olympic team because coach Bengt-Ake Gustafsson had seen him at all levels of international play, from U18 in 1999 to U20 the next two years, and two years at the senior World Championship in 2003 and 2005.

Kronwall's Olympic dream seemed to end early, though, when he withdrew from the 2006 Olympics because he was dissatisfied with the progress of his knee. However, during the Olympics in Turin, another defenceman, Mattias Ohlund, was injured and Kronwall was asked to fill in. His recovery progressing nicely since he had withdrawn, he accepted the late invitation, and played two games, the semi-finals against the Czech Republic and the finals against Finland.

Kronwall recorded an assist in an easy 7–3 win over the Czechs in the semis and then scored the go-ahead goal midway through the second period of the gold-medal game against Finland. That score made it 2–1 for Tre Kronor, and although the Finns tied the game a short time later, Nicklas Lidstrom scored the gold-medal winner early in the third to give Kronwall his first Triple Gold Club championship.

After the Turin Olympics, Kronwall returned to the Red Wings and began to establish himself as a top-six defenceman. He played with more confidence and more effectiveness on a team loaded with European talent. Just a few weeks later, however, the Red Wings lost to Edmonton in six games in the first round of the NHL playoffs, and Kronwall happily accepted an invitation to don a Tre Kronor sweater again for the World Championship in Riga, Latvia.

Sweden beat all comers, finishing with a 4–0 win over the Czechs in the gold-medal game to become the first nation ever to win Olympic gold and World

Not only did Kronwall win Olympic and World Championship gold in the same year (2006), but he was also named tournament MVP in the latter event.

Kronwall took the Stanley Cup home after winning with the Detroit Red Wings in 2008.

Although the 2007 playoffs were disappointing for Detroit, who was eliminated in the conference finals, the second season a year later was just the opposite. The Red Wings went all the way, beating Pittsburgh in a six-game finals to win their fourth Cup of the last 12 years, the closest thing to a dynasty the NHL has seen since the Oilers in the 1980s.

With the win, Kronwall, Zetterberg, and Samuelsson all became members of the Triple Gold Club. None, however, was faster than Kronwall. On February 23, 2006, he wasn't even thinking about the Olympics. On June 4, 2008, he was the 20th member of the Triple Gold Club.

A calm and patient defenceman, Kronwall was not a superstar but was spectacularly consistent and reliable.

Championship gold in the same year. Eight players did the double for Sweden that year, and two of Kronwall's Swedish teammates – Henrik Zetterberg and Mikael Samuelsson – also were two-thirds on their way to Triple Gold Club members as a result.

In the process of his amazing 2006 run, Kronwall became the only player to score a goal in an Olympic final and a World Championship final in the same season. That both goals contributed to gold medals is all the more relevant.

Starting in 2006, Kronwall became a full-time and important member of the Red Wings. He became respected and feared around the league for his hip checks along the boards against oncoming forwards, an old-school skill that required speed, strength, and perfect timing. The trick of the play was that Kronwall had to allow the puck carrier to feel he could skate by the defenceman along the boards, and then when the attacker had committed to the play, Kronwall would close the gap and hammer his victim into the boards, easily relieving him of the puck in the process.

21

HENRIK
ZETTERBERG

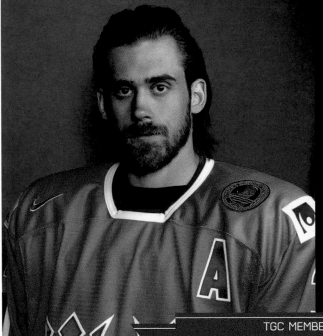

BIRTH PLACE: Njurunda, Sweden,
BIRTH DATE: October 9, 1980
POSITION: Left wing—shoots left
HEIGHT: 5'11" (1.80 m)
WEIGHT: 190 lbs. (88.5 kg)

TRIPLE GOLD CLUB HONOURS

OLYMPICS 2006 (Sweden)
WORLD CHAMPIONSHIP 2006 (Sweden)
STANLEY CUP 2008 (Detroit Red Wings)

TGC AGE
27 YEARS, 239 DAYS

TGC MEMBER AS OF
JUNE 4, 2008
STANLEY CUP WIN VS. PITTSBURGH

NHL		Regular Season					Playoffs				
Season	Team	GP	G	A	P	PIM	GP	G	A	P	PIM
2002–03	DET	79	22	22	44	8	4	1	0	1	0
2003–04	DET	61	15	28	43	14	12	2	2	4	4
2005–06	DET	77	39	46	85	30	6	6	0	6	2
2006–07	DET	63	33	35	68	36	18	6	8	14	12
2007–08	DET	75	43	49	92	34	22	13	14	27	16
2008–09	DET	77	31	42	73	36	23	11	13	24	13
2009–10	DET	74	23	47	70	26	12	7	8	15	6
2010–11	DET	80	24	56	80	40	7	3	5	8	2
2011–12	DET	82	22	47	69	47	5	2	1	3	4
2012–13	DET	46	11	37	48	18	14	4	8	12	8
NHL Totals		714	263	409	672	289	123	55	59	114	67

• Conn Smythe Trophy (2008)

Olympics						
Year	Team	GP	G	A	P	PIM	Finish
2002	SWE	4	0	1	1	0	5th
2006	SWE	8	3	3	6	0	G
2010	SWE	4	1	0	1	2	5th
Totals		16	4	4	8	2	G

World Championship						
Year	Team	GP	G	A	P	PIM	Finish
2001	SWE	9	1	3	4	2	B
2002	SWE	9	0	7	7	4	B
2003	SWE	9	3	4	7	2	S
2005	SWE	9	2	4	6	4	4th
2006	SWE	8	2	3	5	6	G
2012	SWE	8	3	12	15	4	6th
Totals		52	11	33	44	22	G,S,2B

Henrik Zetterberg receives his TGC honours
at the inaugural ceremony in Vancouver.

Even among the many low Detroit draft choices who turn out to be gems, Henrik Zetterberg is an incredible example of head European scout Hakan Andersson's ability to identify talent. "Z" was selected 210th overall by Detroit in 1999, one of the greatest low selections in Entry Draft history. And, like Niklas Kronwall and Mikael Samuelsson, he earned his Triple Gold Club honours in record time—two years.

Like many Swedes, Zetterberg developed with one club, moving from lower levels to Elitserien under the same umbrella organization. In his case that club was Timra, and he and teammate Fredrik Modin virtually grew up and developed together with the team.

In Zetterberg's case, he remained with Timra for a full three years after that draft day in 1999, but by the time he came to Detroit's training camp in the fall of 2002, he was nearly 22 years old with significant experience. His first international tournament came at the 2000 World Junior Championship, and a year later, still only 20 years old, he was named to the senior Tre Kronor team for the World Championship, winning a bronze medal.

Incredibly, he was also named to the team for the Olympics in Salt Lake in 2002, one of only two Swedes not already playing in the NHL. Just a few months later, he played at the World Championship again, in Germany, winning a bronze medal.

By this time there was little left for him to do in Sweden, so he moved to Detroit to begin a career in the NHL. He scored 22 goals and had 44 points as a rookie and was runner-up to Barret Jackman for the Calder Trophy. But Zetterberg had greater years ahead of him compared with the St. Louis defenceman, whose career never developed as the Calder Trophy suggested. Although Zetterberg was slowed the next year by a broken leg, it was clear he was a special player. His puckhandling skills were exceptional, and his commitment to team play and defence made him a valuable asset. Not big, he had a powerful stride and was difficult to knock off the puck. He was equally dangerous as both a shooter and a passer.

Zetterberg returned to Timra for the lockout year of 2004–05, and when the NHL was back on, so was Zetterberg. Despite reaching personal-best stats that included 39 goals and 85 points, he and the Red Wings lost in the first round of the playoffs. The season was far from a disaster for him, though. During the Olympics break in February 2006, he helped Tre Kronor win gold, with a goal and an assist in the 3–2 win over Finland.

He returned to Europe after the early departure from the NHL playoffs to win gold again at the World Championship in Riga, Latvia, where he became one of only eight players to win Olympic gold and World Championship gold in the same season. Zetterberg had started the season as a promising player, and by the end of the season he had blossomed into an NHL superstar and had won two-thirds of his Triple Gold Club membership.

At this point, the Red Wings were very much a European, if not a Swedish team, and Zetterberg often played with what was termed the "Swedish five," which referenced the "Russian five" of Detroit's earlier Cup wins in 1997 and '98 and the old Soviet Union's propensity not for developing three-man forward lines and two-man defensive pairings but rather a group of five players who played together shift after shift. The Detroit version of the Swedish five consisted of forwards Zetterberg, Tomas Holmstrom, and Mikael Samuelsson and defencemen Nicklas Lidstrom and Niklas Kronwall.

The Red Wings made it as far as the conference finals in 2007, and in 2008, led by Zetterberg's offence, the team won the Stanley Cup. He had 43 goals and 92 points in the regular season, and in the playoffs he led the team with 13 goals and 27 points

Few players in the modern game have the hand-eye skills of Zetterberg, whose puck wizardry is the stuff of legend.

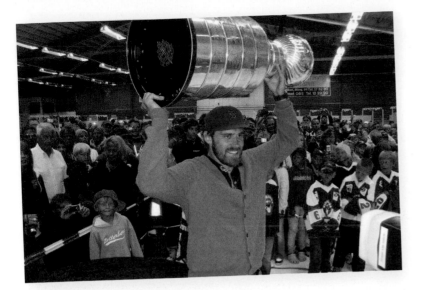

The 2008 Detroit Red Wings had more Europeans (12) than any other Stanley Cup-winning team in NHL history, Zetterberg being one of the finest of that group.

in 23 games. He scored the Cup-winning goal in the decisive game six against Pittsburgh, and he was named winner of the Conn Smythe Trophy for his incredible playoff performance. He was only the third non-Canadian to win the honour after Brian Leetch (USA, 1994 with the Rangers) and teammate Nicklas Lidstrom (SWE, 2002).

The Red Wings almost repeated their great season in 2008–09, but the finals, another Detroit–Pittsburgh clash, saw the Sidney Crosby–led Penguins prevail in seven games. On a personal note, though, Zetterberg made history by signing a 12-year, $73 million contract extension, the richest in team history.

When Zetterberg was named to Team Sweden for the 2010 Olympics, it marked his third straight Olympics honour, and in 2012 he played in his sixth World Championship. As well, when Lidstrom retired in the summer of 2012, the Red Wings had a huge void to fill both on defence and in leadership. After a lockout cancelled the first half of the 2012–13 season, Zetterberg was named captain of the Red Wings to succeed Lidstrom, another mark in Z's illustrious career.

Still active, Zetterberg is sure to represent Sweden for years to come and has plenty of time to add to his TGC honours.

22 MIKAEL SAMUELSSON

BIRTH PLACE: Mariefred, Sweden
BIRTH DATE: December 23, 1976
POSITION: Right wing—shoots right
HEIGHT: 6'2" (1.88 m)
WEIGHT: 213 lbs. (96.6 kg)

TRIPLE GOLD CLUB HONOURS

OLYMPICS 2006 (Sweden)
WORLD CHAMPIONSHIP 2006 (Sweden)
STANLEY CUP 2008 (Detroit Red Wings)

TGC AGE
31 YEARS, 164 DAYS

TGC MEMBER AS OF
JUNE 4, 2008
STANLEY CUP WIN VS. PITTSBURGH

NHL			Regular Season					Playoffs			
Season	Team	GP	G	A	P	PIM	GP	G	A	P	PIM
2000-01	SJ	4	0	0	0	0			DNP		
2001-02	NYR	67	6	10	16	23			DNQ		
2002-03	NYR/PIT	80	10	14	24	42			DNQ		
2003-04	FLO	37	3	6	9	35			DNQ		
2005-06	DET	71	23	22	45	42	6	0	1	1	6
2006-07	DET	53	14	20	34	28	18	3	8	11	14
2007-08	DET	73	11	29	40	26	22	5	8	13	8
2008-09	DET	81	19	21	40	50	23	5	5	10	6
2009-10	VAN	74	30	23	53	64	12	8	7	15	16
2010-11	VAN	75	18	32	50	36	11	1	2	3	8
2011-12	VAN/FLO	54	14	17	31	20	7	0	5	5	2
2012-13	DET	4	0	1	1	0	5	1	1	2	2
NHL Totals		673	148	195	343	364	104	23	35	60	62

Olympics						
Year	Team	GP	G	A	P	PIM	Finish
2006	SWE	8	1	3	4	2	G

World Championship						
Year	Team	GP	G	A	P	PIM	Finish
2005	SWE	9	1	4	5	4	4th
2006	SWE	8	4	5	9	4	G
Totals		17	5	9	14	8	G

O f the three Swedes to become Triple Gold Club members at the same time (alongside Niklas Kronwall and Henrik Zetterberg), Mikael Samuelsson is the atypical player. A low draft choice? Yes. Stanley Cup winner with Detroit? Yes. But that's where any predictable pattern ends. He was drafted 145th overall in 1998, but it was San Jose, not Detroit, that made the sage selection. More to the point, he simply didn't seem like a top prospect or a player who would have a long professional career in the NHL. To wit, he was nearly 22 years old before the Sharks selected him. He had never played at the World Juniors or had any significant international experience.

Although he stayed two more years in Sweden after being drafted, he was a rarity in that he did not stay with the same club his entire Elitserien career. Indeed, he played for Sodertalje, Frolunda, and Brynas in successive seasons, and not many scouts or managers saw much NHL, or Tre Kronor, potential in the young forward.

When he came to the NHL, Samuelsson was not an instant success. He played most of his rookie season with the AHL's Kentucky Thoroughblades. He was called up on two occasions to play a total of four games, but he had no points and didn't impress. He was 24 years old now, and still didn't look like he would pan out. The Sharks traded him during the summer, to the New York Rangers, and again he was assigned to the minors to start the 2001–02 season.

This time, though, he sparkled in the AHL and the Rangers called him up, keeping him for the year and using him to kill penalties and in defensive situations. He stayed with New York for the new season, but at the trade deadline he was on the move again, this time to Pittsburgh, and the next summer he was traded again, this time to lowly Florida.

That 2003–04 season was a disaster. Samuelsson played only 37 games thanks to a broken jaw and then a broken hand. By the summer of 2004, he was a free agent, the league was in disarray and about to shut down for a year, and Samuelsson was without a team. He played in Switzerland and Sweden and at the end of the season was invited to play for Tre Kronor at the World Championship. At that point Hakan Andersson, Detroit's super scout, took an interest in Samuelsson and convinced the Red Wings to sign him.

In one fell swoop, Samuelsson's fortunes started to change. He signed a one-year deal with the Red Wings, and his first year with the team was so successful they signed him to a three-year contract extension even before the season ended. As well, he was named to Sweden's Olympic roster for Turin. Playing on a line with Henrik and Daniel Sedin, he helped Tre Kronor win gold in only his second major international tournament.

Although he scored only one goal, it was the third-period game winner in a 2–1 win over the United States. At the end of the season, he was again called upon to represent his country after the Red Wings were eliminated in the playoffs in the opening round against Edmonton. This was the first time Samuelsson had appeared in the playoffs.

Samuelsson enjoyed a quiet moment with the Stanley Cup in his backyard in Sweden.

Off he flew to Riga, Latvia, for the World Championship. Samuelsson had nine points in eight games, including four goals, two of which came against Russia in a 3–3 tie in the qualifying round. Sweden went on to win gold, and Samuelsson was one of only eight players from that unique double-gold season of 2006. A year earlier he was without a contract, and now he was two-thirds on his way to being a member of the Triple Gold Club.

The next three years saw Samuelsson establish himself as arguably the best third-line centre in the league. A nightmare to play against because of his defensive tenacity, he was also a capable offensive threat who bought into the Detroit system and perfected its use. In his next three seasons, he played

Samuelsson was one of the more unheralded players from Sweden's golden double in 2006, when the team won both Olympic and World Championship gold.

63 playoff games and went to the conference finals once and the Stanley Cup finals twice.

Samuelsson completed his Triple Gold Club honours by winning the Stanley Cup with Detroit in 2008, contributing offensively by scoring twice in game one of the finals against Pittsburgh. After one more year, he was a free agent again and signed a three-year contract with Vancouver. It was a calculated gamble on his part. While he had fantastic success in Detroit, he looked to be no more than a third-line player because the Red Wings were so deep in talent on the first two lines. He wanted a greater role, so he chose the Canucks, but although he responded, he never enjoyed the same team success as he had with the Red Wings.

Just as 2005–06 was a phenomenal year for Samuelsson, 2009–10 was his *annus horribilis*. Team Sweden left him off its 2010 Vancouver Olympics roster, and he publicly declared his utter disdain with the decision. Retribution might have been his because the Swedes finished out of the medals, but the Canucks traded him a year later to Florida, and in the summer of 2012 he signed a new deal with the Red Wings.

Now, in the twilight of his career, Samuelsson is a Triple Gold Club member and has outlasted thousands of other players drafted higher than him who didn't pan out. His career started slowly, but like a fine wine it got better with age.

23

ERIC
STAAL

BIRTH PLACE: Thunder Bay, Ontario, Canada
BIRTH DATE: October 29, 1984
POSITION: Centre—shoots left
HEIGHT: 6'4" (1.93 m)
WEIGHT: 205lbs. (93.0 kg)

TRIPLE GOLD CLUB HONOURS

STANLEY CUP 2006 (Carolina Hurricanes)
WORLD CHAMPIONSHIP 2007 (Canada)
OLYMPICS 2010 (Canada)

TGC AGE
25 YEARS, 122 DAYS

TGC MEMBER AS OF
FEBRUARY 28, 2010
OLYMPIC FINAL WIN VS. UNITED STATES

NHL		Regular Season					Playoffs				
Season	Team	GP	G	A	P	PIM	GP	G	A	P	PIM
2003–04	CAR	81	11	20	31	40			DNQ		
2005–06	CAR	82	45	55	100	81	11	2	8	10	12
2006–07	CAR	82	30	40	70	68	25	9	19	28	8
2007–08	CAR	82	38	44	82	50			DNQ		
2008–09	CAR	82	40	35	75	50			DNQ		
2009–20	CAR	70	29	41	70	68	18	10	5	15	4
2010–11	CAR	81	33	43	76	72			DNQ		
2011–12	CAR	82	24	46	70	48			DNQ		
2012–13	CAR	48	18	35	53	54			DNQ		
	NHL Totals	690	268	359	627	531	43	19	24	43	12

Olympics						
Year	Team	GP	G	A	P	PIM	Finish
2010	CAN	7	1	5	6	6	G

World Championship						
Year	Team	GP	G	A	P	PIM	Finish
2007	CAN	9	5	5	10	6	G
2008	CAN	8	4	3	7	6	S
2013	CAN	8	0	3	3	4	5th
	Totals	25	9	11	20	16	G,S

The name *Staal* is to the NHL of the 21st century as the name *Sutter* or *Hextall* was to the 20th century. And instead of Viking, Alberta (clan Sutter), or Winnipeg, Manitoba (clan Hextall), it's Thunder Bay, Ontario, that can rightfully lay claim to the four hockey-playing brothers, three of whom have blossomed into NHL stars and a fourth who is trying to join them.

The eldest is Eric, who first played in the NHL in 2003 but whose reputation started growing much earlier. In fact, he was only 15 years old when he started his major junior career, playing for the Peterborough Petes in the OHL. After three years in which he developed and improved by leaps and bounds, he was drafted second overall by Carolina at the 2003 NHL Entry Draft behind only Marc-Andre Fleury, the goalie who was selected by Pittsburgh.

Staal made the Hurricanes at his first training camp, and the 18-year-old continued to excel despite the tougher competition of the NHL. Although the records show that he had 31 points as a rookie and 100 points in his second season, there is a critical in-between step that led to this extraordinary acceleration. The lockout of 2004–05 forced Staal to play the season with the team's AHL affiliate in Lowell, Massachusetts, and it was there he started to develop into a superstar. Like so many other top prospects, this extra season of learning at the lower level played a crucial role in his ascent. Who knows if he would have developed as much if his second NHL season followed his first right away.

When the NHL resumed play for 2005–06, Staal was physically stronger and mentally more prepared. He had 45 goals and hit the century mark in points, and the Hurricanes won the Stanley Cup, one of the most improbable wins in recent decades. Staal's 100 points was seventh best in the league, and the Hurricanes finished the season with a 52–22–8 record, good for 112 points and tied for third overall. This was the best season ever for the Hartford/Carolina franchise.

The 'Canes started their march to the finals by beating Montreal in six games. Trailing 2–0 in the series, they won game three 2–1 thanks to Staal's overtime goal. They then easily eliminated New Jersey in five games to face Buffalo in the Eastern Conference finals. The series went the distance, Carolina prevailing 4–2 in the seventh game, a game that marked the first time since the opening night of the playoffs that Staal didn't record a point. His 15-game playoff-point streak fell shy of Bryan Trottier's 19-game record.

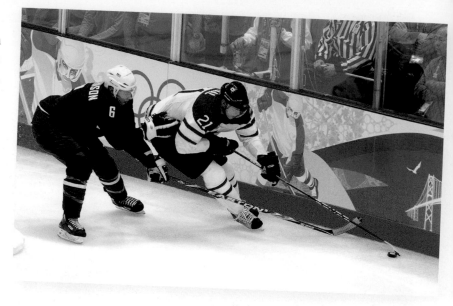

Staal's long reach and enormous upper-body strength allow him to shield the puck well while looking for a pass or shot.

In the finals, against Edmonton, Carolina eked out a 3–1 win again in the seventh game to win the Cup, giving Staal his first Triple Gold Club championship. Surrounding this win was a more dubious fact of hockey history that also helped Staal fulfill TGC criteria number two. The Hurricanes became the first team in NHL history to miss the playoffs one year, win the Cup the next, then miss the playoffs the following year.

But by virtue of missing the postseason in 2007, Staal was able to accept an invitation to play for Canada at the World Championship in Moscow. As well, the Pittsburgh Penguins lost a five-game series to Ottawa to start the playoffs, and this allowed Jordan, Eric's younger brother, to play as well. The Staals were stars as Canada went on to win gold with a 4–2 win over Finland in the gold-medal game. Eric finished second in team scoring with ten points and Jordan was a standout two-way player. Just 22 years old, Eric already was two-thirds toward his Triple Gold Club membership.

Over the next three years it was clear that Eric was among the best young players in the world. Big and strong, he had a great shot, tremendous passing ability, and, perhaps most important of all, seemed to be a natural leader. He led by example on-ice and off, marrying in the summer of 2007 even though he was still just 22. By the time Canada's general manager and his team of administrators and consultants sat down to select the 2010 Olympic team, there was no question Staal's name would be on the list.

The oldest of four pro brothers, Eric won the Stanley Cup in his second season with the Carolina Hurricanes and earned all his TGC honours in only four years.

Between his being named to the team and Canada's first game in Vancouver, though, another giant step in his career took place in Raleigh. On January 10, 2010, Staal was named the Hurricanes team captain, replacing Rod Brind'Amour. The decision was made simply because it was clear with a long-term contract in place Staal was the face and leader of the team. Early in 2008 he had signed a seven-year deal worth some $57 million soon after he had helped Canada win a silver medal at the World Championship in Quebec City.

Once Staal and his Canadian teammates arrived in British Columbia for the 21st Olympics, though, it was all business. Canada was always the favourites when playing best on best, but there was now the overwhelming pressure of home expectation as well. Playing a mostly checking role, Staal was one of 23 sensational elements that helped Canada win gold. Wearing number 21 so that the more senior Jarome Iginla could take Staal's usual number 12, Eric scored just once (in a 5–3 preliminary round loss to the United States) but had a great offensive game in the qualifying round, collecting three assists in an elimination 8–2 win over Germany.

(Left to right) Scott Niedermayer, Eric Staal, and Chris Pronger smile for the cameras in the dressing room after winning Olympic gold in Vancouver.

But in the playoff round, Staal was effective in the faceoff circle and was a key penalty killer and role player, using his size and speed to his advantage. When Sidney Crosby scored the golden goal on the afternoon of February 28, 2010, to give Canada a 3–2 overtime victory against the Americans, Staal was the newest member of the Triple Gold Club (along with coach Mike Babcock).

Staal will almost certainly be on the 2014 Olympic team for Canada, and at only 29 years of age he still has plenty of time to add to his Triple Gold Club credentials. One of the most consistent and dominating players of his era, he is a role model and superstar who has earned his TGC status through skill and determination. And with brother Jordan having earned a Stanley Cup with Pittsburgh in 2009 to go with the 2007 World gold, he is also only one Olympic gold away from becoming the first brother combination in TGC history.

24

JONATHAN TOEWS

BIRTH PLACE: Winnipeg, Manitoba, Canada
BIRTH DATE: April 29, 1988
POSITION: Centre—shoots left
HEIGHT: 6'2" (1.88 m)
WEIGHT: 210lbs. (95.3 kg)

TRIPLE GOLD CLUB HONOURS

WORLD CHAMPIONSHIP 2007 (Canada)
OLYMPICS 2010 (Canada)
STANLEY CUP 2010 (Chicago Blackhawks)

TGC AGE
22 YEARS, 41 DAYS

TGC MEMBER AS OF
JUNE 9, 2010
STANLEY CUP WIN VS. PHILADELPHIA

NHL Season	Team	Regular Season GP	G	A	P	PIM	Playoffs GP	G	A	P	PIM
2007–08	CHI	64	24	30	54	44	DNQ				
2008–09	CHI	82	34	35	69	51	17	7	6	13	26
2009–10	CHI	76	25	43	68	47	22	7	22	29	4
2010–11	CHI	80	32	44	76	26	7	1	3	4	2
2011–12	CHI	59	29	28	57	28	6	2	2	4	6
2012–13	CHI	47	23	25	48	27	23	3	11	14	18
NHL Totals		408	167	205	372	223	75	20	44	64	56

Olympics Year	Team	GP	G	A	P	PIM	Finish
2010	CAN	7	1	7	8	2	G

World Championships Year	Team	GP	G	A	P	PIM	Finish
2007	CAN	9	2	5	7	6	G
2008	CAN	9	2	3	5	8	S
Totals		18	4	8	12	14	G,S

It's almost impossible to believe how successful Jonathan Toews has been. He wins virtually every tournament he participates in and is often the best player in the process.

Toews believed in the importance of an education. As a result, he attended Shattuck–St. Mary's prep school in Faribault, Minnesota, and eschewed major junior hockey in Canada in favour of NCAA hockey. He played at the University of North Dakota, and during a sensational freshman year he also played for Canada at the 2006 World Junior Championship, winning gold. He was then drafted third overall by Chicago in the summer of 2006 (behind only Erik Johnson [St. Louis] and Jordan Staal [Pittsburgh]).

Toews stayed at UND for one more year, leading the team to a second straight appearance in the Frozen Four. Again, midway through the season he represented Canada at the U20, and Canada's gold this time – for a fifth year in a row – was in large part to a record-setting performance by Toews. In the semi-finals against arch-rivals United States, Toews scored three goals in the shootout (international rules allow shooters to take more than one shot after the initial round), the last one the game winner, and Canada advanced to the gold-medal game. In that game the team beat Russia 4–2, and Toews had a goal and an assist.

Because of his two phenomenal seasons of combined NCAA and U20 hockey, Toews received a rare invitation for a non-NHLer when Hockey Canada asked him to play at the World Championship, held in Moscow that year. Toews not only competed – he was a star player, scoring two goals and seven points in nine games just after his 19th birthday. More impressive, Canada won gold, and so Toews had yet to play a game in the NHL yet already had earned one component of the Triple Gold Club honours. He also became the first Canadian to win gold at the U20 and senior World Championship in the same year.

That sealed the deal. In the summer of 2007 he signed an entry-level contract with the Blackhawks. Toews scored a goal on his first shot in his first game – October 10, 2007, against San Jose – and accrued a point streak of ten games to start his NHL career, the second-longest such streak of all time.

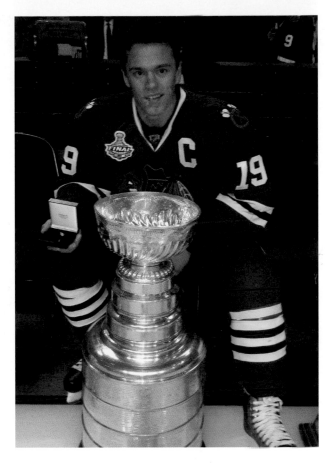

The Chicago Blackhawks' young captain, Jonathan Toews, poses with the Stanley Cup and his TGC pin after winning the Cup in 2010 to complete his membership into hockey's prestigious club.

The only bad news during Toews's rookie season was a sprained knee, which cost him 16 games and, likely, the Calder Trophy. He finished with the year with 24 goals and 54 points, but the Hawks missed the playoffs. He accepted an invitation to play for Canada again at the World Championship, this time winning a silver medal. Later that spring, Toews finished second in the voting for the Calder Trophy to teammate Patrick Kane, but on July 18, 2008, he made more history when the Hawks named him team captain.

Just 20 years old and the third-youngest captain in NHL history (after Vincent Lecavalier and Sidney Crosby), Toews donned the "C" with expected excellence. He was nicknamed "Captain Serious" because of his professional demeanour, but he fulfilled his duties the way few young men have done in league history.

Toews first rose to prominence at the 2007 World Juniors when he scored three shootout goals in the semi-finals against the United States.

Chicago lost to Detroit in five games of the conference finals in 2008–09, but Toews had 34 goals and 69 points, improving with almost every game he played. Graceful, slick, and quick, he was a threat every time he skated into the offensive zone, with or without the puck. He had a great shot, eyes in the back of his head, and a hockey sense few could match.

The 2009–10 season, his third in the league, was one for the history books. At the end of the 2009 calendar year Toews was named to Canada's roster for the Vancouver Olympic the following February, along with teammates Brent Seabrook and Duncan Keith, and Toews's play lived up to his top billing. He scored only one goal, but that came in the gold-medal game, and his seven assists tied for the tournament lead. His eight points was tops on a team that included Sidney Crosby, Rick Nash, Joe Thornton, and Jarome Iginla. He was named Best Forward of the tournament.

The players returned to their NHL teams, and the three Olympic-Hawks led Chicago to a remarkable double victory. Chicago defeated the Philadelphia Flyers in six games in the final, the winning goal

His Chicago teammates call him "Captain Serious" because despite his youth Toews is remarkably mature and responsible.

coming from Kane in overtime, and with the win Toews, at age 22, became the youngest player to join the Triple Gold Club.

Toews, Keith, and Seabrook, meanwhile, became three of only six players to win the Cup and Olympic gold in the same year. He also became the second-youngest captain (after Crosby) to win the Cup. As well, his remarkable play earned him the Conn Smythe Trophy.

The next three seasons were impressive for Toews, and in 2013 he captained the Hawks to their second Stanley Cup, adding to his TGC trophy case. Indeed, he seems destined to play for Canada again at Sochi, and at 25 years old he might well win another set of TGC honours before his career is over a decade and more from now. A natural leader and born to win, Jonathan Toews is entering the prime of his career as one of the best players of his generation.

Toews had just turned 19 when he played on Canada's World Championship–winning team in 2007.

25 PATRICE BERGERON

BIRTH PLACE: L'Ancienne-Lorette, Quebec, Canada
BIRTH DATE: July 24, 1985
POSITION: Centre—shoots right
HEIGHT: 6'2" (1.88 m)
WEIGHT: 194lbs. (88 kg)

TRIPLE GOLD CLUB HONOURS

WORLD CHAMPIONSHIP 2004 (Canada)
OLYMPICS 2010 (Canada)
STANLEY CUP 2011 (Boston Bruins)

TGC AGE
25 YEARS, 326 DAYS

TGC MEMBER AS OF
JUNE 15, 2011
STANLEY CUP WIN VS. VANCOUVER

NHL				Regular Season					Playoffs		
Season	Team	GP	G	A	P	PIM	GP	G	A	P	PIM
2003–04	BOS	71	16	23	39	22	7	1	3	4	0
2005–06	BOS	81	31	42	73	22			DNQ		
2006–07	BOS	77	22	48	70	26			DNQ		
2007–08	BOS	10	3	4	7	2			DNP		
2008–09	BOS	64	8	31	39	16	11	0	5	5	11
2009–10	BOS	73	19	33	52	28	13	4	7	11	2
2010–11	BOS	80	22	35	57	26	23	6	14	20	28
2011–12	BOS	81	22	42	64	20	7	0	2	2	8
2012–13	BOS	42	10	22	32	18	22	9	6	15	13
NHL Totals		579	153	280	433	180	83	20	37	57	62

Olympics							
Year	Team	GP	G	A	P	PIM	Finish
2010	CAN	7	0	1	1	2	G

World Championships							
Year	Team	GP	G	A	P	PIM	Finish
2004	CAN	9	1	0	1	4	G
2006	CAN	9	6	8	14	2	4th
Totals		18	7	8	15	6	G

The most recent addition to the Triple Gold Club, Patrice Bergeron became TGC member number 25 in a most unique way. Indeed, he is the only player in hockey history to win World Championship gold *before* he won World *Junior* Championship gold.

A product of the Quebec juniors, Bergeron played two years for the Acadie–Bathurst Titan before being selected by Boston 45th overall at the 2003 NHL Entry Draft. He attended Bruins training camp in the fall of 2003, at which time Bruins management were certain they were going send him back to the QMJHL. Bergeron had other thoughts, though, and so impressed the coaching staff that he made the club for opening night. He played the year with the Bruins, scoring 16 goals and 39 points in 70 games.

The Bruins were eliminated in the first round of the 2004 playoffs, losing to Montreal in the seven-game series 4–3 despite holding a 3–1 lead at one point. The early exit meant a quick summer for Bergeron, but Hockey Canada extended an invitation to the still 18-year-old to play at the World Championship in the Czech Republic.

Given a lesser role, the youngster contributed one goal and helped Canada win gold. The next season was marred by a year-long lockout, forcing the Bruins to send Bergeron to the minors. He played with Providence for the entire season, scoring 21 goals and averaging nearly a point a game. Midway through the year, he was loaned to Canada's junior team in North Dakota, and it was there he made history.

Bergeron played on a line with Sidney Crosby and Corey Perry, and the troika proved to be one of the finest forward combinations in U20 history. Bergeron led the tournament in scoring and was named MVP, and Canada took home a gold by remaining undefeated and becoming one of the greatest U20 teams ever. It was Canada's luck that the lockout made Bergeron available to the team, and he made history with his unique U20 gold after winning the senior gold first.

The NHL resumed for the 2005–06 season, and almost immediately Bergeron's role on the team increased dramatically. The Bruins traded their top player, Joe Thornton, to San Jose, and Bergeron

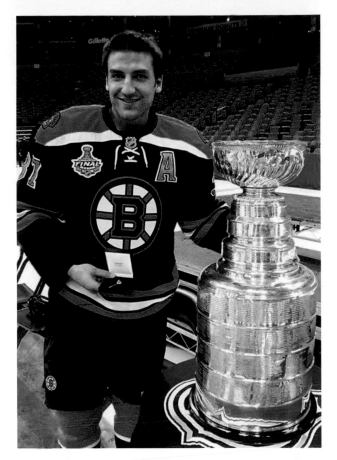

Bergeron earned his final TGC requirement In June 2011 when he helped the Boston Bruins win their first Stanley Cup since 1972.

moved to the number-one line to play with Marco Sturm and Brad Boyes. Bergeron responded with a season of 31 goals and 73 points, but the Bruins missed the playoffs.

This allowed Bergeron to go to the World Championship again, alongside Crosby, and the two paired at the senior level with equally amazing play as they had a year and a half earlier at the junior level. The pair was nothing short of sensational, and Bergeron's 14 points were second overall, but Canada finished in fourth.

Since then Bergeron's career has been complicated by concussion problems. Despite being a gifted player and sensational offensive talent, he has been the victim of vicious hits and bad luck. On October 27, 2007, he was hit from behind into the boards by Randy Jones, rendered unconscious by the force of the blow against the end glass.

He was carried off on a stretcher and missed the remainder of the season – 72 games in all – because of post-concussion syndrome. Typical for the injury, he felt better several times during the year, but as soon as he started rigorous skating or activity, his condition worsened and he was forced to stop.

Finally, by the start of the 2008–09 season, Bergeron felt well enough to play, but just before Christmas he collided with Dennis Seidenberg and was concussed again. This time his absence was limited to one month. The next two years were relatively injury-free for the centreman, and in late December 2009 he was named to Canada's Olympic team.

He was the only player on the team not invited to the summer orientation camp the previous year, mostly because of his concussion issues, but his strong

Bergeron is the only player in hockey history to win gold at the World Championship (2004) before winning gold at the World Junior Championship (2005).

start to the 2009–10 season assuaged team general manager Steve Yzerman as to Bergeron's health. Unfortunately, Bergeron strained his groin in the first game of the Olympics and fell down the depth chart, but he was still part of the team that captured gold on home ice in dramatic fashion when Crosby scored in overtime of the gold-medal game.

A year later, Bergeron completed his Triple Gold Club credentials by helping the Bruins win the 2011 Stanley Cup. The opening round of the playoffs, against Montreal, ended spectacularly. After dropping the first two games at home, the Bruins rallied,

Bergeron teamed so well with Sidney Crosby during the 2005 U20 that Bergeron led the tournament in scoring (13 points) and was named MVP.

the first period – the game winner, as things turned out – and added a short-handed goal late in the second, and the Bruins won 4–0. This marked the first time a team had won three, seven-game series en route to the Stanley Cup.

Bergeron had achieved his Triple Gold Club status on his own, something only three players had done previously (Scott Niedermayer, Chris Pronger, Jonathan Toews). He added to his list of victories midway through the 2011–12 season, again thanks to a lengthy lockout. Over Christmas 2012, he helped Canada win the Spengler Cup.

Over the course of the last few years Bergeron has demonstrated a remarkable tenacity and perse-verance, coming back from three concussions and playing skilled hockey for winning teams. Although thousands of players have tried to join the Triple Gold Club, and hundreds have come close, Bergeron is only the 25th man to achieve victory at the three most important hockey events to be competed for.

forced game seven, and won it in overtime thanks to Nathan Horton. In the second round they swept Philadelphia in four straight games, and in the final game of the series Bergeron suffered another concussion. It was deemed mild, however, and he was back in the lineup after a two-game absence.

The conference finals against Tampa Bay were another seven-game nail-biter. Again the Bruins won, 1–0, and again it was Horton with the game-winner.

The finals pitted Vancouver against the Bruins, and neither side could win a game in the opponent's building. Six games; six wins by the home side. But in game seven, in Vancouver, things changed. Bergeron scored the opening goal midway through

An all-round gifted player, Bergeron can pass and shoot with equal skill and success.

26 MIKE BABCOCK

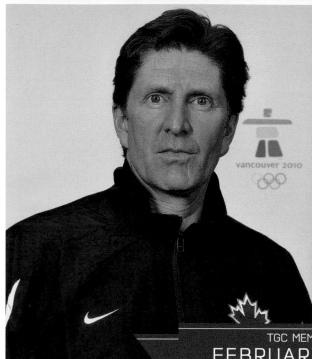

BIRTH PLACE: Saskatoon, Saskatchewan, Canada
BIRTH DATE: April 29, 1963

TRIPLE GOLD CLUB HONOURS

WORLD CHAMPIONSHIP 2004 (Canada)
STANLEY CUP 2008 (Detroit Red Wings)
OLYMPICS 2010 (Canada)

vancouver 2010

TGC MEMBER AS OF
FEBRUARY 28, 2010
OLYMPIC FINAL WIN VS. UNITED STATES

NHL

Year	Team	GP	W	L	T	OTL	W	L
			Regular Season				Playoffs	
2002–03	ANA	82	40	27	9	6	15	5
2003–04	ANA	82	29	35	10	8	DNQ	
2005–06	DET	82	58	16	–	8	2	4
2006–07	DET	82	50	19	–	13	10	8
2007–08	DET	82	54	21	–	7	16	6
2008–09	DET	82	51	21	–	10	15	10
2009–10	DET	82	44	24	–	14	5	7
2010–11	DET	82	47	25	–	10	7	4
2011–12	DET	82	48	28	–	6	1	4
2012–13	DET	48	24	16	–	8	7	7
NHL Totals		786	445	232	19	91	78	55

Olympics

Year	Team	GP	W	OTW	OTL	L	Finish
2010	CAN	7	4	2	0	1	G

World Championships

Year	Team	GP	W	T	L	Finish
2004	CAN	9	7	1	1	G

That there are 25 players who have succeeded in joining the Triple Gold Club and only one coach speaks volumes for the difficulty of winning the three greatest hockey championships. Much of this statistical fact is the reality that every team has 20 skaters, two goalies – and only one head coach. So, if it's difficult to be considered one of the 20 best players from a particular nation to participate in the Olympics, it is that much more difficult to be named the one and only head coach of the team.

Like many great coaches, Mike Babcock started his life in hockey as a player, and like most great head coaches, he was nothing more than a middling skater. In his case, he was a defenceman first with Saskatoon of the WHL. From there he went to the University of Saskatchewan, where Dave King was coach, and after a year he moved east to attend McGill University in Montreal.

After graduating in 1986 with a degree in physical education, Babcock did graduate studies in sports psychology for a year and then moved to England, where he was a playing coach for the Whitley

Warriors. From there he returned to Canada and began a coaching career in earnest, first with Red Deer College in Alberta, where he stayed for three years. In his first season the team won the provincial championship, and he was named coach of the year, and in 1991 he moved up to the WHL as head coach of the Moose Jaw Warriors.

Two years later, he was coach of the unsung University of Lethbridge, where he guided the team to a national title. In 1994, Babcock returned to the WHL, this time with Spokane, and it was there he settled in for the next six years. The Chiefs averaged 38 wins a year in the 72-game schedule under Babcock, and he established a rapport with the players that was part paternal, part taskmaster. Twice he was named coach of the year in the WHL, 1995–96 and 1999–2000, after taking the Chiefs to the league finals both times.

During his WHL career, Babcock was named head coach for Canada's entry at the 1997 World Junior Championship in Switzerland. With a roster that included Joe Thornton, Daniel Briere, and Chris Phillips, Babcock led Canada to a gold medal, the fifth successive gold in what was now the greatest U20 dynasty.

As a result of his success in the WHL, the Mighty Ducks signed him as their minor-league coach, and from 2000–02, Babcock was bench boss for the Cincinnati Mighty Ducks. In the summer of 2002, he finally made the big time. The Ducks replaced Bryan Murray with Babcock. He wasted no time in establishing himself as a top coach, leading the Ducks to the Stanley Cup finals in his first season. The Ducks lost in game seven to New Jersey, but Babcock's reputation had been firmly established at the highest level.

The Ducks missed the playoffs the next year, and that afforded Babcock a second chance to coach Team Canada. This time it was with the senior team at the World Championship in the Czech Republic. With a roster that included four future Olympians in 2010, Babcock again struck gold, becoming the first

Babcock's poise and focus are his greatest attributes, enabling him to communicate with players under the most pressure-filled circumstances.

Canadian coach ever to win top prize at both the U20 and Worlds.

The 2004–05 season was washed out because of the lockout. Now without a contract, Babcock decided not to sign with the Ducks and instead took the head coaching job with Detroit, which was open after the firing of Dave Lewis. Babcock became the 26th Red Wings coach on July 14, 2005, and to say he started out like gangbusters does not do justice to the effect he had on the team.

While Lewis, who took over for his mentor, Scotty Bowman, played a careful lock system that was generally unsuccessful – or, at least, failed to maximize the team's potential – Babcock came in and revolutionized the team. In his first season the Wings won a staggering 58 games, but they lost in the first round of the playoffs, being eliminated by Edmonton in six games.

A year later, this time after a 50-win season, the Red Wings went to the conference finals before losing, but in 2007–08, everything worked perfectly.

The coaching staff poses with their Olympic gold medals in Vancouver (left to right): Jacques Lemaire, Mike Babcock, Lindy Ruff, and Ken Hitchcock.

The Olympics came down to strategy, and Babcock proved to be the superior coach. Canada faced the Americans for the gold, and a late goal by U.S. forward Zach Parise tied the score 2–2 and sent the game to four-on-four, sudden-death overtime. Babcock met with his players in the dressing room. He explained they were going to go with their top offensive players, and play to win. The Americans were stunned by the onslaught and generated little in the way of offence, and at 7:40 of the extra period Crosby scored to give Canada the victory.

With the win, Eric Staal became the 23rd member of the Triple Gold Club – and Babcock became the first and only coach to win the top three championships. He did so in his first Olympics and his first World Championship, and he won the Cup in just his fifth NHL season. Historic – and fast. And likely to be alone in this category for a long time yet.

Nicklas Lidstrom, now captain of the team after the retirement of Steve Yzerman the previous summer, led the Wings to an historic Cup victory, winning the Stanley Cup in a six-game battle with Sidney Crosby and the Pittsburgh Penguins and becoming the first European to captain a Cup team.

In 2008–09, the scene was the same, but the outcome reversed. Crosby led the Pens to a stunning game seven win on Detroit ice to become the youngest captain in NHL history to hoist Lord Stanley's silverware. Nevertheless, it was clear Babcock was the top coach in the league, and when Canada's Olympic general manager, none other than Yzerman, had to choose a coach in the summer of 2009, there was little reason he'd choose anyone other than Babcock, who was young, energetic, mentally tough, highly competitive, and a winner wherever he went.

The 2010 Olympics were the highlight of Babcock's career. Played on home ice, in Vancouver, he faced enormous pressure to win. He even met with his family before the Games began to explain to them the pressures, but that win or lose the family would always be strong and important and could withstand whatever the fallout was from Vancouver.

Babcock runs a practice during the Vancouver Olympics.

SILVER
United States

GOLD
Canada

BRONZE
Czechoslovakia

CANADA MAKES HISTORY

The introduction of hockey to the Olympics was significant because it marked the start of truly international hockey, with teams from Europe and North American playing each other. Despite the mutual participation, though, the two continents were miles apart in terms of the game's development. The Stanley Cup had been introduced in 1893, pro hockey early in the 20th century, and the National Hockey League (NHL) in 1917. Hockey was evolved and sophisticated in North America. In Europe, though, the IIHF had been established only in 1908, and by 1920 bandy (hockey on a soccer field using field hockey sticks) was still the dominant form of the game. In Antwerp, not surprisingly, the two North American nations fought for gold, and Canada emerged victorious thanks to a 2–0 win. The impression Canadians made on and off the ice was critical to the establishment of a formal Olympic Winter Games four years later.

There were two reasons that led to hockey finally being made an Olympic event. First, the IOC was able to secure commitments from at least five European nations to participate – Belgium, France, Switzerland, Sweden, and the newly created Czechoslovakia (formerly Bohemia). And second, the managers of Antwerp's Le Palais de Glace arena refused to allow their building to be used for figure skating unless hockey was included. Because these two issues took time to arrange, it was not until mid-January 1920 that the competing nations (the five Europeans, as well as Canada and the United States) were informed of the event's inclusion in the Belgian *Summer* Olympics.

The event changed the course of international hockey. While the Canadian version of the sport had made inroads in Europe, it was still second to bandy in popularity. As well, rules varied widely from country to country, team to team, game to game even, making it difficult for fans to understand the game and for organizations to present a unified code and standard of play from one day to the next.

For 1920, the rules called for seven-man hockey (the six modern positions as well as a rover), and games were divided into two 20-minute halves separated by a ten-minute intermission. In North America, the NHL had already done away with the seventh, the rover, who skated between the defence and forwards, and created three periods of 20 minutes each separated by 15-minute intermissions.

Tie games went to overtime in ten-minute increments until a winner was decided. No substitutes were allowed, and if a man were injured and couldn't play, one from the other team had to come off the ice in a spirit of fairness.

The first game of the Olympics featured Sweden and Belgium, a game officiated by William Hewitt. The father of the famous *Hockey Night in Canada* broadcaster Foster, William was a long-time secretary and administrator with the Canadian Amateur Hockey Association (CAHA) and was in Antwerp as

The Winnipeg Falcons represented Canada at the 1920 Olympics, winning gold easily.

Canada's general manager. His officiating of what turned out to be a rough-and-tough game between two teams that knew little about the sport drew immense praise and convinced the IIHF to adopt Canadian rules immediately after the Olympics, including the elimination of the rover, shifting games to three periods of 20 minutes, and calling penalties as Hewitt called them.

There were a total of ten games played in 1920, and only two were close – the Canada–United States match for the gold medal and the Czechoslovakia–Sweden game for the bronze medal. The North American teams romped through their games, winning by dozens of goals cumulatively, while even within Europe there was a clear hierarchy between those teams that knew how to play the game (Sweden, Czechs) and those that didn't (Belgium, France, Switzerland).

Canada was represented by the Falcon Hockey Club of Winnipeg, a team that was made up of mostly Icelandic Canadians. They started playing in 1908 when the Viking and Athletic Clubs joined forces. The team disbanded after only one season, but four players reunited to create a younger version of

the team in 1912: H. A. Axford, Bill Fridfinnson, John Davidson, and Harvey Benson.

Olympic participants pose for a group photo in Antwerp.

The team won the Independent Intermediate League in its first year and moved up to the more skilled Independent Senior League a year later. Again, it won the championship, and for the 1915–16 season it played in Division II of the Patriotic League. The entire team then joined the army in 1916 and played hockey for the 223rd Battalion. When the players returned from overseas they captured the championship for Western Canada.

Four members from the 1912 team helped the Falcons win gold in 1920: Frank Fredrickson, Bobby Benson, Wally Byron, and Connie Johannesson.

The Falcons were elected to represent Canada because the Canadian Olympic Committee felt that the group of amateur players most deserving to represent Canada – and the team most likely to win – would be the best amateur team in the country – the Allan Cup champions. To qualify for the Allan Cup finals, the Falcons whipped the Fort William Maple Leafs in Winnipeg by scores of 7–2 and 9–1 before carrying on to Toronto to play Varsity (the University of Toronto team) in a two-game total-goals series for the Allan Cup and the right to travel to Belgium.

The Falcons breezed to an opening game 8–3 win on March 28 and stunned the locals after eking out a 3–2 win in the second game, earning the right to represent Canada in this historic Olympics.

The Americans, meanwhile, made unfriendly neighbours with Canada by submitting a roster that included no fewer than four Canadian-born players: Herb Drury, Frank Synott, and brothers Joe and Larry McCormick. The Belgian Olympic Committee, however, signed off on the list based on several criteria: only amateur athletes could compete; athletes must be a native of any given country or a naturalized citizen to represent that country; whoever takes part in the Olympic Games as a citizen of any given nation cannot be admitted in any future Olympiad as a candidate for any other nation, even if he has been naturalized in that country (save and excepting cases of conquest or the creation of fresh states duly ratified by treaty). The American team passed the smell test in these regards and was allowed to compete as it was formed.

The Swedes came to the tournament familiar primarily with bandy. As a result, they were elegant skaters but had little ability to stop and start like the Canadians and even less experience in the art of body-checking. They were, however, coached by Raoul Le Mat, who had attended Georgetown University in Washington, D.C. The players dressed like soccer players, wearing virtually no upper-body padding, no shin guards, and crude hockey gloves. The goalie wore what Hewitt described as "a cross between a blacksmith's apron and an aviator's coat." The team improved immensely over the first few days in Antwerp – most notably in the players' ability to check and control the puck – by watching the Canadians practise.

The Czechs, meanwhile, were dismissed by Hewitt out of hand: "They run on their skates with clumsy movements and use wrist shots and their play is all individual." Nonetheless, they were somewhat skilled in the art of skating and stickhandling, which placed them above some of the competition. The other teams provided little skill and were not integral to the success of the competition this year.

The game that decided gold was won 2–0 by Canada over the United States, a game of such speed and skill that it was regarded as the best game ever witnessed by fans in Europe to that time. The first half was scoreless, but Frank Fredrickson (the only player on the team to go on to play in the NHL) and Connie Johannesson scored in the second to give Canada the victory.

The bronze-medal game featured great goal-tending from Czech Karel Walzer, who was perfect in the 1–0 victory. Captain Josef Sroubek scored the only goal of the game early in the first half, but the Swedes dominated the rest of the game, only to be foiled time and again by Walzer. Indeed, one Swedish newspaper, *Dagens Nyheter*, counted the shots on goal in Sweden's favour by 16–2 and 32–0 in the two halves, yet the team was on the losing end.

The Czechoslovakians beat Sweden, 1–0, to win bronze in 1920.

RESULTS

TOURNAMENT FORMAT

The tournament format was called the Bergvall system, a unique knockout system in which teams that won games in the opening round went on to compete for the gold medal; those that lost games to the champion – Canada – played another knockout series for the silver; and, those that lost games to the silver medalists – the United States – went on to play for the bronze. France received a bye in the first round and thus qualified right away for the gold-medal round.

GOLD MEDAL ROUND

April 23	Sweden 8	Belgium 0
April 24	United States 29	Switzerland 0
April 24	Canada 15	Czechoslovakia 0
April 25	Sweden 4	France 0
April 25	Canada 2	United States 0
April 26	Canada 12	Sweden 1

SILVER MEDAL ROUND

April 27	United States 7	Sweden 0
April 28	United States 16	Czechoslovakia 0

BRONZE MEDAL ROUND

April 28	Sweden 4	Switzerland 0
April 29	Czechoslovakia 1	Sweden 0

FRANCE
CHAMONIX 1924
JANUARY 25–FEBRUARY 5

1ST OLYMPIC WINTER GAMES

SILVER
United States

GOLD
Canada

BRONZE
Great Britain

WATSON WITHOUT COMPARE

In June 1922, the French Olympic Committee invited representatives from around the world to a special meeting outlining plans for an International Sports Week in Chamonix in early 1924 involving tournaments in hockey, skating, and skiing. Officially, the original title of the competition was "Semaine internationale des sports d'hiver." The poster for this event included neither the five Olympic rings nor the word *Olympic*, but on May 29, 1925, the IOC amended its mandate to be more inclusive. As a result, the 1924 "semaine internationale" is now considered the first Olympic Winter Games.

Canada won gold at the first official Olympic Winter Games, a victory led by scoring sensation Harry Watson, who recorded 36 goals in five games, including 13 in a single game against Switzerland.

The Toronto Granites represented Canada at the tournament. It was a team formed by ex-servicemen from the First World War. From the time they began competing in the Ontario Hockey Association (OHA) in 1919–20 until they disbanded (after Chamonix), the Granites were virtually unbeatable. They won the John Ross Robertson Cup in 1920, 1922, and 1923 (OHA Senior champions) and were runners-up to the University of Toronto in 1921.

The team qualified as Canada's Olympic representatives by winning the Allan Cup in successive seasons. In 1922, the Granites beat the Regina Victorias 6–2 and 7–0 in games played in Toronto, and in 1923 they beat the University of Saskatchewan 11–2.

The Granites left Toronto on Monday, January 6, 1924. They took a train to New Brunswick and departed aboard the *RMS Montcalm* on January 11, arriving in Liverpool on January 18. They continued on to London and Paris, reaching Chamonix on January 22, where they booked into the Chamonix Palace Hotel.

In an attempt to get first-hand information for its readers, the *Toronto Telegram* hired left-winger Harry Watson to write two highly enjoyable journal-style reports for the paper, one while crossing the Atlantic, the other from Chamonix. Watson's coverage was both playful and evocative.

Modest Opening Ceremonies kick off the 1924 Olympics in Chamonix.

Jan. 11, 1924 – Today is a memorable day in the lives of the Canadian Olympic team for, having finished up our Canadian tour, we are finally on our way on the *RMS Montcalm* for Chamonix to defend the world's championship against all comers from Jan. 29 to Feb. 5, 1924.

The trip started in a not too promising manner as the Bay of Fundy was on its bad behaviour and certainly showed its mean disposition with a wind, rain, and fog storm from the time we set sail till the morning of Jan. 12. The result was that most of us remained on deck till pretty late. Hooley Smith had bet me $10 that he wouldn't be seasick, but about 11 p.m. was counted out by Referee P.J. Mulqueen. At this time Hooley's main cry was "And we've got to come back!"

Breakfast on the 12th was a very sad affair, as Jack Cameron, Ramsay, Rankin, and myself were the only members to appear. This was the day of Dunc Munro's famous quotation: "Why the – don't they hold the games at Oakville?" He was afraid he was going to die; the next day he was afraid he wasn't going to die.

Tuesday the 15th, the boys were all feeling pretty well, so a little exercise was indulged in, throwing the medicine ball, skipping, and a few jogs around the deck to finish off. Still perfect weather.

Wednesday the 16th was celebrated with a repetition of Tuesday's training and a concert by the crew in aid of Seamen's Charities. The concert was very good and ended in Mr. Mulqueen auctioning an autographed picture of the team for $25 to Mr. Scott of the Montreal Gazette. Hooley told Mr. Scott he was crazy, as he would have sold him a dozen for $5.

Friday the 18th – At 5:30 this morning we passed the Fastnet Lighthouse and so are practically in port. We dock at Liverpool early tomorrow and from there to London. It has been a wonderful and delightful trip, and our only hope now is that we can get to Chamonix at the earliest opportunity, so that we may start heavy training again and justify the confidence that has been placed in us and retain for Canada supremacy in the hockey world.

The two groups of the preliminary round were dominated by the North Americans. In Group A, Canada thrashed its three opponents by a cumulative score of 85–0, while in Group B the Americans won with nearly equal ease, outscoring their three opponents 52–0. The Granites were led by Watson, who scored 36 goals in the five games Canada played. Amazingly, he never turned pro after the Olympics, went into business, and later became the first and only true amateur inducted into the Hockey Hall of Fame.

Three of his teammates went on to win the Stanley Cup – Dunc Munro, with the 1926 Montreal Maroons; Hooley Smith, with the 1927 Ottawa Senators; and, Bery McCaffery, with the 1930 Montreal Canadiens.

The three teams in Canada's group were Sweden, Czechoslovakia, and Switzerland. All are world-class hockey countries now, but in 1924 they were no match whatsoever for Canada. In the other group, though, the Americans faced Great Britain, Belgium, and France, all of which have become second-tier hockey nations.

The two stars on the U.S. team were Herb Drury and "Taffy" Abel, both of whom produced the bulk of the offence for the team.

Interestingly, *players* often served as referees for matches they didn't play in. For instance, Canada's Dunc Munro refereed the Belgium–United States game, while Beattie Ramsay handled both the France–Great Britain match and the France–United States game.

Although the medal round included four teams, it was patently obvious the quest for gold was between the North Americans. On the final day, however, Great Britain rallied from a goal down to score the only two goals of the third period to beat Sweden 4–3 and claim the bronze medal.

Harry Watson scored six goals in Canada's 22–0 win over Sweden en route to gold. (top) and then Great Britain by a 19–2 score (below).

All games were played outside on a European-sized rink quite unfamiliar to the Canadians, who were used to smaller confines that created a more physical game. The boards were only about a foot high, thus preventing the Canadians from using them with the skill they did back home, particularly for hitting and passing. Additionally, netting was put up at both ends to prevent the "loss" of pucks in snowbanks. Ice conditions were often so poor that the boards had to be relocated almost daily to ensure the best possible patch of ice was being used.

The gold-medal game was even more intense both before and during the game (though perhaps not as much on the scoreboard). Both William Hewitt and W. S. Haddock, managers for the Canadians and Americans respectively, refused the official proposal to draw the referee's name from a hat. In the end, Hewitt proposed Paul Loicq of Belgium, and Haddock wanted La Croix of France. A coin toss settled the argument, and Loicq became the referee.

The weather for the game was perfect. The United States won the right to choose which end it preferred after Loicq ruled that that choice belonged to the team whose captain was older! Irving Small bested Dunc Munro in that department and elected to defend the west end, meaning Canada had to play into the sun for the first and third periods.

There was an obvious air of animosity to the game, created in part by Watson's remark earlier in the tournament that Canada would win by 10 or 12 goals. Less than two minutes after the opening faceoff, Watson was bleeding from the nose and American Willard Rice had been knocked unconscious by a Rod Smylie slash. By the end of the game, the Americans were exhausted and gasping for breath, and the Canadians were tired but victorious thanks to the heroic and skilful play of their star forward trio of Watson, Smith, and McCaffery. Watson led the way with a hat trick in what was to be his final international game.

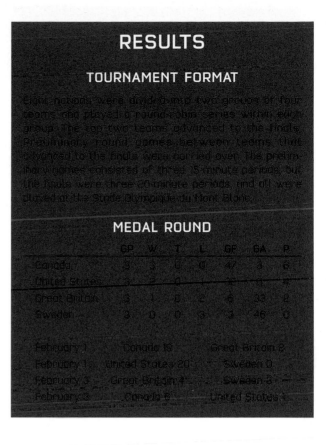

RESULTS

TOURNAMENT FORMAT

Eight nations were divided into two groups of four teams and played a round-robin series within each group. The top two teams advanced to the finals. Preliminary round games between teams that advanced to the finals were carried over. The preliminary games consisted of three 15-minute periods, but the finals were three 20-minute periods, and all were played at the Stade Olympique du Mont Blanc.

MEDAL ROUND

	GP	W	T	L	GF	GA	P
Canada	3	3	0	0	47	3	6
United States	3	2	0	1	38	6	4
Great Britain	3	1	0	2	6	33	2
Sweden	3	0	0	3	3	46	0

February 1	Canada 19	Great Britain 2
February 1	United States 20	Sweden 0
February 3	Great Britain 4	Sweden 3
February 3	Canada 6	United States 1

Canada won gold with ease in 1924, beating Switzerland 33–0

SWITZERLAND
ST. MORITZ 1928
FEBRUARY 11–20

2ND OLYMPIC WINTER GAMES

SILVER
Sweden

GOLD
Canada

BRONZE
Switzerland

OVERWHELMING VICTORY

Such was Canada's dominance and reputation that the nation was given a bye directly to the medal round. Once there, they played to expected form by winning all three games while not allowing a single goal and scoring 38.

Canada's representatives in St. Moritz were the University of Toronto Graduates, a group of players who graduated from the U of T and went on to establish themselves in the senior Ontario Hockey Association (OHA). After winning the OHA title, the Grads travelled to Vancouver to meet Fort William in the Allan Cup finals, the winner earning the right to represent Canada at the 1928 Olympics. They won this too, although the scores were close, the first a 2–2 tie, then a 3–2 overtime loss, followed by a 4–1 win to force an unusual, tie-breaking, fourth game, which the Grads won 2–1 (after 20 minutes of overtime).

To prepare for international competition, the Grads played the University Club of Boston in Boston before returning to Canada to play teams en route to Halifax, where they set sail for St. Moritz. In all, they lost only once all month, the second game against Boston, and this marked but the third time in two years the team had been beaten.

The last game in Canada, in Halifax, was particularly satisfying for the team. The players were roused by an enormous crowd of 8,000 packed into the new Forum. The Grads played an all-star team from the Maritimes and won handily, and the fans were further treated to a speed-skating race featuring Dave Trottier and Ross Taylor of the Grads against two Maritimers. The next day, January 22, they set sail aboard the SS *Arabic*.

Controversy ensued after coach Conn Smythe tried to add two players – Wes Kirkpatrick and Dick Richards – to the Olympic roster. Two of his players – Joe Sullivan and Hugh Plaxton – lobbied over Smythe's head to get their relatives on the squad instead, threatening to boycott the Games if their brothers were not selected to the Olympic team. Smythe was livid and refused to go overseas without the men to whom he had promised positions. However, Frank Sullivan, Bert Plaxton, and Rogers Plaxton were put on the team, and Kirkpatrick

Canada's hockey team leads the 1928 contingent during the Opening Ceremonies.

and Richards were left off. Smythe stayed in Canada rather than travel with the team after this insult.

The Canadians trained while on the ship, mostly by jogging around the deck. They stayed in Belgium while the rest of the Canadian Olympic team carried on to Switzerland, and it was there that they practised daily at the Palais de Glace in Antwerp, the same sheet where the Canadians had won the 1920 gold medal.

On the final day, the team's regulars and substitutes put on a spectacular Blue and White exhibition game at the Palais for the Belgian Olympic Committee, a hugely successful evening. The Grads arrived in St. Moritz on February 5, staying at the palatial Grand Hotel, from which many events of the Games could be seen from the balconies.

Team Canada players practise outside during an off day in picturesque St. Moritz.

The opening ceremonies for the Olympics were accompanied by bitter cold and a snowstorm. A mere 300 spectators welcomed the competitors from 25 nations as the parade proceeded to the hockey rink where the athletes took the Olympic oath. Just four days later, however, conditions were so mild that all events were postponed and organizers feared the Games might have to be cancelled. The ice on the rink had been reduced to slush, which wreaked havoc with the half-completed 10,000-metre speed-skating event. Within 48 hours, though, the cold returned and the Games were completed without further disruption.

Dave Trottier spent much of his spare time sizing up the opposition and wrote this report for the *Toronto Star*: "These European teams play a rough and ready game of close checking and that means that it will be hard to score against them if they can match our speed. Some of these players are exceptionally fine skaters, especially those from Switzerland and Norway, but their stickhandling and the finer points of hockey team play, fast snappy passing, pokechecking, dodging a man, drawing a defence or goaler out – all these, instinctive in a Canadian player, are as yet an undeveloped art with the Europeans. . . . Our team should have no difficulty in beating anything I have seen but we are going to take no chances, and a game is never won until the final whistle blows."

The 1928 Olympics lacked drama because the United States hadn't sent a team. Thus, the silver medallists from the first two Olympic hockey competitions were not on hand to challenge the Canadians, giving the Grads a virtual clear path to gold. The medal round robin consisted only of Canada with Sweden, Switzerland, and Great Britain, and, as Trottier predicted, none was a formidable opponent.

Canada outscored the three European nations by a cumulative 38–0 score after wins of 11–0 (Sweden), 14–0 (Great Britain), and 13–0 (Switzerland). There was no high drama in the victory, no challenge for the Canadians.

After the gold-medal triumph, the Grads played exhibition games in Vienna, Berlin, Paris, and London before heading home. Exactly one week later, the Grads docked at Halifax and were promptly whisked off to an arena for another exhibition game. They travelled to Toronto via Quebec City and Montreal, and were met at Union Station by a huge procession of University of Toronto students who marched them up Bay Street through a ticker-tape parade to City Hall.

Canada's dominance continued unchecked in 1928 as the nation didn't allow a goal in three games.

RESULTS

TOURNAMENT FORMAT

All ten European teams were placed in three divisions to play round-robin preliminary matches. One team from each division moved on to the medal round. Because of the team's universally acknowledged superiority, Canada received a bye directly into the medal round, which again was set up as a round-robin schedule for the four finalists.

MEDAL ROUND

	GP	W	T	L	GF	GA	P
Canada	3	3	0	0	38	0	6
Sweden	3	2	0	1	7	12	4
Switzerland	3	1	0	2	4	17	2
Great Britain	3	0	0	3	1	21	0

February 17	Canada 11	Sweden 0
February 17	Switzerland 4	Great Britain 0
February 18	Canada 14	Great Britain 0
February 18	Sweden 4	Switzerland 0
February 19	Canada 13	Switzerland 0
February 19	Sweden 3	Great Britain 1

UNITED STATES
LAKE PLACID 1932
FEBRUARY 4-13

3RD OLYMPIC WINTER GAMES

III Olympic Winter Games

Lake Placid, USA
February 4-13, 1932

SILVER
United States

GOLD
Canada

BRONZE
Germany

SMALL TOURNAMENT OFFERS FEW SURPRISES

Canada won its fourth straight gold medal after holding arch-rivals the United States to a tie in the deciding game. The double round-robin event saw teams play only six games, and that tie was the only blemish on an otherwise perfect record for the Winnipegs, Canada's representatives in Lake Placid.

In the first three Olympics, Canada had no trouble winning the gold medal each time. The teams representing the country were dominant and performed with the brilliance that was expected of them. However, the nomination of the Winnipeg Hockey Club to represent Canada in Lake Placid did not arouse the usual optimism. Indeed, the Winnipegs, as they were called, were seen as a weak team.

Yes, they had won the Allan Cup convincingly over the Hamilton Tigers a year before and were current senior Canadian champions, but they lacked star power, an intimidating talent that had marked the quality of previous Olympic teams. There was no Mike Goodman, Harry Watson, or Bert Plaxton, no scoring sensation who could win games single-handedly. This was a *team*, a cohesive group that played solid hockey without flair.

The Canadian Olympic Association was so worried about the team's lack of scoring ability that it made the radical suggestion to add players from other teams to the Winnipegs, and these sentiments increased in strength after the team lost two games 1–0 and tied another 0–0 in the weeks leading up to the Games during competition in the Winnipeg City League in which they played. On the other hand, they were considered the finest defensive team ever to play in Canada.

In the end, Walter Monson and Norm Malloy, of the Senior A Selkirk Fisherman, and Bert Duncanson, a noted Junior A star, were added to bolster the offence, as were Norm Malloy and Clifford Crowley.

As a final tuneup for the Games, the 'Pegs played a unique exhibition double-header in Toronto just before leaving for Lake Placid. The game consisted of two 30-minute periods – one against the National Sea Fleas, the other the Marlboros. The 'Pegs played true to form, and the media were relentless in their criticism after the team lost to the former, 1–0, and played to a scoreless draw against the latter.

Lou Marsh's column was brilliantly derisive, beginning with: "Goals were as scarce as watercress in the Gobi desert up at the Gardens last night. When the statisticians got through adding up the counters they hadn't any more goals than One Eye Connelly has optics. The only one on the sheet was credited to the National Sea Fleas and there were three teams out there on the ice. The Canadian Olympic team drew a blank."

The Winnipegs, Canada's representatives in Lake Placid, 1932.

The team had little trouble in getting to Lake Placid, but the location ensured that only two European teams made the cross-Atlantic journey – Germany and Poland – leaving the hockey portion of the Olympics with only four participants.

Given the limited tournament, it seemed certain that the two games between the North American countries would determine gold. As a result, there was a little psychological gamesmanship between the two leading up to the Olympics.

In preparation, the U.S. team played an exhibition game against the Boston Bruins, for which fans paid for their tickets and the Olympic team pocketed a large portion of the receipts.

"I am of the opinion that under the amateur rules the United States team has professionalized itself by playing against the Boston Bruins," said P.J. Mulqueen, chairman of the Canadian Olympic Committee. The Americans argued by way of explanation that without this revenue they could not afford to go to the Games.

Marsh pointed out that team Canada could have done the same thing in Toronto but knew this would

The main hockey venue was indoors and vastly preferred by players to the outdoor venue, the quality of which was subject to winter's conditions.

be a serious violation of the rules and so declined. He observed that, "You can bet your last centime that if the shoe was on the other foot – and the Canadian team had played a pro club for any object where a gate was taken – there would be a protest!!"

The next flap came when the Olympic schedule was sent to the Canadian team and the 'Pegs discovered they were being asked to play nine games in eleven days. Organizers had pre-sold tickets to hockey games based on eight nations participating. When only four registered, they didn't want to refund money to purchasers; instead they committed the competing teams to play two additional "exhibition" games (one against a group of Lake Placid all-stars, the other against a visiting McGill University team), proceeds going to the U.S. Olympic Association. The Canadians sent their subs to play those games to ensure the top players had sufficient recovery time between Olympics games.

The village of Lake Placid featured two hockey venues, an inferior outdoor rink with a seating capacity of 8,000 and the other indoors with excellent ice but with a capacity less than half that. The outdoor rink was actually set up *inside* the speed-skating oval! Spectators had limited views of these games, and the extreme cold only hurt the spectator appeal of the games. Yet, despite the poor weather, horrible outdoor ice conditions, and extremely poor attendance (average of 1,500), most of the tournament was played outside. Superior conditions favour the superior team; inferior conditions help to minimalize the skill differences between the top and lower teams.

American goalie Frank Farrell wore glasses and a mask. Prior to the first Canada–United States game, the opening faceoff was delayed while he had his

Canada and the United States played two fiercely-contested games, the former coming out on top by one goal to win gold (top). Only four teams competed in Lake Placid because of high travel costs for European nations (bottom).

goalie pads strapped tightly so that they were of legal width. The rules stated that when a goalie's knees were together the pads could not be more than 20 inches wide. While Canadian goalie William Cockburn's were well within the limit (18.5 inches), the Americans, Poles, and Germans were all 21.5 inches.

The two games between the North Americans were intense and close. In the opener, Doug Everett gave the home side a 1–0 lead early in the second period. It took a late goal from "Hack" Simpson to send the game into overtime, and Vic Lindquist scored the winner for Canada at 7:14 of the extra period.

As expected, the final game of the Olympics determined gold. Everett and Simpson scored again, in the first, to make it 1–1, and Winthrop Palmer gave the Americans a 2–1 lead late in the second period. Canada tied the game, this time with only 50 seconds left in regulation. Romeo Rivers scored the goal, which turned out to be the gold-medal goal. Teams played three extra periods of ten minutes, after which referees decided to call the game a tie, giving Canada first place by the narrowest of margins.

GERMANY
GARMISCH-PARTENKIRCHEN 1936
FEBRUARY 4-13

4TH OLYMPIC WINTER GAMES

SILVER
Canada

GOLD
Great Britain

BRONZE
United States

IVᵉˢ JEUX OLYMPIQUES D'HIVER
GARMISCH-PARTENKIRCHEN
DU 6 AU 16 FEVRIER 1936

COMITE D'ORGANISATION DES IVᵉˢ JEUX OLYMPIQUES D'HIVER 1936
GARMISCH-PARTENKIRCHEN (BAVIERE)

CONTROVERSIAL WIN FOR GREAT BRITAIN

The Olympics went from record low to record high. While Lake Placid had only four participating teams, Garmisch had an incredible 15 nations, a clear indication that hockey fever was sweeping through Europe and replacing bandy as the number-one ice sport on the continent. Amid great controversy and confusion, an early 2–1 victory by Great Britain over Canada proved to be the deciding result to give a country other than Canada an Olympic gold for the first time.

As was customary in Canada, the 1935 Allan Cup champions, the Halifax Wolverines, were selected to represent the nation at the 1936 Olympics. By late 1935, however, the Wolverines barely resembled the team that had been crowned amateur champions of Canada several months earlier. As a result, the Allan Cup finalists, the Port Arthur Bear Cats, were thought to be the next best choice to go to the Olympics, although several players were added to the roster to bolster the team.

Canada's first hockey game of these Olympics – an 8–1 win over Poland – was played outside, on frozen Lake Riessersee, under horrible conditions. Fewer than 300 fans braved a blinding snowstorm to see a game frequently stopped while the ice was cleared. The puck was often lost among the deep snowbanks. At one point, the game was delayed several minutes before it was discovered under the foot of an attendant.

Early on, Canada protested the status of two players on the Great Britain team, Jimmy Foster and Alex Archer. The CAHA believed these two were professional players and should not be allowed to participate in the Olympics. Both had been ruled ineligible by the IIHF the night before the Games opened, but the British, feeling they had done no wrong, were prepared to withdraw from the Olympics were Foster and Archer not permitted to play.

The CAHA justified its stance by noting that the players had (a) played in Canada, (b) were Canadians by birth, and (c) had transferred to British teams without the consent of the CAHA, as rules demanded. As a result, they were automatically suspended in Canada and, by extension, in any other national federation that was run in accordance with the IIHF. The ruling affected not only these two but 16 other Canadians currently playing in British leagues who may have hoped to play internationally for Britain at some point.

William Hewitt, secretary of the CAHA, continued: "We wrote the international association early last fall detailing the situation regarding all

Carl Erhardt (middle) collects Great Britain's gold medals while Canada (left) and United States receive silver and bronze, respectively.

players who had migrated to England without official permission. Surely it is the prerogative of a national governing body in sport to control its players? If the situation hits the English team, it is their own fault because they knew our attitude in plenty of time."

The Olympic rule stated that: "A competitor at the Olympic games must be an amateur in accordance with the rules of the international federation which governs his respective sport . . . and only those who are nationals or naturalized subjects of a country are eligible to represent that country in the Olympic games . . . the naturalized subject must give proof that he was an amateur in his native country at the time of changing his nationality."

To this end, the association in each country for each sport must certify that each athlete is in good standing not only within that country but also within the international federation governing that sport.

Goalie Jimmy Foster was the difference for Great Britain, as his stellar play led the nation to a remarkable gold medal.

The Great Britain team had three other Canadians – Art Child, Jimmy Chappell, and Archie Stinchcombe – who had secured the CAHA's permission to leave Canadian hockey and were playing without problem. Three days later, in a spirit of Olympic sportsmanship, the CAHA withdrew its protest.

The tournament format called for three rounds of round-robin play, each round eliminating some teams until only four were left to play for the medals. Canada cruised along in the first round, but in the middle stage it played Great Britain in what was a politically charged and emotional game.

On February 11, 1936, the most shocking result in international hockey to that date was recorded when the Brits beat Canada 2–1. Gerry Davey scored just 20 seconds into the game for the underdogs, but Canada calmly took over and Ralph St. Germain tied the game later in the period. But the British goalie, Jimmy Foster, who had grown up and learned the game in Canada, played with remarkable poise, thwarting every Canadian shot the rest of the way. And then, with just 12 seconds left in the third period, Edgar Brenchley beat Canadian goalie Dinty Moore with a shot to give the British a stunning victory.

That score was at first a shocker but without long-term implications. Then, it changed the course of these Olympics when tournament officials announced only *after* the second round was over that second-round matches would count in third-round standings, thus overturning the original rules under which all teams were thought to have been playing.

This ruling virtually eliminated Canada from gold-medal contention. Canadian official P. J. Mulqueen called it "one of the worst manipulations in sporting history," and the *Times* editorial agreed,

Japanese goalie Teiji Honma played with a mask in the style of a baseball catcher's.

TOURNAMENT FORMAT

The 15 entries were divided into four divisions (three of four teams, one of three teams) and played a round-robin series within each division. The top two countries then advanced to a semi-final round and the top two from that advanced to the finals. Any ties in the groupings would be decided by total number of goals scored in the Games. Games consisted of three 15-minute periods and each team could dress only ten players. Three substitutes per game were allowed.

An extremely important rule for the final round stated that any team that had beaten another in a previous round did not have to play against that same team in the finals. Instead, they were automatically given two points for the earlier win (the one win, therefore, counted as two points in both the semi-final and final rounds for Britain at these Olympics). Thus, Canada's loss to Great Britain in the semi-finals virtually assured them of losing the gold medal, for they couldn't play the English in the final round to avenge the earlier defeat.

MEDAL ROUND

	GP	W	T	L	GF	GA	P
Great Britain	3	2	1	0	7	1	5
Canada	3	2	0	1	9	2	4
United States	3	1	1	1	2	1	3
Czechoslovakia	3	0	0	3	0	14	0

February 14	Great Britain 5	Czechoslovakia 0
February 15	Canada 7	Czechoslovakia 0
February 15	Great Britain 0	United States 0*
February 16	Canada 1	United States 0

* 30:00 OT

saying euphemistically, "it is regrettable that the Olympic hockey committee didn't publicly announce the regulations governing the tournament."

Canada won its last two games, but Foster continued his incredible play, posting two shutouts in the medal round to earn Great Britain an improbable gold. The final game was a 0–0 tie with the United States that included 30 minutes of overtime, but the Americans couldn't beat Foster, who would certainly have been named tournament MVP had such an honour existed in 1936.

Upon returning home, however, most of the Canadian players placed responsibility for the format confusion on their own officials. Left winger Ralph St. Germain said plainly: "The Olympic rules state that the hockey may be played either on an elimination or point system or both. Either through carelessness or dumbness, the [Canadian] officials neglected to find out what system was being used until after we were defeated by England."

Teammate Hugh Farquharson agreed: "No one realized, and the officials at least should have, that to lose that first game meant probable loss of the title. It would have made a big difference if that were known when we went into our game with England. That pool system has been in use over there for many years. There is no excuse for not completely understanding it before a Canadian team left Canada."

The damage had been done. Canada, winner of Olympic gold in 1920, 1924, 1928, and 1932, was now silver medallists thanks to a single 2–1 loss to an inferior opponent outside the medal round.

SWITZERLAND
ST. MORITZ 1948
JANUARY 30–FEBRUARY 8

5TH OLYMPIC WINTER GAMES

JEUX OLYMPIQUES D'HIVER
1948 ST MORITZ SUISSE

SILVER
Czechoslovakia

GOLD
Canada

BRONZE
Switzerland

MILITARY GOLD FOR CANADA

The CAHA had long been displeased with the IIHF over a number of critical issues: the way amateur problems had been dealt with and unfair rules that had been applied specifically against Canada (i.e., the controversy at the 1936 Olympics). Indeed, Canada boycotted the 1947 World Championship. In the spring of 1947, however, the IIHF attended CAHA meetings in Canada and agreed to alternate its own presidency between North America and Europe. In return, Canada returned to international competition.

It was not until October 15, 1947, however, just 107 days before the first game of the 1948 Olympics was scheduled, that the CAHA agreed to send a hockey team to St. Moritz. Because of the lateness of the decision, it was impossible to invite the Allan Cup champions or to organize a team in any traditional way.

The Royal Canadian Air Force (RCAF), which sported some of the finest "pure" amateurs in the country, volunteered its services, and the CAHA gladly approved, promising to pay for the players' expenses both to St. Moritz and while in training at the Auditorium in Ottawa (though costs toward the latter would

be minimal, as the players stayed at the Princess Alice Barracks on Argyle Street, right next door to the arena).

Corporal Frank Boucher, coach of the RCAF team in the Ottawa City League, was named coach for the Olympics. He had plenty of NHL experience (14 years) and also was a member of the RCAF overseas team that was highly regarded in amateur circles.

Boucher's father, George "Buck" Boucher, was put in charge of selecting and inviting players to training camp. Buck acted as coach and chose the final team in Ottawa, and Frank took over the coaching duties in Switzerland. On October 19, the first players began arriving in Ottawa for tryouts.

Hopes for the team as it was first chosen were all but destroyed on December 14, 1947, in an exhibition game. The McGill Redmen thrashed the RCAF Olympic team 7–0 in the team's first match. Boucher immediately called replacements for a tryout, obtaining four players from New Edinburgh of the Senior City Hockey League: Ted Hibberd, Reg

The RCAF Flyers celebrate moments after winning gold in 1948.

Schroeter, Ab Renaud, and Pete Leichnitz. These additions clearly made a difference, and the Flyers skated to a convincing 8–4 win over Belleville of the OHA Intermediate league soon after.

Boucher kept tinkering. Just ten days before the team was to set sail, three new additions were included after impressive tryouts: defenceman Andre Laperriere, from the University of Montreal, and forwards George Mara and Wally Halder. Also added was goalie Dick Ball, who took over as the number-one man. Thus, in the two weeks leading up to the Games, the team had changed personnel almost completely.

But the problems were far from over. Just three days before sailing, Ball was diagnosed by team doctors with a lung condition that rendered him unable to travel and forced him to leave the team. A new goalie was needed instantly, and Ball himself

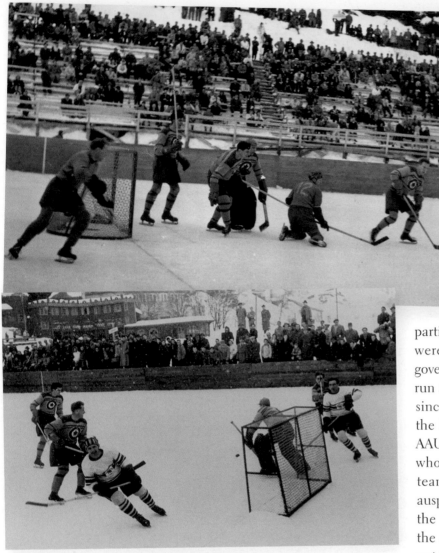

Canada's goalie Murray Dowey was sensational, posting five shutouts in eight games, but the Czechs nearly took home the gold thanks to a remarkable team effort.

a couple of days before the closing ceremony.

The conflict involved two American hockey bodies – the American Hockey Association (AHA), a professional group, and the Amateur Athletic Union (AAU), a strictly amateur one, as its name suggests. The conflict between these two groups was complicated and, in some respects, defied logic, but it was a serious one all the same.

The IIHF had always stated that athletes could not participate in the Olympics unless they were endorsed by their own country's governing body. In this case, the AAU had run amateur hockey in the United States since 1930, but it had been expelled by the IIHF the previous year because the AAU had refused to support those players who made up the Americans' national team, all of whom played under the auspices of the "professional" AHA. But the IIHF recognized the AHA and not the AAU, and thus welcomed the AHA, *not* the AAU, to St. Moritz, even though it was a league that *paid* its players.

The AAU refused to acknowledge these players because, according to their pamphlet, "the AHA players were openly paid salaries. Beyond the continued use of the name 'amateur' in connection with its hockey, there were few pretensions."

Avery Brundage, chairman of the U.S. Olympic Committee, the American governing body that controlled all amateur sports in the country, threatened the AHA with total withdrawal of American athletes from the Games if it sent its team over. The IIHF countered by threatening to withdraw all other hockey teams from the Games if the AHA were banned.

To complicate matters, the Swiss Olympic Organizing Committee had formally accepted the

suggested Murray Dowey of the Barkers in the Toronto Mercantile Hockey League. It was perhaps the most important decision the team made during the whole process. Dowey arrived just in time to take the train to New York, where the RCAF team sailed for England.

While the Canadians were sorting out their difficulties in trying to piece together a team, the Americans were embroiled in a much different and greater controversy that almost cost the world the cancellation of the whole Olympics and eventually relegated hockey to a non-official event until only

Three top Czech stars in 1948 were (left to right) Oldrich Kucera, Josef Malecek, and Jiri Tozicka.

RESULTS

TOURNAMENT FORMAT

With nine teams entered, all were placed together with a simple round-robin format used as a schedule. Teams received two points for a win, one for a tie. For the first time, all games now consisted of three 20-minute periods. In the case of a tie in the standings after the round robin, goal average would decide the final positions. This meant dividing the goals scored by goals against. For instance, Canada scored 69 and gave up 5, for a figure of 13.8. The Czechs, by comparison, scored 80 but surrendered 18, for an average of just 4.3. That is how Canada won the gold in St. Moritz.

STANDINGS

	GP	W	T	L	GF	GA	P
Canada	8	7	1	0	69	5	15
Czechoslovakia	8	7	1	0	80	18	15
Switzerland	8	6	0	2	67	21	12
United States	8	5	0	3	86	33	10
Sweden	8	4	0	4	55	28	8
Great Britain	8	3	0	5	39	47	6
Poland	8	2	0	6	29	97	4
Austria	8	1	0	7	33	77	2
Italy	8	0	0	8	24	156	0

AHA application, while the executive committee of the IOC suggested that both U.S. entries be denied. A month before the Games were to begin, the U.S. Olympic Committee voted 68–6 in favour of withdrawing all American athletes from the Games if the AHA were allowed to participate.

Just before the United States was to play its first game of the Olympics, the IOC relegated hockey to an "unofficial" event. Then, on February 7, a compromise was reached whereby only the U.S. entry would be considered unofficial by the IOC. The team – the AHA team – would play all opponents and be placed in the standings, and other teams' results versus the United States would count, but the Americans were not allowed to win a medal.

The controversy put the RCAF Flyers clearly in the background but also ensured Canada was the prohibitive favourite to win gold. The team played all of its games outdoors, and this caused havoc on a couple of occasions when snowstorms almost forced the cancellation of matches already under way.

The RCAF Flyers beat the U.S. team easily, 12–3, and had only one close game all tournament: a scoreless tie against the Czechoslovaks, a game in which the two goalies – Dowey and Bohumil Modry – stole the show. The result also foreshadowed the first wave of European counties to catch up to Canada. The previous year it was the Czechs that won World Championship gold when Canada did not participate, and now they proved they were world class with this tie against Canada. In fact, both teams had identical records in St. Moritz, Canada receiving favourable placing only because of a superior goal average.

Dowey, the last-second replacement, recorded a remarkable five shutouts in eight games. Early in the tournament, he went 226:07 minutes without allowing a goal, and he finished off with 196:10 of shutout minutes.

OSLO 1952

FEBRUARY 14–25

6TH OLYMPIC WINTER GAMES

DE VI. OLYMPISKE VINTERLEKER

14. FEBRUAR OSLO 1952 25. FEBRUAR

SILVER
United States

GOLD
Canada

BRONZE
Sweden

CANADA'S SIXTH AND LAST GOLD FOR 50 YEARS

It was impossible to have imagined at the time, but Canada's dominant win in Oslo was to be its last for half a century. Despite the Canadians winning six of the first seven Olympic games, the arrival of the Soviets in 1954 turned the hockey world upside down and gave the motherland of the game a fierce rival. But in 1952, the Edmonton Mercurys brought gold home, as was expected of them.

At the same time, the fourth-place finish by the Czechs, while not wildly out of the ordinary, was in large part due to tragic events two years earlier. Indeed, Czechoslovakia was arguably the best national team in the world in the years immediately following the Second World War. The team won the 1947 and 1949 World Championships and lost the 1948 Olympic gold to Canada only on goal ratio.

But it was their own government that prevented this great team from defending its title at the 1950 World Championship in London, England. Just before the national squad was about to board the plane for Great Britain on March 11, 1950, the players

Canada's Edmonton Mercurys won gold in 1952, the last Olympic title for Canada for half a century.

were handcuffed by the national state security police and taken to jail.

Seven months later, on October 7, the players appeared in court on charges of treason. The security police presented "intelligence information" about plans by the players to defect in London during the World Championship. The main argument was that in December 1948, the players of LTC Praha (most of whom played for the national team) had discussed the option of defecting in Switzerland after the Spengler Cup tournament in Davos.

Yes, there had been earlier defections by Czechoslovakian hockey players to the west, but none of the accused players had ever seriously considered taking this step, even when they had their chance. They could have stayed in Sweden after the 1949 World Championship or in Vienna where they prepared for the 1950 event in London. The players, of course, pleaded not guilty.

Their fate, however, was predetermined by authorities who ruled the totalitarian regime, and

12 members of the national team were sent to jail. Goaltender Bohumil Modry was sentenced to 15 years in prison; forward Gustav Bubnik to 14 years; forward Stanislav Konopasek got 12; Vaclav Rozinak and Vladimir Kobranov each got ten years; and Josef Jirka got six years. Six other players were given sentences ranging from eight months to three years: Mojmir Ujcik, Zlatko Cerveny, Jiri Macelis, Premysl Hajny, Antonin Spaninger, and Josef Stock.

Modry, the best goaltender in Europe of that era, died in 1963, at the age of 47, from prison-related complications. Most of the players were released after five years, but their lives and families were shattered. So was a great hockey team. Czechoslovakia would have to wait 23 years, until 1972, before it won another World Championship gold medal.

Game action from Sweden's 5–2 win over Switzerland, a result which helped Tre Kronor win the bronze medal.

In 1952, its roster didn't remotely resemble the one that had won gold at the 1949 Worlds, and the results showed.

The participation of the Edmonton Mercurys as Canada's representatives, meanwhile, was the result of the efforts of one man – Jim Christianson, a car dealer who provided the $100,000 needed for the Canadians to tour Europe and participate in the Olympics. As team owner, he named the Mercs after a top-selling brand of Fords.

The Mercs had not a single player who had played or would go on to play in the NHL. It was as purely amateur as one could get. Nevertheless, the Mercs put on a dominating performance worthy of their predecessors. Of the eight games the team played, only three were close. On February 19, the team beat the Czechs by a 4–1 margin. Canada's other two close games included a 3–2 win over Sweden and a 3–3 tie with the Americans. But the United States had also lost to Sweden 4–2, giving Canada the gold and the Americans silver. Sweden

beat the Czechs to take bronze, but the larger picture that emerged from Oslo was a sense that Canada was no longer the dominant force it had been.

In the years immediately after the war, the Czechs had proved they were closing in on Canada, and in 1952 the Swedes were also closing the gap. Indeed, Doug Grimston noted that, "European teams have improved considerably the last few years and, with some proper coaching, could be mighty troublesome to Canada. European teams lack stamina, especially on power plays, and they are timid when it comes to bodily contact." But, he warned, if these problems could be eradicated, many countries could become superior hockey-playing nations. By the time the next Olympics arrived, his words had proved prescient.

While in Norway with the Mercs, owner Jim Christianson contracted a virus and was ill for most of the trip. Upon his return to Canada, his illness

Swiss players watch the game from their bench. They won four of eight games and finished in fifth place.

worsened, and he died a short time later. But the connection between owner and players didn't die with him. Indeed, it started a new relationship that has, remarkably, endured to this day.

The Ford Motor Company appointed a dealer principal of Christianson's dealership, but about ten years later Mercs defenceman Al Purvis inherited the position. Purvis then recruited several of his Olympic teammates as shareholders (Miller, Gauf, and Dawe) and employees, each managing a division of the operations. Over the years, Purvis bought back their shares, and half a century later the Waterloo Mercury dealership in Edmonton celebrated 50 years of operation with Purvis still in charge.

SILVER
United States

GOLD
Soviet Union

BRONZE
Canada

CANADA FINISHES THIRD AS SOVIETS WIN FIRST GOLD

The Soviets were the big story in Cortina thanks in large part to the events of March 7, 1954. On that day, the hockey landscape changed irrevocably and forever. The Soviets entered their first international tournament ever, the 1954 World Championship, and they proceeded to go through the round-robin event undefeated, a 1–1 tie with Sweden the only blemish.

On the final day of the Worlds they hammered Canada 7–2, ensuring gold, stunning the world, and giving the Canadians a rivalry that would endure year after year, from that day to this. As a result, the names of Puchkov and Bobrov, Babich and Kuchevski, were familiar by the time teams arrived in Cortina. And Canada was perhaps co-favourite for this event, but no more than that after reclaiming the World title in 1955 by beating the Soviets 5–0 on the final day.

Canada was represented by the Kitchener–Waterloo (Ontario) Dutchmen, the team that had won the Allan Cup the past two years. The team competed in the five-team OHA Senior A league, but for the purposes of Cortina replacements had to be made because of players' amateur status required by Olympic rules. For instance, Clare Martin, Bud Kemp, Joe Schertzel, Jack Hamilton, and Jack White were all professionals who had been reinstated for amateur play, which was fine for Senior OHA hockey but not for the Olympics.

As a result, the Dutchies signed forwards Bob White and Jim McBurney to replace the pros in November, and in early January they added Elmer Skov, George McLagan, and Art Hurst as possible final reinforcements for the Olympic tournament. Unfortunately, these were players from Senior B and Junior B teams, not significant levels in Canada but considered good enough for international competition. In retrospect, the CAHA overvalued the lower leagues in Canada and devalued the top European players, and by 1956 it was no longer possible to win with that perspective as the guiding light.

Kitchener–Waterloo played its last OHA game on January 14, 1956, flew to Prestwick, Scotland, the next day, and played their first exhibition game that night. The mood in the Canadian hockey world was that they'd be back soon enough with another gold medal. "We didn't come over here to lose" was how manager Ernie Gorman put it when asked of his team's chances. And since no one contested his optimism the feeling was clearly that the loss to the Soviets was a blip on the screen, one eradicated in 1955 and one not to be repeated at the more important Olympic Winter Games.

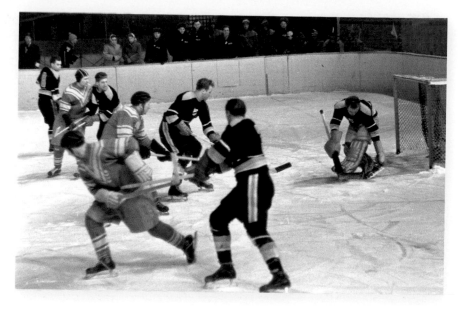

The Soviets won gold in their first Olympic tournament, finishing with a perfect 7–0–0 record.

Italian and German players pretty much conceded top spot to the Canadians, and even Louis Lecompte, a Canadian referee at the Games, could see no reason for Canada to lose at the hands of the Soviets: "I don't think the Russians are as strong as last year [at the World Championship] and a number of other teams are much stronger," he suggested. "The Canadians look like a happy gang of kids on the ice, and can they ever go. The Russians often carry the puck within ten feet of the net and then pass instead of shoot. You can't get goals that way."

The refereeing of Lecompte's colleague in Italy, Germany's Hans Unger, however, left a lot to be desired and sparked a controversy that didn't go away. Up until the medal round, the most surprising result for Canada was its narrow 3–1 win over their lowly hosts, the Italians. The previous day, the Dutchies had beaten Austria 23–0, a team Italy had managed to tie 2–2 two days earlier. Surely Canada would pummel Italy with equal ease?

Over the first two periods, though, Unger whistled Canada for ten penalties to Italy's two. The games still used a two-referee system, and of Canada's infractions, nine were called by Unger. Twice

The Soviets beat Sweden, 4–1, en route to gold, while Tre Kronor settled for fourth place.

Hotel. Inside that building, there was a similar ceremony where the inhabitants mourned the passing of an era. In the hotel was housed the Kitchener–Waterloo hockey team and all those other Canadians who aspired to Olympic heights in the field of amateur competition. There was no joy there, no happy words, no jubilation, for last night Canadian amateur hockey suffered a blow to its prestige from which it may never recover. The Kitchener–Waterloo team was beaten fairly and squarely by a team which would never make the junior finals in Canada. If you think saying that is easy, then you are greatly mistaken."

This "end of the world" shock was balanced by the rest of the medal round results. Ten teams were whittled down to six for the chance to win medals, and the standings of that round look as they might today, in the 21st century. But some 60 years ago, this was the very dawn of hockey's modern era, and the standings were extraordinary.

Sweden beat the Czechs while the Soviets beat Sweden. On the final day, all medals were still up for grabs as Canada played the Soviets and the United States played the Czechs. The Americans won easily, 9–4, giving them eight points and a share of first place with the Soviets. If Canada won its game, there would be a three-way tie and Canada would likely have won silver.

But no one got the chance to do the math to break such a three-way tie. Yuri Krylov scored in the second period and Valentin Kuzin early in the third. Nikolai Puchkov was perfect in goal, and the Soviets produced a gold-medal effort in a 2–0 win. The gold at the 1954 Worlds was no fluke, and the Americans had also vaulted over the Canadians into second place.

Canada was down five men to three, and at one time Italy had seven men on the ice. Rather than call a too-many-men penalty, Unger blew play dead and ordered Italy to send a man to the bench.

Canadian coach Bobby Bauer called Unger "disgraceful," and Jimmy Dunn, president of the CAHA, immediately protested Unger's involvement in any further games involving Canada. Walter Brown of the IIHF agreed and never assigned Unger a Canada game thereafter.

A game that had as stunning a result without any controversy was Canada's 4–1 defeat by the United States on January 31, 1956. The loss virtually ensured Canada would not win gold, an unfathomable situation given Canada's superiority from 1920 and on.

Thom Benson of CBC Radio reported the result with appropriate solemnity: "Today, in this small mountain village, there was a funeral. The bells of the ancient church told the passing of a procession. The mourners chanted prayers as they trudged up the steep hills behind the coffin bearers. Those who were left were saying their farewells to a robust and lively friend. The cortege wound its way through narrow and twisted streets up past the Concordia

The 1956 Olympics were considered a dismal failure for Canada and an historic triumph for the Soviets. Bronze was a medal, a medal that symbolized failure. It was the worst placing a Canadian team had achieved in 36 years of Olympic hockey. It also ushered in a new era of the game, and with it a new controversy that would rage for the next two decades as the Soviets rose to prominence and then became unbeatable.

Soviet official Roman Kiselev was asked by one Canadian reporter how much professional hockey players were paid in the Soviet Union, and he answered tersely: "There are no professionals in Russia." So, while the Soviets operated a league of their own and trained their Olympians 11 months of the year, Kiselev was suggesting the players didn't actually earn a salary of any size, shape, or form.

All the same, the Canadians in charge of the country's Olympic representatives were again questioning the concept of sending a team to international events, suggesting again that a best-of-the-best format would be better, if not essential, if Canada were to remain competitive in the years ahead, especially if the Soviets were going to send their best of the best to the Olympics and World Championships.

Further, it wasn't just a discussion of amateur versus professional or league team versus all-star collection that mattered. The larger issue was that the Soviets trained year-round specifically for the top IIHF events while the CAHA forced its players to gather at the last minute to prepare for events that clearly were gaining in prestige and importance. It was getting impossibly tough to ask Canadians to play under these conditions and skate away with the gold medal. The Soviets were using this to their advantage.

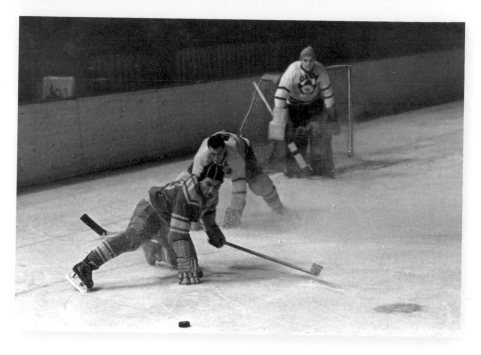

Canadian goalie Keith Woodall watches a teammate fight off a Soviet in CCCP's crucial 2-0 victory.

RESULTS

TOURNAMENT FORMAT

Ten teams were divided into three groups, each playing a round-robin schedule within that group. The top two teams from each section then advanced to a six-team finals round. The team with the most points during the six (two points for a win, one for a tie) won the gold, with goal differential being the deciding factor in the event of a tie. If still tied, goals against average would be the last method to decide the winner. Tie games after 60 minutes of play would not be decided by overtime.

MEDAL ROUND

	GP	W	T	L	GF	GA	P
Soviet Union	5	5	0	0	25	5	10
United States	5	4	0	1	26	12	8
Canada	5	3	0	2	23	11	6
Sweden	5	1	1	3	10	17	3
Czechoslovakia	5	1	0	4	20	30	2
Germany	5	0	1	4	6	35	1

UNITED STATES
SQUAW VALLEY
1960
FEBRUARY 19–28

8TH OLYMPIC WINTER GAMES

SQUAW VALLEY CALIFORNIA   FÉVRIER 1960

LES VIIIème JEUX
OLYMPIQUES D'HIVER

SILVER
Canada

GOLD
United States

BRONZE
Soviet Union

THE QUIET MIRACLE

These Olympics turned out to be quite possibly the most dramatic for hockey ever played. Canada had regained its inside position as favourites, thanks to winning gold at the 1958 and 1959 World Championships, but the competition from other top countries was intensifying every year. By the end of the event, Canada and the Soviets took a back seat to the Americans, who produced one of the most dominant, surprising, and impressive showings in international hockey history.

An important development occurred when the 1959 Allan Cup champion Whitby Dunlops declined the invitation to represent Canada at Squaw Valley, thus paving the way for the Kitchener–Waterloo Dutchmen to appear in their second successive Olympics. As in 1956, they were at a disadvantage right off the bat because three of their number – Bill Kennedy, George Gosselin, and Dick Mattiussi – were professionals and thus ineligible. Given this, and the fact that the Dutchmen had placed third at Cortina, it was clear the team needed to augment its roster. As a result, the Dutchies got Bob Attersley, Fred Etcher,

George Samolenko, and Harry Sinden from the Whitby Dunlops; Moe Benoit from the Belleville MacFarlands; Don Head from the Windsor Bulldogs; and Jack and Jim Connelly from the Chatham Maroons. The Montreal Canadiens also made superstar prospect Bobby Rousseau available.

Rousseau's inclusion was the result of a surprising turn of events. On January 12, 1960, K–W manager Ernie Gorman announced that 19-year old St. Michael's College star centre (and future Maple Leafs captain) Dave Keon would be given a one-game trial the next night when K–W played a home game against the Windsor Bulldogs. Keon was spectacular that night, scoring once and creating numerous chances while displaying his trademark stickhandling wizardry. He had, more or less, made the Olympic team based on the strength of his play.

St. Mike's, however, was prepared to loan him to the Olympians for the shortest of time, such was his value to the team. Wren Blair, a key member of the Olympic team's player committee, felt that in fairness to the other players, Keon would be needed for six weeks, not three as St. Mike's had suggested.

St. Mike's coach, Father David Bauer, sympathetic but resolute, suggested Bobby Rousseau of the Brockville Canadiens, the Habs' farm team, to replace Keon. Montreal general manager Frank Selke consented to the loan. Keon returned to St. Mike's, and Rousseau joined the Olympians.

The Olympics were fraught with controversy again. The schedule, for starters, was cruel. Teams were being asked to play eight games in ten days. As well, the indoor rink was booked virtually day and night for figure skaters to practise and compete on, leaving all hockey teams to practise outside. But outdoors, there was little ice due to a pleasant thaw that had arrived in time for the games.

Television interests produced a series of heated discussions that ended up in a weird and wacky final

Jubilant Americans celebrate a most improbable gold after defeating all comers in 1960.

weekend of play. CBS, which had paid $1 million to broadcast the Games, wanted the United States and Canada to play on the final afternoon because it would draw huge ratings. The Soviets, though, wanted to play Canada at that same time because, they argued, this was surely to be the game to decide gold.

In the end, it was agreed that no games, save consolation-round matches, would be played outdoors. The three games that were scheduled for opening day would begin in the evening, producing a ridiculous situation in which the CCCP–Germany game started at midnight. And Canada and the United States would play Thursday night – a good TV night – paving the way for a gold-medal showdown Sunday afternoon between the Canadians and the Soviets. The Americans would play the Czechs at 8 a.m., much earlier in the day on Sunday.

The preliminary round produced no surprises. The top two teams from three groups advanced to a round-robin finals group, and it was there that the fun began in earnest. The opening night provided games between the three top teams

Bill Christian scores the winning goal against the Soviets in the third period.

though, the Americans did it again. Bill Cleary scored early in the opening period to give the Americans a 1–0 lead, but the Soviets answered with two quick goals.

The lead held until midway through the second period when Bill Christian tied the game, and with 5:01 left in the third he got his second of the night, which turned out to be the game winner. For the second time in three days the Americans poured off the bench and mobbed McCartan, and now, incredibly, the Canada–CCCP game on Sunday afternoon was the penultimate of the Olympics. Now, the game that mattered most was the U.S.–Czech game, and organizers couldn't believe that this game was scheduled for Sunday 8 a.m.

There have probably never been so few spectators for so important a game in Olympic hockey history, but those who were there witnessed a remarkable contest. The first period featured six goals and ended in a 3–3 tie, and the Czechs got the only goal of the middle period from Miroslav Vlach. Coach Jack Riley gave the talk of his life in the second intermission, his team trailing 4–3 and that close to gold. One apocryphal tale has it that the Soviets, so eager were they to have the Americans win gold instead of the Canadians, came into the dressing room and advised the Americans to use oxygen to boost their recovery for what promised to be a frenetic final 20 minutes.

Whatever happened, worked. The Americans scored an incredible six goals in the final period and waltzed to a 9–4 win to capture gold. This marked the only time to this day that one of the top six nations beat four other top nations to win gold. In this case, the United States beat Canada, Sweden, the Czechoslovaks, and the Russians – and won gold. It was the first "miracle" win for the nation, the first Olympic gold in hockey, and a thoroughly unexpected result. Later that day Canada blitzed the

against the underdogs, with unsurprising results. The Soviets outscored the Czechoslovaks 8–5; the Americans beat the Swedes 6–3; and Canada hammered Germany 12–0.

Two nights later came the first shocker, as Tre Kronor tied CCCP 2–2. All goals came in a wild third period. Nisse Nilsson gave the Swedes an early lead, but the Soviets scored twice in the middle part of the period to take control. But with just 1:28 left in the game, Nilsson scored again to give the Swedes a critical point in the standings (and, more important, take one point away from the Soviets' tally).

The next night, Thursday, it was the home team that provided one of the most shocking results in Olympics history when they beat Canada 2–1. The Americans built a 2–0 lead through 40 minutes and sustained a formidable attack in the final minute to preserve the win. Goalie Jack McCartan was spectacular – the main reason Canada didn't win the game with room to spare.

This marked the second Olympics in a row that the Canadians had lost a game to the Americans, but with the U.S.–CCCP game yet to be played, Canada still held hopes for gold. Two days later,

Soviets 8–5 to win silver, but silver was the colour of failure.

This second-place showing was indicative of two factors, both of which would have to be addressed if Canada were ever to remain atop the international hockey heap. First, the idea of taking a single club to represent the country no longer seemed possible. After all, this K–W team, an excellent amateur team, had, in the end, only eight original members on the final Olympic roster.

Furthermore, it was also clear that the players competing for communist countries, most notably the CCCP, were the 17 best players in that country. Had the finest 17 Canadians in 1960 – Gordie Howe, Terry Sawchuk, Henri Richard, George Armstrong, Jean Beliveau – been permitted to represent Canada, it would surely have won the gold.

CAHA representative Gordon Juckes commented that: "In my opinion, there are a number of lessons for Canada in the 1960 Winter Olympic Games. Compared to other teams, ours was not banded together soon enough as a team unit. The CAHA's draft regulations, which we and Kitchener both hoped would provide our team with reinforcements well in advance, broke down for a number of reasons. It was the beginning of February – with the Olympics barely two weeks away – before Canada's complete Olympic team came together finally and conclusively."

The main venue in Squaw Valley had stands on all four sides but was an open-air arena by virtue of the corners which were exposed to the elements.

RESULTS

TOURNAMENT FORMAT

The format remained unchanged from the one used in Cortina d'Ampezzo in 1956. The nine competing countries were divided into three pools of three teams, each pool playing round-robin games with the others in their division. The top two teams from each pool then advanced to a six-team finals round robin, the gold medal going to the team with the most points (two for a win, one for a tie). In the event of a tie in the standings, goal differential would decide the winner.

MEDAL ROUND

	GP	W	T	L	GF	GA	P
United States	5	5	0	0	29	11	10
Canada	5	4	0	1	31	12	8
Soviet Union	5	2	1	2	24	18	5
Czechoslovakia	5	2	0	3	21	23	4
Sweden	5	1	1	3	19	19	3
Germany	5	0	0	5	5	45	0

AUSTRIA
INNSBRUCK 1964
JANUARY 29–FEBRUARY 9

9TH OLYMPIC WINTER GAMES

SILVER Sweden

GOLD Soviet Union

BRONZE Czechoslovakia

SOVIETS BEGIN TO DOMINATE

These Olympics marked the beginning of the second dynasty in hockey history at the Games. Whereas Canada dominated from 1920 to 1952, winning gold six of seven times, the Soviets were now on their way to winning seven of the next eight. They did so with a unique style of play. Coach Anatoli Tarasov was a huge fan of Lloyd Percival, a Canadian who espoused modern training regimens, careful attention to diet, and skating and passing skills above all.

Tarasov combined Percival's beliefs with his own style of coaching in which players were grouped as five-man units rather than forward lines and defensive pairings. And players were instructed not to wantonly give up possession of the puck. If an opening didn't present itself during a rush, turn back and try again. Don't shoot on goal until a clear scoring chance had been created. And don't just dump the puck in and chase it.

As for Canada, the influence exerted by Father David Bauer guided the nation's teams. In June 1962, when the CAHA held its summer meetings in Toronto, Father Bauer proposed a setup that included uniting the top amateurs in university hockey with Senior A players and letting them compete together for a year with the sole ambition to prepare for major tournaments, notably the Olympics and World Championships.

The CAHA embraced the concept and agreed that the first team would centralize at the University of British Columbia (with which Father Bauer had become affiliated after leaving St. Mike's). With little fanfare, Father Bauer officially began his term as Canada's "national team" coach on August 21, 1963, when players gathered at UBC to begin preparations for the 1964 Olympics in Innsbruck.

Sweden's captain, Sven "Tumba" Johansson, celebrates his team's silver medal in 1964, only the nation's third Olympic medal ever.

Father Bauer was drawing talent from a pool that lacked that very ingredient he most required. Canada's university students and senior players were, quite simply, not the country's best. Thus, the best thing Father Bauer's concept had going for was that by playing together for an extended period, the players would be a more cohesive unit and be more effective than if they were assembled with greater haste.

In the end, the medals were decided by the games one would imagine. In the first week and a half the Swedes beat the Americans for only the second time in 34 years, a 7–4 decision, while the Soviets beat the Czechs 7–5. The Soviets built up a 4–0 lead after the first period, and although the Czechoslovaks fought back, they were too far down to mount a comeback. Both Canada and the Soviets started out with wins in their first five games and the Czechoslovaks and Swedes had but one loss.

Canada beat Sweden by a 3–1 score on the second day of games, and that game included an incident that almost sparked a riot. Carl Oberg, a Swedish forward, broke his stick during play and in frustration tossed the tattered twig in the Canadian bench as he skated to his own bench to get a new one. The stick hit an unsuspecting Bauer in the forehead, opening a cut. The Canadian players were incensed, but Bauer restrained his players.

IIHF president Bunny Ahearne suspended Oberg for one game, and Gennaro Olivieri, the Swiss referee who failed to give Oberg a penalty on the play, was also suspended for a game. In an expression of sportsmanship, Father Bauer invited Oberg to be his guest the next night to watch the Czechoslovakia–Soviet game, a gesture that earned international acclaim.

At the end of the Games, Father Bauer was awarded a special gold medal for "the control he exercised over his players" during the stick-throwing incident, which easily could have turned into a full-scale brawl. Oberg's actions were stupid and irresponsible, of course, but he had no intention of actually hurting Bauer or any player on the bench.

All of the drama for medals centred on the final two days of the tournament with all possibilities still open for the top teams. In the Canada–Czechoslovak

The Soviets started the 1964 Olympics with a 5–1 win over the United States en route to a perfect 7-0-0 record and the gold medal.

game – throughout the Olympics, in fact – Canada's goalie Seth Martin was brilliant, and with fewer than ten minutes remaining in the game, his team still had a 1–0 lead, thanks to Rod Seiling's second-period goal. The game turned, though, when a Czechoslovakian player collided with Martin on a rush. The goalie tumbled to the ice, clutching his left leg.

Martin was determined to continue, but two minutes later he was forced to accept the fact that his injury compromised his ability to stop the puck. He skated to the bench, and backup Ken Broderick took his place. With no warmup and almost no Olympic experience to his credit, he was hardly prepared for the pressure of this situation. Jan Klapac tied the game at 11:10; captain Jiri Holik got the go-ahead goal two and a half minutes later; and Josef Cerny put the icing

on the cake with a final tally at 19:01. A game Canada controlled ended in heart-breaking defeat.

The Soviets, meanwhile, got by Sweden 4–2 in a game equally close. The score was tied 2–2 in the third period, but early goals from Leonid Volkov and Viktor Kuzkin ensured victory. As was always the case with CCCP, it had the ability to strike quickly and frequently. A close game was never over until the final buzzer, and the Swedes paid the price for being too content with the tie score instead of pouncing on a situation in which the Soviets were vulnerable.

One day later, gold was decided when Canada played the Soviets in one of the great battles between the teams in the 1960s. George Swarbrick got the only goal of the first period to give Canada the lead, but Yevgeni Mayorov tied the score midway through the second. Undaunted, Bob Forhan put Canada in front three minutes later, but Vyacheslav Starshinov tied the score again late in the period. One period left for gold.

Father Bauer put Martin back in goal for the third period after Broderick had played the first 40 minutes, hoping the injured goalie would provide some motivation for his players. But Veniamin Alexandrov scored just 1:36 into the final period to put the Soviets ahead, and although Canada had a late power play, CCCP held on for the victory to claim the title.

The disappointment didn't end there. It was the CAHA's understanding that in the case of a tie in the standings, the superior position would be decided by goal differential versus games involving the top four teams only. Thus, at the end of the final day of competition, a problem occurred when there was a second-place tie among three teams – Canada, the Swedes, and the Czechoslovaks.

Accordingly, Sweden was set to claim the silver medal (11 goals for, 10 against, +1 overall in games versus Canada, Soviets, and Czechoslovakia), and Canada the bronze because it had a -1 goal differential. The Czechs were -5 and would finish fourth. However, the IIHF later announced later that the tiebreak would be decided by goal differential against *all* teams, thereby pushing the Czechs into third and dropping Canada to fourth.

Not having heard this new ruling, the Canadian players walked into the Ice Palace for the awards ceremonies, learning only then that they had been denied a medal. "Come on, fellas," said Father Bauer, "let's get out of here. We're not getting anything."

Opening Ceremonies for the 9th Olympic Winter Games, in Innsbruck, Austria.

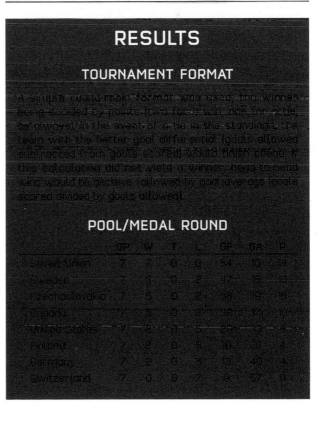

RESULTS

TOURNAMENT FORMAT

A simple round-robin format was used, the winner being decided by points (two for a win, one for a tie, as always). In the event of a tie in the standings, the team with the better goal differential (goals allowed subtracted from goals scored) would finish ahead. If this calculation did not yield a winner, head-to-head wins would be decisive followed by goal average (goals scored divided by goals allowed).

POOL/MEDAL ROUND

	GP	W	T	L	GF	GA	P
Soviet Union	7	7	0	0	54	10	14
Sweden	7	5	0	2	47	18	10
Czechoslovakia	7	5	0	2	38	19	10
Canada	7	5	0	2	32	17	10
United States	7	2	0	5	29	33	4
Finland	7	2	0	5	10	31	4
Germany	7	2	0	5	13	49	4
Switzerland	7	0	0	7	9	57	0

FRANCE

GRENOBLE 1968

FEBRUARY 6–17

10TH OLYMPIC WINTER GAMES

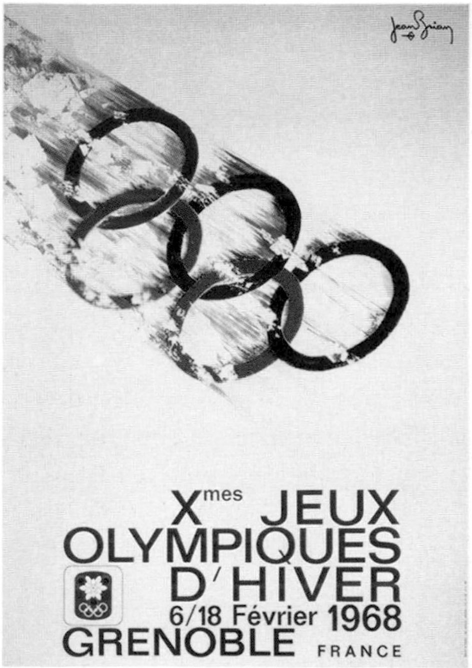
Xmes JEUX
OLYMPIQUES
D'HIVER
6/18 Février 1968
GRENOBLE
FRANCE

SILVER Czechoslovakia

GOLD Soviet Union

BRONZE Canada

TWO IN A ROW

The gold-medal win by the Soviets marked the first time a nation had won consecutive titles since Canada in 1948 and 1952, but although it was an impressive victory, it was not emphatic. The Soviets beat the four weaker teams easily but lost to the Czechoslovaks 5–4 and eked out a 3–2 win over Sweden. On the final day, the gold medal hanging in the balance, the Soviets hammered Canada 5–0, winning gold and relegating Father Bauer's national team to bronze. There was a clear hierarchy between the top four teams and bottom four, the United States joining Finland and the two Germanys in the latter category this year.

In the years following the team's disappointing fourth-place finish at the 1964 Games in Innsbruck, Canada had finished fourth, third, and third again at the World Championships won each year by the Soviet Union. Father Bauer's team concept might have been the best Canada could hope for, but it was still made up of mostly of Canadian university students and not likely able to defeat the experienced Soviets any time soon.

One change saw the national team divided into two groups, one in Winnipeg in the Western Canadian Senior League and the other in Ottawa playing in the Quebec Provincial Senior League. Coach Jackie McLeod felt that this structure would give the greatest number of players the greatest opportunity to show their skills and prove themselves worthy of the final Olympic roster. By the same token, though, it prevented the final team from getting to know one another on ice, which was a significant point to the creation of the national team in the first place.

Team Canada's most important pre-Olympic test, however, came at a tournament in Grenoble at the newly built Olympic Stadium, featuring four countries – Canada, Czechoslovakia, Soviet Union, and the United States. The national team won the tournament, beating its top three opponents on the eve of the Games.

The ever-present conversation that remained in the air during these Olympics continued to be about amateur status. As Canada struggled to put together a truly amateur team of players who were not paid but who were of high calibre, its two greatest opponents – the Soviets and Czechoslovaks – assembled teams that played year-round and were professional in every sense of the word. Canada tried to be diplomatic, but that line of reasoning got nowhere.

As a result, Father Bauer's main concerns for the long-term future of the national program, as he admitted, remained unsolved: "We set up the national team concept four years ago on a four-year program. . . . Now we must plan ahead as to whether we will continue to develop. The team can't go on living from hand-to-mouth year after year. Also, we must do something to counter the attractive offers some of our players are receiving from professional clubs."

The early games in Grenoble had two significant surprises. The first was a close 4–3 win by Sweden over the Americans, and the second was a more

The Czechs beat the Soviets, 5–4, in a bitterly-contested game between two communist enemies.

devastating 5–2 win by Finland over Canada. The Finns scored early and built a 2–0 lead midway through the opening period and got some fine goaltending by Urpo Ylonen to contain the Canadian attack. The loss pretty much scuppered Canada's chances for gold without beating the Soviets and gave the Finns hope of their first Olympic medal.

Canada clawed its way back into contention with a crucial 3–2 win over the Czechoslovaks, a win that was due in large part to an odd play at a critical time. Canada had surged to an impressive 3–0 lead after two periods. However, the Czechs came out flying to start the third and scored twice in the first three minutes to make it a 3–2 game. They continued to press Ken Broderick's net for the tying goal, and then Danny O'Shea, on his way to the bench for a line change and furious with himself after having missed a breakaway, smashed his stick against the Plexiglas by Canada's bench. The glass shattered and the game was held up ten minutes while it was replaced.

The Czechs built a 5–2 lead against the Soviets early in the third, just enough to withstand a rally and hold on to a one-goal victory.

McLeod used the unplanned timeout to settle down his players. Canada held on to win 3–2 and remained tied with the Czechs for second place at that point in the tournament. The coach later admitted that the break was fortuitous. "The guys somehow got their signals mixed, and on both Czech goals we were caught with three men deep. After that delay, though, they settled down and played it right."

Entering the 1968 Olympics, the Soviets had played 32 consecutive championship games without a loss dating back to March 8, 1963 (World Championships and Olympics). In Grenoble, they extended their record to 37 games before taking on their biggest rivals, Czechoslovakia, on February 15.

That game proved to be a classic. Boris Mayorov gave the Soviets the lead after just 28 seconds, but the Czechoslovaks bounced back, scoring three unanswered goals in less than four minutes. For the rest of the evening the teams played arguably the best international game to date. The pace and emotion was spectacular as the Soviets found themselves in the unique position of having to play come-from-behind hockey.

The CSSR squad had a 4–2 lead going into the final period, and when Jaroslav Jirik (who one year later would become the first player from inside the Iron Curtain to play in the NHL) scored the fifth goal with four minutes left, everyone in the Olympic arena thought the game was as much as over. But the Soviets had one more comeback in them. Viktor Polupanov and Mayorov scored within one minute to make it a 5–4 game as the champions staged a furious assault on goaltender Vladimir Dzurilla.

And, indeed, goaltending proved to be the difference. While Dzurilla was superb, the Soviets' Viktor Konovalenko had a poor game, having surrendered two weak goals. The Soviets could not manage to score the tying goal, and the Czechoslovaks celebrated as if they had won gold.

On the morning of February 17, the final day of hockey games, the standings were as tight as one could have imagined. Three teams were tied for first place with ten points – Canada, the Soviets, and the Czechoslovaks – and Sweden had eight points. The afternoon game saw the Swedes and Czechoslovaks tie 2–2, so for a brief time Czechoslovakia was in first place with 11 points. The winner of the Canada–Soviet Union game would win gold; the loser would have to settle for silver. A tie would give Canada silver because it had beaten the Czechoslovaks. Sweden was now in fourth.

More than 15,000 people packed the Stade de Glace in Grenoble to see the final game of the 1968 Olympics. While both Canada and the Soviets maintained a blistering pace, CCCP got the upper hand when Anatoly Firsov scored short-handed late in the first period.

The 1–0 score lasted for 18 minutes until Yevgeni Mishakov doubled the lead at 12:44. The score was in greater thanks due to goalie Viktor Konovalenko, who stopped Fran Huck close in and then Morris Mott and Herb Pinder in quick succession. A third goal early in the final period was the dagger in Canada's heart, and two later goals made it a lopsided 5–0 result. Gold for the Soviets; bronze for Father Bauer's national team.

Despite losing to the Czechs, CCCP won its second straight Olympic gold in 1968 while their adversaries finished second.

RESULTS

TOURNAMENT FORMAT

The top eight teams were grouped into a medal round section, each playing a round-robin schedule. The top team in the standings (two points for a win, one for a tie) would win the gold medal. In the event of a two-way tie, the winner of the head-to-head game would get the gold. If there were a tie between more than two teams, goal differential (goals against subtracted from goals scored) would be the deciding factor.

POOL/MEDAL ROUND

	GP	W	T	L	GF	GA	P
Soviet Union	7	6	0	1	48	10	12
Czechoslovakia	7	5	1	1	33	17	11
Canada	7	5	0	2	28	15	10
Sweden	7	4	1	2	23	18	9
Finland	7	3	1	3	17	23	7
United States	7	2	1	4	23	28	5
West Germany	7	1	0	6	13	39	2
East Germany	7	0	0	7	13	48	0

JAPAN
SAPPORO 1972
FEBRUARY 5–13

11TH OLYMPIC WINTER GAMES

SILVER
United States

GOLD
Soviet Union

BRONZE
Czechoslovakia

SOVIETS DOMINATE IN AN HISTORIC YEAR

Although the 1972 Olympics turned in a predictable result, the year was one of the most significant in the history of hockey. It produced three different champions of sort – Olympics, World Championships, Summit Series – each one important for a variety of reasons. To start, though, the Soviets dominated the six-team field in Sapporo, winning gold, while the underappreciated Americans beat the Czechoslovaks and took the silver.

As well, this year marked the first time that the IIHF had held a World Championship tournament in the same season as the Olympics. The experiment lasted only this year and 1976 before being abandoned until 1992, after which there has been a World Championship every year regardless of the Olympics.

But the Sapporo Olympics were noteworthy also because Canada did not send a team. This remarkable statement by Hockey Canada stemmed from the ongoing concern, which had escalated into a fight, over the so-called amateurs from the Eastern Bloc. Indeed, Canada had withdrawn entirely from international hockey in 1970 just as it was about to host the Worlds for the first time.

The backstory represents a pivotal moment in the sport's history. After winning the 1968 federal election, Prime Minister Pierre Trudeau fulfilled a campaign promise by commissioning a Task Force on Sports aimed at understanding amateur hockey in Canada and why its programs had become increasingly unsuccessful over the past decade. The committee concluded that one organizing body should be created to oversee all levels of amateur hockey and control all national and international competitions participated in by Canada.

Hockey Canada, formed on February 24, 1969, felt that since Canada was hosting the World Championship in 1970 (Winnipeg and Montreal), its goal should be to make it one in which Canada's professionals could compete. When the IIHF met in Switzerland in July 1969, the question of professional participation was at the top of the agenda. The IIHF agreed to allow nine non-NHL pros into each tournament for one year, after which a full review would decide the long-term future of the practice. It wasn't all Hockey Canada had hoped for, but it was something.

The first significant tournament under the new arrangement was the Isvestia, in Moscow at Christmas 1969. Canada used only five pros and finished a close second, and as a result the IIHF held an emergency meeting on January 3, 1970, immediately after the tournament's conclusion. At this time, president Avery Brundage rescinded the rule and declared that any players competing against

J.P. Parise is barely able to contain his emotions during Game 8 of the Summit Series against referee Josef Kompalla.

Canada's pros would be forfeiting their amateur status and would not be eligible to compete at the Olympics. Hockey Canada was livid.

Earl Dawson, president of the CAHA, declared that if the non-NHL pros agreement were not re-established, Canada would not host the Worlds, would withdraw from international competition, and would not send teams on goodwill exhibition tours through Europe. The IIHF was nonplussed, and Hockey Canada followed through on its threat.

John Munro, federal minister of national health and welfare, praised the tough decision: "Our country has not been able to ice the best teams because of farcical regulations which made it impossible to use players with the same experience as those other countries used. Canada has *some* pride."

David Molson, president of the Montreal

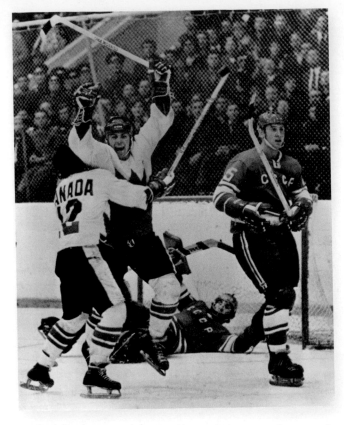

Paul Henderson celebrates the goal that won the Summit Series for Canada with 34 seconds left in Game 8.

That game was an anomaly as the Soviets squandered a 3–1 lead in the third period and settled for a tie. Sweden, however, lost to the Czechoslovaks and Finns and finished fourth, unable to take advantage of taking that important point from CCCP.

While Soviet victory was a given at the Olympics, the silver medals won by the United States were anything but. In fact, the Americans' performance was almost as stunning as in 1960. The team had been doing so poorly that it competed in B Pool for the World Championship later in the year after a dismal showing in 1971, but it qualified for the Olympics and surprised even itself. The team included Henry Boucha and Robbie Ftorek, two players who went on to play in the NHL, but beyond those names it was an anonymous and trivial roster.

Although the United States lost to Sweden 5–1 and to the Soviets 7–2, it beat Czechoslovakia 5–1. The Czechoslovakians scored early in the game, but the Americans tied it later in the period and then scored three times in the second to pull away for the win. Just a few weeks later, practically this exact Czechoslovakian team won gold at the World Championship.

The Americans, meanwhile, beat Finland and Poland later in the Games. The Americans and Czechoslovakians tied for second place with 3–0–2 records, but the Americans received the higher placing because of head-to-head results. It wasn't until 1975 that they returned to A Pool at the Worlds, but for this one Olympic year they produced a special and memorable result.

The end of the Olympics usually signalled the pinnacle of the international hockey season, but in 1972 it merely signalled the start of much more important hockey still to be played. After beating Canada 5–0 in the 1968 Olympics, Soviet coach Anatoli Tarasov boasted that his team could beat any in the NHL.

By 1972, it became clear that such an opportunity would be beneficial for everyone concerned, and so Hockey Canada negotiated an eight-game tournament in which the very best players in Canada would play any team that the Soviets could put together. The first four games would be played in Canada, the

Canadiens, was equally supportive. "I'm in full agreement with the decision," he said. "We should have done it 10 years ago. I'm glad we stood up to them and did not compromise. It is a matter of principle." Abroad, praise was equally high for the Canadians' stance. In Sweden, the newspaper *Dagens Nyheter* said that, "[IOC president Bunny] Ahearne has conducted this confused affair so badly that he should now leave his post. Otherwise there is a great risk that the cold war will be protracted." In Finland's *Ilta Sanomat*, the editors concurred: "It is no longer reasonable to distinguish between professionals and amateurs. The Russian world champions are no less professionals than the Canadians. It is unnecessary to speak of 'pure amateurs' in any country."

Two years later, the disagreement no closer to a resolution, Canada didn't go to Sapporo. The top pool of the Olympics, then, consisted of only six teams playing a single round robin, only 15 games in total. The Soviets, of course, won gold, winning four games easily and tying the other 3–3 with Sweden.

last four in Moscow. The dates were September 1 to 28, 1972.

The most revealing fact about the Summit Series was that the Soviets' roster included 13 players who had played at the Sapporo Olympics earlier in the year and, incredibly, seven players from the 1968 Winter Olympics at Grenoble. Team Canada had not one player for the Summit Series who had played at these Olympics, full proof that Canada's best amateurs and pros represented two distinct pools of talent while the pros and amateurs of the Soviet Union were identical.

The series proved to be a defining moment in Canada's cultural and sporting history and changed the international game forever. Canada's narrow victory heralded both pride within and respect for an opponent that was clearly better than Canada had given it credit for. In the short term, though, the Summit Series was an isolated event. The IOC and IIHF were no closer to allowing professionals to join the Olympics, and Canada continued to boycott all international competitions.

RESULTS

TOURNAMENT FORMAT

The six teams were grouped into one section, each playing a round-robin schedule. The top team in the standings (two points for a win, one for a tie) would win the gold medal. In the event of a two-way tie, the winner of the head-to-head game would get the gold. If there were a tie between more than two teams, goal differential (goals against subtracted from goals scored) would be the deciding factor.

POOL/MEDAL ROUND

	GP	W	T	L	GF	GA	P
Soviet Union	5	4	1	0	33	13	9
United States	5	3	0	2	18	15	6
Czechoslovakia	5	3	0	2	26	13	6
Sweden	5	2	1	2	17	13	5
Finland	5	2	0	3	14	24	4
Poland	5	0	0	5	9	39	0

The Americans stunned the hockey world by winning silver at the 1972 Olympics despite being in the B Pool in World Championship play.

AUSTRIA

INNSBRUCK 1976

FEBRUARY 6–14

12TH OLYMPIC WINTER GAMES

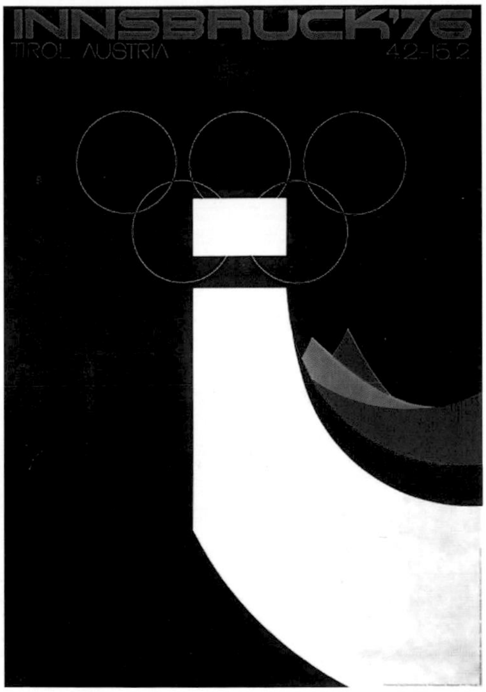

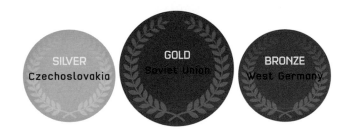

SILVER Czechoslovakia

GOLD Soviet Union

BRONZE West Germany

SOVIETS ROLL ALONG

The 1976 Olympic hockey tournament was a virtual replica of the one held four years earlier. Canada didn't compete; the Soviets won a six-team event with just 15 total games; and the Games were only a prelude to a more important event later in the year. The top story to come out of these Olympics that was not expected was surely the bronze medal won by West Germany, the first medal it had won since a bronze in 1932. More impressive, German forward Erich Kuhnhackl tied for the tournament lead with ten points.

The Soviets won gold on the final day of the Olympics against their greatest rivals of this era, the Czechoslovaks. The CSSR had lost earlier to Poland because of a doping violation committed by Frantisek Pospisil, so they needed to win to get the gold. A tie would give the Soviets gold.

The Czechoslovaks started off with incredible tenacity and led 2–0 by the end of the first period, but the Soviets scored the only two goals of the middle 20 minutes to tie the score and set up one period of hockey to decide Olympic gold. Eduard Novak scored midway through the third for the Czechoslovaks, but two goals within 24 seconds late in the period gave the Soviets a 4–3 win and their fourth straight Olympic title.

Canadian hockey fans watched the event from the outside,

more concerned about other goings-on at the IIHF that were to have a greater and long-lasting impact. Several months earlier, in the summer of 1975, the IIHF replaced Bunny Ahearne with Gunther Sabetzki as president.

Sabetzki declared that getting Canada back into competition was his top priority. He met with Alan Eagleson to try to resolve the ongoing fight over amateur and pro status, and the men focused on two events, the inaugural 1976 Canada Cup, a best-on-best among six nations, and Canada's participation in the 1977 World Championship in Vienna.

The IIHF agreed to endorse the Canada Cup and was, in turn, guaranteed a flat fee of $25,000, 5 per cent of TV revenues generated by the five non-Canadian entries, and a $100,000 bond guaranteeing Canada's commitment to play at the 1977 Worlds. The last of these was a moral victory but not a victory on ice per se. The IIHF agreed that Canada could use professionals at the World Championship, but the tournament was still held in early spring at a time when the NHL playoffs were in full swing. As a result, the only real pros who could participate were those on NHL teams that did not make the playoffs or were eliminated quickly. They would be pros but not necessarily the best of the best.

The Canada Cup was the first truly international tournament featuring "best on best" from the best countries in the world, culminating with a best-of-three finals between the top two teams. Canada, the Soviet Union, Czechoslovakia, Sweden, Finland, and the United States came to play a round-robin series followed by a best-of-three finals between the top two teams in the standings. While it was no surprise to see Canada finish in first place,

The Soviets were at their dominating best in 1976, going 5-0-0 and winning gold for the fourth straight Olympics.

it was a surprise to see the Soviets in third place and the Czechoslovakians ahead of them to qualify for the finals.

That being said, the Soviets, leery of the event and possible defections, sent an "experimental" team over with young coach Viktor Tikhonov. Although they didn't make the finals, the Canada–Czechoslovakia matchup for the Canada Cup was thrilling all the same, as the Toronto Maple Leafs' Darryl Sittler proved the hero with his overtime goal in game two to win it for the home side.

The Czechs had handed Canada its only loss in the five games of the round robin, a 1–0 decision highlighted by the shutout goaltending of Vladimir Dzurilla. In the finals, however, he wasn't quite so invincible. Canada won the first game by a 6–0 score in Toronto, but the second game, in Montreal, was much closer. In fact, Canada had leads of 2–0 and 3–2 in the game, but it needed a late goal by Bill Barber to send the game into overtime.

In the fourth period, Sittler provided the heroics, faking a slap shot with Dzurilla well above his crease

The medal ceremonies saw the Soviets and Czechs take first and second place, respectively, and the West Germans claim the bronze.

and shooting it in the open net to give Canada the 5–4 win.

Although the win was great publicity for Canada, the tournament proved such a success that it became clear that fans around the world were ready to see the best play the best in a new event. There is a clear line between the series of Canada Cup tournaments that followed – in 1981, 1984, 1987, and 1991 – to the World Cup in 1996 and on to the NHL participation of 1998 and then greater NHL presence at the annual World Championship.

The 1976 Canada Cup proved that Canada had the best team, but like the wakeup call in 1972, it also proved there were several other nations close to the top or able to beat Canada on any particular day. The 1976 Canada Cup was the maturation of international hockey, the event that took international hockey out of a "European" context and into a global context of best on best, the winners crowned, in one sense, true world's champions.

The Soviets blitzed the Americans and goalie Jim Warden to the tune of 6–2 to open the 1976 Olympics.

SILVER
Soviet Union

GOLD
United States

BRONZE
Sweden

MIRACLE ON ICE

No tournament had as shocking a result as the 1980 Olympics. A group of American university students upset the mighty Soviets to claim gold and inspired a new generation of players to take up the game. The U.S. victory transformed hockey in that country and had an everlasting effect on the developmental programs, while the Soviets suffered the most ignominious defeat in their history.

And equally uncontested was the Soviet Union's status as overwhelming favourites to win a fifth Olympic gold. The team, coached by Viktor Tikhonov, won the World Championship every year since the Innsbruck Olympics, and the core of the team had been together for years. The great Vladislav Tretiak was in goal; the defence was led by a young Slava Fetisov; and the forwards were a vast array of speed and skill, notably the KLM line of Vladimir Krutov, Igor Larionov, and Sergei Makarov.

The Czechoslovaks won gold at the 1976 and 1977 World Championships and were runners-up to the Soviets the next two years. They, too, had a veteran roster that was clearly going to be the main rivals to CCCP for gold. Canada still couldn't use NHLers, and its university lineup posed little threat to the top teams, and the same was said for the Americans.

Coached by Herb Brooks, who played at the 1964 and 1968

Olympics for the United States, the team was gutsy and skilled but without any top-level international experience save Buzz Schneider, the only player from Innsbruck. Brooks, who coached at the University of Minnesota, had nine of his own on the team, and in the final exhibition game before the Olympics, on February 9, 1980, the Soviets humiliated the Americans 10–3 at Madison Square Garden.

In the round-robin preliminary round in Lake Placid, the Soviets dominated their group by winning all five games, although two were close. Finland led the Soviets 1–0 in the second period and 2–1 in the third, but the CCCP attack counted three goals in just 79 seconds late in the game to claim a 4–2 win.

The Soviet–Canada game was even more dramatic. Although Father David Bauer's dream of a national junior team endured from 1963 to 1969, Canada's withdrawal from international hockey pretty much ended the need for such a team. However, with Canada's return to the World Championships in 1977 and the Olympics in 1980, Father Bauer was able to convince Hockey Canada to reinstitute his idea at least for one Olympic cycle. Still, the problems were the same. Father Bauer brought together the best university students in Canada; the Soviets iced the best 20 skaters in their country.

Despite this discrepancy, Canada scored early and pulled ahead 3–1 early in the second period of their clash. But in hockey everyone knows how critical a late goal can be, and the Soviets brought the game within reach with just 13 seconds left in the second period when Alexei Kasatonov scored to make it 3–2. Early in the third, the teams combined for three quick goals. The Soviets scored within

No greater upset has there been than the Americans' 4–3 win over CCCP at the 1980 Olympics.

12 seconds to turn a one-goal deficit into a one-goal lead, Alexander Golikov scoring the fourth Soviet goal.

Controversy ensued when Team Canada players alleged that the Soviet forward had scored using an illegal stick. Stelio Zupancich skated to the Soviet bench to get Golikov's stick by force to show referee Jim Neagles, but Zupancich was stopped at the gate by coach Viktor Tikhonov. Shoving ensued; Neagles decided to ignore the accusation; and the game carried on.

"What we should have done," suggested Canadian forward Ron Davidson afterward, "was tackle Golikov and grab his stick before he got off the ice."

Exactly one minute later Dan D'Alvise tied the game for Canada, but captain Boris Mikhailov got the go-ahead goal at 8:41 and Golikov made it 6–4 at 16:51.

While the Canadians may have lost on the scoreboard 6–4, their performance might well have kept Father Bauer's national team alive. "I think our objectives have been partially realized," he opined, "but we have to hope that playing for their country doesn't obscure the other values to be derived from this experience. The whole rationale was to provide another option wherein some form of education could be involved, wherein some experiences other than hockey might be a part of human growth. These fellows have received pretty good coaching; they've improved their skills; hopefully this experience broadened their horizons. I think the game against the Russians brought all of these together."

In the other pool, the Americans drew inspiration from their first game and never let up. Playing the heavily favoured Swedes, they proved resilient and then successful. Sweden took an early lead that held up for a period and a half, but Dave Silk scored with just 28 seconds left in the second period to tie the game 1–1. The Swedes scored again early in the third and held the lead through the last minute of play, but Brooks pulled his goalie, Jim Craig, and with the extra attacker Bill Baker scored. The goal came with just 27 seconds left in the game, and the feeling of "we believe" was born.

Coach Herb Brooks, a former player for the U.S., was masterful behind the bench in February 1980.

Two days later, the Americans played the even more heavily favoured Czechoslovaks, and a mini-miracle took place when the home side skated to an impressive 7–3 win. The score was tied 2–2 after the first period, but the United States scored four of the five goals in the second and added another in the final period to move them improbably to the top of the standings in their pool. More expected wins against Norway, Romania, and West Germany put them in the medal round.

The medal round was a mini-round robin among the four teams, but previous games between teams counted toward the standings. Thus, the U.S.– Sweden tie carried forward, as did the Soviet win over Finland.

Every great hockey country has a defining moment, a moment when the course of its future changed, when history was made, when an event spurred a momentous development in the game. For the United States, that date was February 22, 1980. The game started at 5:06 Eastern Time and was not even shown live by ABC. The Americans faced off against the Soviets, and another 10–3 score would surely not have been a surprise to anyone. Yet, taking encouragement from their earlier results, being led by coach Brooks and fantastic goaltending from Jim

Craig, the Americans continued to believe in themselves.

Vladimir Krutov scored midway through the opening period, but Schneider tied the game 1–1. Sergei Makarov put the Soviets ahead again, and then the course of hockey started to change. Mark Johnson tied the game at 19:59, a single second left on the clock before the end of the first period. The teams skated off believing the period was over – the scoreclock showed no time remaining – but referee Karl Kaisla ruled that a goal couldn't be scored unless there was a second remaining, so he called the teams back out to "play" that final second.

Incredibly, backup goalie Vladimir Myshkin took Tretiak's place in the crease. Tikhonov had been so incensed by the tying goal, blaming Tretiak, that he took out the most dominant goalie in international hockey history and replaced him with the vastly more inexperienced Myshkin. Early in the second period, Alexander Maltsev gave the Soviets their third lead, and the game stayed that way for a long time.

The longer the Soviets failed to increase their lead, the greater confidence the Americans developed. Johnson tied the game at 8:39, and then, just 81 seconds later, Mike Eruzione put the Americans ahead 4–3. Craig held the fort, and with ten seconds remaining in the game Al Michaels, doing the play by play, asked viewers rhetorically, "Do you believe in miracles?"

Two days later, at 11:00 a.m., the Americans played Finland with gold on the line. If the United States won or tied, gold would be theirs. Finland tried to play the spoiler, taking a 1–0 and 2–1 lead by the end of the second period, but the Americans stormed out for the third period and scored three times to win 4–2. The gold medal inspired a new generation of hockey in the United States and can be seen as the very reason the country is now a major hockey power.

"Do you believe in miracles!?" The U.S. celebrates its greatest international triumph.

RESULTS

TOURNAMENT FORMAT

Twelve teams were divided into two groups and played a round-robin schedule within each division. The top two teams from each then advanced to a four-team medal round round robin. Results carried over from earlier rounds. In case of a tie in the standings, the winner of the head-to-head meeting would be awarded the superior position.

MEDAL ROUND

	GP	W	T	L	GF	GA	P
United States	3	2	1	0	10	7	5
Soviet Union	3	2	0	1	16	8	4
Sweden	3	0	2	1	7	14	2
Finland	3	0	1	2	7	11	1

SILVER
Czechoslovakia

GOLD
Soviet Union

BRONZE
Sweden

XIV Олимпийские зимние игры Сараево 1984   XIV Olympic Winter Games Sarajevo 1984   XIVémes jeux olympiques d'hiver Sarajevo 1984

Sarajevo '84

BACK ON TRACK

The Soviets presented arguably their most impressive performance in history, making amends for the loss to the United States four years earlier and winning gold easily. The lack of drama at this year's Olympics can certainly be blamed on the Americans' Miracle on Ice four years earlier. The Soviets' stunning loss "woke the giant," as they say, and the team went on a scoring and winning rampage that lasted the better part of the decade. CCCP didn't lose one game at the World Championships during the three years between Olympics, and their 13–1 win against Sweden to clinch gold in 1981 was the most lopsided such score in IIHF history. As well, they beat Canada 8–1 in a one-sided Canada Cup final, ensuring that the team's legacy was further assured (although Canada gained a measure of revenge by ousting the Soviets in the semi-finals of the 1984 Canada Cup in September).

Sarajevo was merely another notch on the team's belt. The only close game was the last of the tournament in which the Soviets shut out the Czechoslovaks 2–0, but they did so by taking the early lead, adding to it quickly in the second period, and playing perfect hockey the rest of the way. In short, the result was never in doubt.

The Czechs beat Finland, 7-3, in the preliminary round in 1984 en route to a silver medal. Suomi, meanwhile, finished sixth and off the podium.

Perhaps the most important noteworthy fact about the Soviets' easy gold was that this event marked the last top-level games for goalie Vladislav Tretiak. Still only 31, his retirement was not because of loss of skill or serious injury but because he had accomplished all he could accomplish many times over – except the one thing he was never allowed to accomplish.

Tretiak was as popular in Montreal as any city in the world outside the Soviet Union. His play in the Summit Series was his coming-out party, and his exceptional play during the famed New Year's Eve game at the Forum, a 3–3 tie on March 31, 1975, earned respect and praise for the hockey aficionados in Montreal. At the 1983 Entry Draft, the Canadiens selected the legendary goalie 138th overall in the hope of one day soon negotiating his release with the Soviets, going so far as to offer the Soviet Union Ice Hockey Federation $500,000 to allow him to play in the NHL.

The Soviets refused to part with their hero,

leaving Tretiak incensed. He had given all he had to his country for 14 years, won three Olympic gold medals and ten World Championship gold – but he was not permitted to represent the Soviets in the NHL for what would have been an historic tour of duty personally and for his homeland. With nothing left to prove and no feeling of further loyalty to the CCCP sweater, he retired.

The Czechs won silver despite not having the Stastny brothers in the lineup. All three had played in Lake Placid in 1980, but four years later all were with the Quebec Nordiques in the NHL. The drama began at the European Cup in Innsbruck, Austria, in August 1980, when Peter and Anton plotted their defection with Nordiques president Marcel Aubut and director of player development Gilles Leger.

The Czechs beat Canada, 4–0, in a game that was fiercely contested from start to finish.

a single goal against the top three teams – the Soviets, Czechoslovaks, and Swedes – its worst drought in 64 years of Olympic competition.

Scoring, though, had been one of the team's weaknesses, and it was for this reason Canada had taken the rare step of adding two juniors to the roster, Russ Courtnall and Kirk Muller, after they had competed in the World Junior Championships in Sweden. But neither of these two 18-year-olds, nor anyone else for that matter, could score in the medal round.

There were significant strides made by the IIHF in the ongoing battle over professional participation in the Olympics. President Gunther Sabetzki negotiated with the IOC to allow pros who had played ten games or less in the NHL to play in Sarajevo, including those players who had appeared for NHL affiliates or who had signed a pro contract but had yet to play a pro game. Four members of the Canadian team fell into this category – Dan Wood (St. Louis Blues), Mario Gosselin (Quebec Nordiques), Mark Morrison (New York Rangers), and Don Dietrich (Springfield Indians of the American Hockey League).

The Americans, however, felt that the IOC and IIHF had agreed to the ten-NHL game plan after they had selected their Olympic team, and William Simon, president of the U.S. Olympic Committee, was adamantly opposed to any pro Canadians participating: "Our stance is well known," he said. "A professional is not allowed to participate in the Olympic games. If they [Canada] play professionals, we will protest."

The Americans increased the intensity of their protest as their first game of the Olympics – versus Canada – approached. The IOC was forced to back

After a post-game meal on August 24, the Slovan team bus was scheduled to depart from the hotel parking lot at midnight. All players were there, except for the brothers. Peter, his wife, and Anton were already in Aubut's car on their way to Vienna, where they arrived early in the morning of August 25. The moments of defection – including an after-midnight search for Anton, who suddenly got lost for an hour in downtown Innsbruck – were in Peter's words "the scariest moments of my life. It was like being part of a John le Carré novel."

When the news broke, the sensational story grabbed headlines around the world. Players from Czechoslovakia had defected before (Vaclav Nedomansky, Richard Farda), but no escape was more dramatic. And no defection would have a bigger impact on hockey than Peter and Anton Stastny's decision to leave Bratislava for Quebec (the third brother, Marian, defected a year later).

Canada finished a disappointing and humbling fourth at Sarajevo. Although the nation qualified for the four-team medal round by winning four of five games in the preliminary round, it ended the tournament in embarrassing fashion by not scoring

Canadians and Finns shake hands after a 4-2 Canada victory in the early going of the 1984 Olympics.

down and decided that players who had appeared in even one NHL game would *not* be allowed to play. As a result, Mark Morrison and Don Dietrich were ruled ineligible, while Gosselin, Wood, and Courtnall were allowed to play.

The amateur-pro controversy was further highlighted later in the year at the 1984 Canada Cup. Only one Canadian player, James Patrick, played for both the Olympic team and Canada Cup team, but 18 members of the 1984 Soviet Olympic team also played in the Canada Cup.

RESULTS

TOURNAMENT FORMAT

The 12 teams were divided into two groups of six, all teams playing a round-robin schedule within each group. The top two teams from each group then advanced to a four country round-robin medal round with the results from the qualifying round between qualifying teams counting in the finals round as well. In the event of a tie in the preliminary round standings, head-to-head results would be the first determining factor. If that game were a tie, then overall goal differential would decide the issue.

MEDAL ROUND

	GP	W	T	L	GF	GA	P
Soviet Union	3	3	0	0	16	1	6
Czechoslovakia	3	2	0	1	6	2	4
Sweden	3	1	0	2	3	12	2
Canada	3	0	0	3	0	10	0

CALGARY 1988

FEBRUARY 13–28

15TH OLYMPIC WINTER GAMES

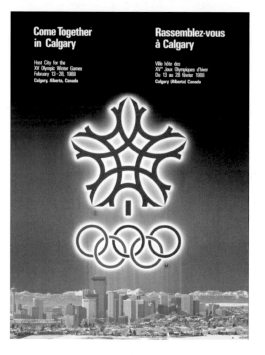

Come Together in Calgary

Host City for the
XV Olympic Winter Games
February 13–28, 1988
Calgary, Alberta, Canada

Rassemblez-vous à Calgary

Ville hôte des
XV⁰ Jeux Olympiques d'hiver
Du 13 au 28 février 1988
Calgary (Alberta) Canada

SILVER Finland

GOLD Soviet Union

BRONZE Sweden

CANADIAN HOSTS SEE SOVIETS WIN

For the first time since the Olympic Winter Games began in 1924, Canada was playing host to the world, but its hockey team put in nothing more than a respectable performance at a time when Soviet dominance remained and Canada's amateurs were having a tough time competing. Nevertheless, most Canadian NHL teams loaned at least one player to the national team to support the nation's Olympic efforts.

If ever there was going to be headway in allowing NHL players to participate in the Olympics, it would be when the Olympics were held in Canada. Seven of the 22 NHL franchises were in Canada, and with the games in an NHL city, players could easily travel to the Olympics. On October 20, 1986, IIHF president Gunther Sabetzki announced that any and all pros would be able to participate in the 1988 Olympics, making Calgary the first truly "open" Games for hockey. The words sounded better than they were.

"There are no restrictions," Sabetzki declared. "Canada can use Wayne Gretzky if it wants to." NHL president John Ziegler, however, made it clear that Gretzky was as unlikely a participant as Gordie Howe: "We put on a thousand events a year," Ziegler said. "Most of our sales are season tickets. I don't think it's fair to the customer if we say, 'You've paid $16 for your ticket – oh, by the way, for the next three weeks you're not going to see the Gretzkys, the Paul Coffeys, and the Bourques and so forth.' What would that do to the integrity of the competition?"

The NHL of 1988 was still overwhelmingly Canadian, so the only team that stood to benefit from the NHL shutting down or loaning players was Canada. Within a decade, the demographics had changed dramatically, but the Calgary Olympics were largely bereft of NHL stars.

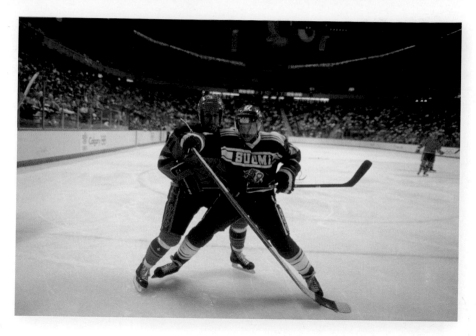

Finland and Sweden battled to a 3-3 tie at the 1988 Olympics, a Games marked by Suomi's first Olympic medal (silver).

Most Canadian-based NHL teams loaned the national team a player in, if nothing else, a symbolic gesture of support. Heading the list was goaltender Andy Moog. A member of the Edmonton Oilers from 1980 to 1987, Moog was a three-time Stanley Cup winner, but he was now sitting out in a contract dispute with Edmonton.

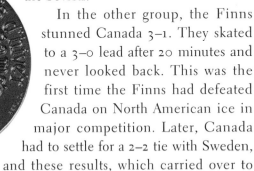

Joining him was Oilers teammate Randy Gregg, who was taking the 1987–88 season off to pursue his dream of an Olympic medal, one that had eluded him when his team finished a disappointing sixth at Lake Placid. Tim Watters was loaned by the Winnipeg Jets; Jim Peplinski and Brian Bradley were loaned by the hometown Calgary Flames; Steve Tambellini was loaned by the Canucks and Ken Yaremchuk by the Leafs.

Having lost the Canada Cup and Izvestia to Canada, the Calgary Cup to the Czechs, and the World Championship to Sweden, the Soviets were going into the Olympics without having won anything of significance in 22 months. Yet they were still the hands-down favourites and played up to that

expectation. They coasted through the preliminary round, winning all five games easily, but the biggest shocker in the early going was West Germany. The team trailed Czechoslovakia 1–0 after the first period of the opening game of this Olympiad but scored once in the second and again in the third to pull off a stunning 2–1 upset. Indeed, the only game they lost was a respectable 6–3 decision to the Soviets.

In the other group, the Finns stunned Canada 3–1. They skated to a 3–0 lead after 20 minutes and never looked back. This was the first time the Finns had defeated Canada on North American ice in major competition. Later, Canada had to settle for a 2–2 tie with Sweden, and these results, which carried over to the playoff round, all but eliminated Canada from gold-medal contention. On the first day of the medal round, Canada played the Soviets in a must-win game for the hosts because of carry-over points, which left Canada with only one and the Soviets with four.

Canada played a solid first period, killing off two penalties and coming out of it scoreless, but just 45

Finns and Swedes shake hands after playing to a tie at the Calgary Saddledome.

than 20 years after having hosted the 1965 World Championship in Tampere, the Finns tried to find ways to get their hands on any kind of a medal, but the Soviet Union, Czechoslovakia, Sweden, and Canada always stood between them and the podium.

Going into the Calgary, Finland was again on the outside looking in. No one gave the Finns any hope, especially after their opening-day 2–1 loss to lowly Switzerland. But that was, in hindsight, the perfect start for the Finns. Being dismissed from the medal expectations, Team Finland was able to fly under the radar. Four days after that fiasco against the Swiss, Finland scored its first major upset, defeating Canada 3–1.

Two days later, Suomi earned an important 3–3 tie against archrival Sweden. In the medal round, however, it seemed as though the Finns were back to their old ways. As soon as the pressure was on, Finland lost to Czechoslovakia 5–2. A medal was still possible, but Finland would have to defeat the Soviet Union.

The final game of the 1988 Olympics, on February 28, 1988, will forever be remembered by the Finnish hockey community for being the first time the national team did not fold under medal pressure. Nineteen-year old Janne Ojanen scored a magnificent goal to get the Finns going, and Erkki Lehtonen scored the winner with 1:40 remaining. Not only did the Finns finally get their medal – a silver, no less – the dramatic 2–1 win was their first ever against the Soviet Union in Olympic or World Championship competition.

On that very day, no one could have foreseen that this game was the last one that the Soviet Union played in an Olympic hockey tournament. While this was the beginning of the end for the "Big Red Machine" under the CCCP flag, the game established Finland as true hockey power – a contender rather than just a pretender.

One of the least-known events at these Olympics was also historically important. For the first time an Olympic hockey game went to a shootout. Norway and France played for 11th place in a game of little consequence, but it turned out to be 6–6 after 60 minutes. Teams took five shots each, and so new

seconds into the second Sergei Yashin scored what proved to be the winning goal. Slava Bykov added another seven minutes later, and Canada failed to score on its two power-play chances. In the third, the Soviets were merciless, scoring three goals and limiting Canada to just three shots. Soviet Union 5– Canada 0.

Two days later, the Soviets crushed Sweden 7–1 to clinch the gold medal, and on the final day they lost to Finland 2–1. The Soviets had now won every gold since 1964 with one exception (1980), but that win on the final day gave Finland the silver medal, its first ever medal in Olympic hockey competition.

Finland had been a serious contender in international hockey since the mid-1960s, but the Nordic nation could never win a medal at either the World Championship or the Olympics. For more

Finland's 2–1 win over the Soviet Union gave it a silver medal, the nation's best Olympic placing ever.

was the format to the statisticians that when France scored the only two goals of the shootout, both skaters were credited with goals! Thus, the official final score from this shootout was 8–6 for France. Derek Haas and Paulin Bordeleau, both Canadian-born, were the scorers.

RESULTS

TOURNAMENT FORMAT

The 12 teams entered in the Olympics were divided into two groups of six and then played a round-robin schedule within each division. The top three teams in each pool then advanced to a medal round in which all previous results against opponents in the medal round counted. The other teams were placed in another pool to determine 7th- to 12th-place rankings. In the case of a tie in the final standings, goal differential would be the deciding factor.

MEDAL ROUND

	GP	W	T	L	GF	GA	P
Soviet Union	5	4	0	1	25	7	8
Finland	5	3	1	1	18	10	7
Sweden	5	2	2	1	15	16	6
Canada	5	2	1	2	17	14	5
West Germany	5	1	0	4	8	20	2
Czechoslovakia	5	1	0	4	12	22	2

FRANCE

ALBERTVILLE 1992

FEBRUARY 8–23

16TH OLYMPIC WINTER GAMES

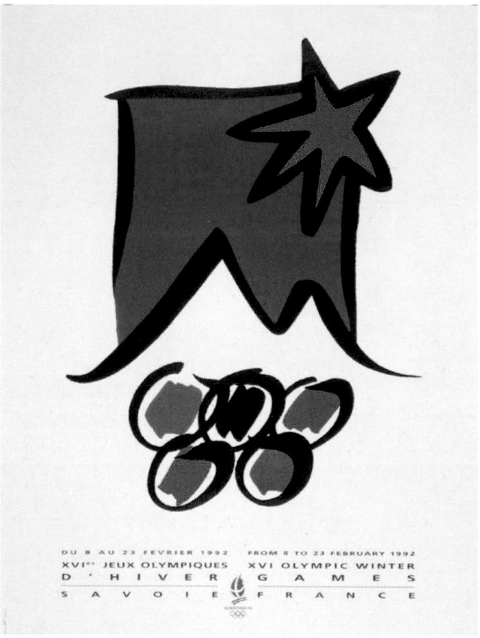
DU 8 AU 23 FEVRIER 1992
FROM 8 TO 23 FEBRUARY 1992
XVIes JEUX OLYMPIQUES
XVI OLYMPIC WINTER
D'HIVER
GAMES
SAVOIE
FRANCE

SILVER
Canada

GOLD
Russia
(Unified Team)

BRONZE
Czechoslovakia

NEW BOSS, SAME AS THE OLD BOSS

The Soviet Union was on its way out and Russia was on its way in, but in the interim the Commonwealth of Independent States won gold with a dramatic win over arch-rivals Canada in the gold-medal game. It marked the seventh time in eight Olympics that the nation won gold, but it remains the most recent victory as well, as the new nation has struggled to emulate its communist success in the democratic era.

In 1992, the tide was turning. More and more players from Europe were in the NHL, being drafted, recruited, signed, and even the Soviet Union and Czechoslovakia, after perestroika, opened their borders. The line between amateur and pro was blurring, but the line between NHL player and international player was also blurring, to the benefit of every tournament, every league, and every fan.

The days of the Soviet hockey superiority were over. Even the Soviet Union as a country had ceased to exist on December 26, 1991, when the USSR dissolved and was replaced by the Commonwealth of Independent States. During the 1992 World Junior Championship in Germany, the Soviet team changed its name from Soviet Union to CIS midway through the tournament, on January 1, 1992, to reflect the country's new political setup.

Roughly one month later, the Olympics were about to begin in Albertville, France. Authoritarian head coach Viktor Tikhonov had lost virtually all the power he had during the 1970s and 1980s, and his famous Green Unit of Fetisov, Kasatonov, Larionov, Krutov, and Makarov were all playing in the NHL.

Tikhonov had to change his approach to coax veterans Vyacheslav Bykov, Andrei Khomutov, and Alexei Zhamnov to play for him while also trying to get the maximum out of whimsical youngsters such as Darius Kasparaitis, Alexei Kovalev, and Yevgeni Davydov.

Despite the absence of superstars, the Soviet/Russian team had problems not with talent but with identity. The famous lettering "CCCP" on the sweaters had been taken away and was replaced by nothing, leaving a generic red sweater in its place. After each victory on ice, there was no national anthem, only the Olympic hymn. Finally, the national red flag with hammer and sickle was also gone. The players were told to salute the Olympic rings instead.

Albertville provided as much drama and excitement as any Olympic hockey tournament ever had, for a myriad of reasons. First, the rosters. The 1988 Calgary Olympics had been a watershed event in officially allowing professionals to participate, but practically speaking only a few were allowed to play. Four years later all of the top teams were recruiting pros with greater energy.

The Swedes were perhaps the most successful in their efforts and thus became the early favourites to win gold. On their blue line was Borje Salming, the

Canada had a chance to win gold in 1992 for the first time in 40 years but came up just short against the Russians.

16-year Toronto Maple Leafs veteran. He was joined by Hakan Loob, Tommy Soderstrom, Mats Naslund, and Bengt-Ake Gustafsson, all seasoned NHLers. The Finns also iced a team that included Kari Eloranta, Simo Saarinen, Hannu Virta, Ville Siren, Hannu Jarvenpaa, Raimo Sumanen, Petri Skriko, and Teemu Selanne. The Czechs were all guaranteed a new car if they brought home a medal, while the Russians were even more blunt about awarding their hockey players' success: a gold was worth $3,000 a player, silver $2,000, and bronze $1,000.

In the leadup to Albertville, one player dominated the headlines more than any other – Eric Lindros. In June 1991, the Quebec Nordiques selected the hugely talented Lindros first overall in the Entry Draft, knowing full well that Lindros had no intention of signing with the Nordiques.

Lindros calmly went back to Junior A with the Oshawa Generals, then played at the World Junior Championships in Fussen, Germany, after which he joined the Olympians. He insisted the Nordiques trade him. If they refused, he would refuse to sign and

The United States beat Italy 6–3 in Pool A action en route to a fourth-place finish. The Italians finished 12th and last.

would re-enter the draft in two years' time, a delay he was willing to wait out.

Goalie Sean Burke and forward Dave Hannan were also on the team, as was another disgruntled star, Joe Juneau. Selected 81st overall by the Bruins in the 1988 Entry Draft, Juneau rubbed Boston general manager Harry Sinden the wrong way by demanding a one-way contract. Sinden refused, and Juneau played with the Olympians. He was instrumental in Canada's silver-medal performance, and the Bruins wound up offering him a three-year deal with a healthy $300,000 signing bonus.

The games themselves were full of surprises and excitement. In Pool A, the United States went undefeated, its only blemish a 3–3 tie with Sweden. Tre Kronor tied the game with just 21 seconds left in the game on a Mikael Johansson goal. Pool B climaxed with a Canada–Russia classic in which the lead

changed several times. Canada trailed 4–2 entering the third period, though, but two goals from Dave Tippett and Dave Hannan tied the game midway through the third. Igor Kravchuk scored the winner a few minutes later, and this 5–4 win gave the Russians some momentum.

Once the preliminary round games had been played, a new format was setup whereby the top eight teams advanced to a simple quarter-finals elimination round. No medal round robin, no losing a game and winning a medal. Now it was win or go home.

The Russians, Czechoslovakians, and Americans all won their games easily, but Canada avoided the ignominy of defeat to Germany only by the skin of its teeth. These Olympics also introduced overtime and shootouts to the playoff format. Canada had leads of 1–0 and 3–2 against Germany but couldn't put the game away, and when the Germans tied it with less than three minutes left in regulation, the teams had to play overtime. Ten minutes settled nothing, so a shootout was necessary. Even then, the shootout went to extra shots.

Canada led the five-shot shootout 2–0 and Germany had taken three of its shots, but amazingly Michael Rumrich and Andreas Brockmann scored to tie it 2–2 after five shots, forcing sudden death. Lindros, who had one of the shootout goals earlier, scored again, and Peter Draisaitl missed, giving Canada the narrowest of victories.

Draisaitl's miss was perhaps the most dramatic in Germany's hockey history. He took a shot as goalie Sean Burke fell to the ice, and the puck skidded through the goalie's pads. Burke thought he had squeezed the puck, but it rolled in behind him only to stop dead right on the goal line! No goal.

Russia and Canada advanced to the gold-medal game with more traditional wins in the semi-finals, setting up a classic showdown between hockey's greatest international rivalry. There were no goals through the first two periods, but the Russians got on the board early in the third when Vyacheslav Butsayev scored. They made it 2–0 late in the game, but then Chris Lindberg made it a 2–1 game at 17:20. Slava Bykov added a late goal, and the new country of Russia won its first Olympic gold. Tikhonov later called this the greatest team he had coached and the most satisfying victory, and Canada's gold drought now extended past 40 years, having last won in 1952.

After the game, Tikhonov didn't want to leave the press conference. He stayed behind after the official question period was over, eager to tell everyone, through an interpreter, that he valued this Olympic gold medal more than all the other wins in his 14 years behind the national team bench. "We had no stars. We won this Olympic gold with youngsters. This is why I am so happy," he said.

This was Tikhonov's last hurrah in international hockey. He would return for the 1994 Olympics and also for the 2003 World Championship, but with no success. Eventually, the IIHF erased all trace of "CIS" in the record books and credited the gold medal to the new nation, Russia.

More important, these Olympics were the beginning of the modern game – format and player participation were changing the Olympics forever.

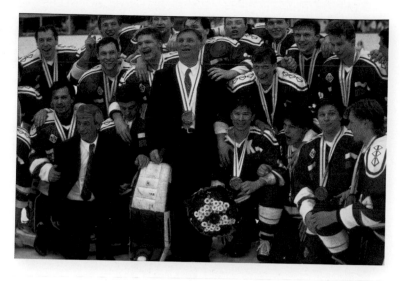

Coach Viktor Tikhonov said the gold victory in 1992 was the most satisfying win of his career.

RESULTS

TOURNAMENT FORMAT

The 12 competing nations were divided into two pools of six teams each and played a round-robin schedule within each group. The top four teams from each then advanced to a playoff round culminating quarter-finals. The top team in group A played the fourth team in group B; the top team in group B played the fourth team in group A; the second team in group A played the third team in group B; and, the second team in group B played the third team in group A. The elimination playoffs (a quarter-finals, semi-finals and finals) represented a new way to bring excitement to the Olympics.

In case of a tie in the standings in the preliminary round, goal differential only in games played between those teams that were tied would be the deciding factor (for example, Canada tied with Unified Team and Czechs but wound up on top). In the elimination playoff round, there would be a ten-minute sudden-death overtime period, then a penalty shot-style shootout after 70 minutes if the game were still tied.

BRONZE MEDAL GAME

February 22   Czechoslovakia 6   United States 1

GOLD MEDAL GAME

February 23   Russia 3   Canada 1

NORWAY
LILLEHAMMER 1994
FEBRUARY 13–27

17TH OLYMPIC WINTER GAMES

SILVER
Canada

GOLD
Sweden

BRONZE
Finland

FORSBERG'S DARING GIVES SWEDEN HISTORIC GOLD

In order to give greater importance to both events, the IOC separated the Winter and Summer Games by organizing an Olympic Winter Games just two years after Albertville to ensure there was an Olympics hereafter every two years.

The first Olympic hockey gold to be decided by a shootout was one for the ages as Sweden beat Canada to win the nation's first Olympic title. The decisive goal came off the stick of Peter Forsberg, whose daring one-handed deke on goalie Corey Hirsch was so unique and memorable the Swedish Post turned it into a stamp.

And 1994 proved historic for several reasons, not the least of which was that Sweden won gold for the first time, beating Canada in the process. Seventy years earlier, Canada beat the Swedes 22–0 at the 1924 Olympics, but in 1994, it was Forsberg's monumental goal in the shootout that gave the Swedes victory.

This victory also gave international hockey its first three members of the Triple Gold Club, although the club, in name, wasn't created for another decade. Tomas Jonsson, Mats

Naslund, and Hakan Loob all had previously won World Championship gold and the Stanley Cup, and with this Olympic victory were the first players to claim all three top hockey prizes.

The 1994 Olympics was also the first that was truly a tournament stocked with former, current, and future NHL stars, very much presaging the next Games in which the NHL shut down for two and a half weeks to allow most of its players to participate in the Olympics. In the case of Sweden, for instance, Forsberg was soon to become one of the best young players in the NHL while his Tre Kronor teammates Naslund and Loob were playing in Sweden after successful NHL careers.

Indeed, Loob scored the first goal of the Lillehammer Olympics for the Swedes, but their opening game was a 4–4 tie with Slovakia. Three more relatively easy wins set up a preliminary round showdown with Canada for possibly top spot in Pool B. Canada won the game 3–2, but Slovakia beat France later in the day to take first while the Swedes settled for third. The Canada–Sweden game featured some 19 minor penalties (11 to Canada), but the decisive goal came midway through the second period when the teams were playing five-on-five. It was scored by Czechoslovakia-born Petr Nedved, whose presence in the Canadian lineup provided one of the controversies of the 1994 Olympics.

Nedved had become a Canadian citizen in July 1993 after spending three years in the Vancouver Canucks organization, but that same summer he was involved in a contract dispute that saw him walk out on the team and refuse to show up for training camp in the fall. Nedved's desire was to play for Canada,

By no means pre-tournament favourites, Sweden won gold thanks to Peter Forsberg's daring shootout goal.

but because of his citizenship change he had to sit on the sidelines until December 26, 1993, before the IIHF finally gave him clearance to play for his new country.

Even with the IIHF's backing, however, many observers weren't thrilled to see Nedved in a Team Canada sweater, feeling that although having pros at the Games was desirable, doing so for contractual reasons, rather than those of pure loyalty, compromised the composition of the team. In fact, he was following in the footsteps of Sean Burke (1992), Andy Moog (1988), and Eric Lindros (1992), who all obviously would have been playing in the NHL than at the Olympics had their contracts been in order. Nedved adamantly refuted this comparison: "The thing is, I feel Canadian. Canada is my home, for now and forever. I wanted to be free, and Canada has made it possible. I am thankful to the country."

Ironically, just as Nedved was figuring to spend the rest of his life in Canada after defecting from Czechoslovakia, his homeland was separating. The 1994 Olympics was the debut for both the Czech

Dejected Canadian players contemplate the bitter taste of defeat after coming so close to the ecstasy of Olympic gold.

Republic 3–2 and Alexander Vinogradov also got a goal in the fourth period to give Russia a 3–2 win over newly created Slovakia.

Kariya's goal came on a power play at 5:54 of overtime with Roman Horak in the penalty box for hooking. Brian Savage scored both regulation goals for Canada, including the tying marker with less than six minutes to play. Vinogradov's goal came with just 1:21 left in the overtime and set up a Russia–Sweden and Canada–Finland pair of semi-finals games.

After a goalless first period, the Finns jumped into an early 2–0 lead against Canada only to have the Canadians rally, tying the game on a Nedved goal with just 36 seconds left in the period. In the third, it was all Canada. In the middle ten minutes of the period, the team jumped into a 5–2 lead, and only a late goal from Jere Lehtinen made the score a little closer.

Sweden looked impressive against the Russians but escaped by the skin of its teeth. After playing tremendous hockey most of the game and building a 4–1 lead, Tre Kronor almost collapsed. The Russians made it 4–2 with 1:11 left in regulation, and just ten seconds later made it 4–3. They pulled goalie Andrei Zuyev in the final minute but couldn't net the equalizer, thus creating a Sweden–Canada game for the gold medal.

Tomas Jonsson scored early in the final game of the 1994 Olympics, and this 1–0 lead held up for more than two periods. But midway through the third Kariya tied the score, and less than three minutes later Derek Mayer put Canada in front. Although Canada has a long and famous history of scoring heroic late goals, it had done unto it what it had so often done unto others. As the clock ticked down, the Canadians seemed in control, but with less than 2:10 to go in regulation Brad Werenka took a hooking penalty, and 21 seconds later the Swedes tied the game.

Ten minutes of overtime settled nothing, so a shootout followed. Canada scored on its first two shots to take a huge 2–0 lead, but the Swedes came back and tied it 2–2 by the time each side had exhausted its five-shooter limit. In the sudden death, both teams missed, then Forsberg scored the greatest shootout goal ever, deking goalie Corey Hirsch to

Republic and Slovakia, and such was the remarkable course of events during one player's lifetime that at age 40 he played for the Czech Republic at the 2012 World Championship, something he could not possibly have foreseen in 1994.

On the other hand, Peter Stastny, who had played internationally for Czechoslovakia, also represented Canada at the 1984 Canada Cup. But with the independence of Slovakia, he was in Lillehammer captaining this historic entry to a highly respectable sixth-place finish.

In the quarter-finals, two teams advanced easily and two teams advanced by the slimmest of margins. Sweden and Finland moved on to the semi-finals impressively, while Canada needed an overtime goal from Paul Kariya to defeat the newly created Czech

one side and slipping the puck to the far side with one hand. Kariya was then stopped by Tommy Salo, and the Swedes claimed gold while Canada's gold-less drought now reached 42 years.

Two photographers caught the goal from directly above Hirsch. Gary Hershorn (Reuters) clicked his shutter just as "Foppa" released the puck, and Al Behrman (Associated Press) did the same a split second later, after the puck had slid under Hirsch's arm and was just inches from crossing the goal line.

Behrman's shot became the "photo." Swedish Post, however, took Hershorn's shot to make a stamp of the historic goal. But there is a slight difference in the philatelic representation of the play. Corey Hirsch is wearing number 11, not 1, and his sweater is blue, not red. When he was asked permission for his likeness to be used, Hirsch was so embarrassed by the goal that he declined, a decision he later regretted. Forsberg, of course, had no trouble agreeing.

Forsberg's goal was captured by Gary Hershorn of Reuters from above, showing the move in all its daring glory.

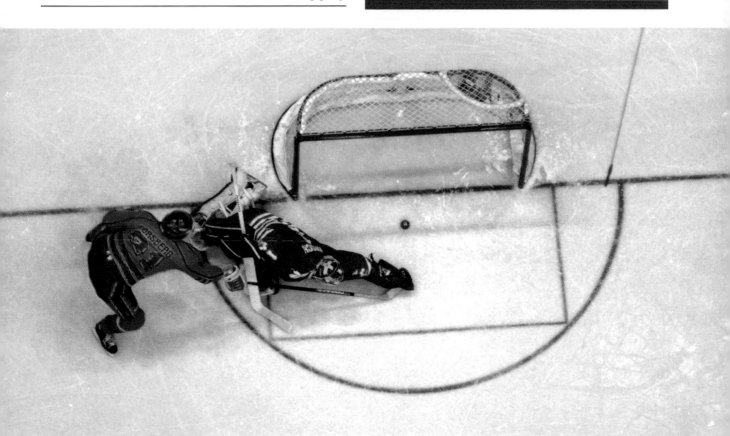

JAPAN
NAGANO 1998
FEBRUARY 7–22

18TH OLYMPIC WINTER GAMES

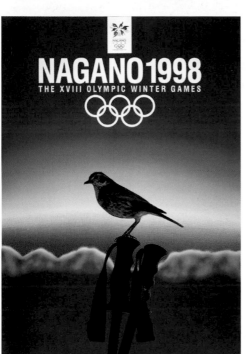

NAGANO 1998
THE XVIII OLYMPIC WINTER GAMES

SILVER
Russia

GOLD
Czech Republic

BRONZE
Finland

DOMINATING CZECHS
(MEN'S TEAM)

The hockey tournaments in Nagano were historic for two reasons. First, there was almost full NHL participation. Never before had the NHL shut down to allow most of its players to participate in the Games, but for two and a half weeks in the middle of the 1997–98 season, that's exactly what happened. This was the final frontier. No more would a Soviet claim for amateur status be relevant, and no more could Canada complain about not being able or allowed to ice its best team. Nagano provided the first inclusive and truly international best-on-best tournament before the largest possible sports audience in the game's history.

As well, Nagano also represented the culmination of many years' efforts to get women's hockey into the Olympics, and for the first time it was a full medal sport. The success of the first Women's World Championship, in Ottawa in 1990, followed by the growing intensity of the Canada–United States rivalry and the growing audience and participation in the women's game the world over, were now coming to fruition in Nagano.

At a time when the NHL had to decide whether to participate, it was locked in a feud with the Players' Association. The Collective Bargaining Agreement (CBA) had expired in the fall of 1994, but a lockout forced the cancellation of nearly half a season. The players wanted to go to Nagano and negotiated this point during CBA talks, so when the two sides finally signed a new agreement in January 1995, it included participation in Nagano and shutting down the league for 17 days.

Given the best-on-best format, Canada was favoured to win the 1998 Olympics leading up to the first game. Of course, having Wayne Gretzky as the first player on the team was a good start, but Canada's depth was so much greater than other countries it couldn't help but be the team to beat. The other top nation was the United States, which had gone from being a small player on the international stage to a team of tremendous significance. The nation's attitude to hockey changed forever after the 1980 Miracle on Ice, and now that generation of kids inspired by the Lake Placid Olympics was in its adult prime. The United States had upset Canada in the best-of-three World Cup finals two years earlier, giving it bragging rights of a sort heading to the 1998 Olympics. A year and a half later, the core of the team intact, the United States looked equally strong. The major differences, of course, were that the Olympics were played on the larger ice and under international rules.

As well, by 1998 the best players from the other top nations were pretty much all playing in the NHL, levelling the playing field for participation. Swedes and Finns had made their way to North America in increasing numbers as during the 1980s, and the early 1990s saw an enormous wave of Russians, Czechoslovaks, and Slovaks come to the NHL.

The first round of the Olympics merely decided

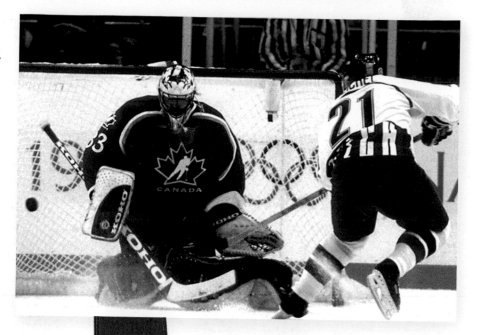

Robert Reichel scored the only goal of the semi-finals shootout en route to an historic Czech gold while eliminating Canada from contention.

the two lowest qualified teams, Kazakhstan and Belarus. The next stage involving the majority of NHL players saw every team play three games in a round robin, no teams being eliminated. This gave the top teams a chance to learn as they played without the pressure of facing elimination. After that, the format reverted to a playoff – win or go home.

Russia, Canada, and the Czech Republic all won their quarter-finals games, as expected. The only tense battle was between arch-rivals Finland and Sweden. There was no scoring through two periods, but the Finns struck twice on a pair of goals from Teemu Selanne. Peter Forsberg scored with just 12 seconds remaining, but that was too little too late. Tre Kronor went home, and the Finns advanced to the semi-finals to face Russia.

The Swedish team was embroiled in controversy unheard of in Olympic history, though, and it started with a most innocent remark. A group of reporters was waiting to interview the Swedes after practise when defenceman Ulf Samuelsson walked by *Sports Illustrated* hockey writer Michael Farber who cracked

a joke to Janne Bengtsson, a Swedish reporter standing next to him: "Why would we give a dirty player like that U.S. citizenship?"

Bengtsson's journalistic instincts went into overdrive. The reporter for *Svenska Dagbladet* was casually aware of a Swedish law, which stated that Swedish citizenship is annulled when a person acquires a foreign passport. Bengtsson immediately started researching. He confirmed that Swedish law didn't allow dual citizenship and that IIHF eligibility regulations stated that in order to represent a country one must be a citizen of his team's country.

Bengtsson approached Rickard Fagerlund, the president of the Swedish Ice Hockey Association and also a member of the IIHF Council: "Do you know that Samuelsson is a U.S. citizen and, as such, is not eligible to represent Sweden?"

Stunned, Fagerlund called team manager Bo Tovland and and told him to ask Samuelsson if Samuelsson did, in fact, hold U.S. citizenship. Samuelsson confirmed that he held an American passport.

Samuelsson was told by Tovland and Fagerlund that his U.S. citizenship nullified his Swedish passport. The player was stunned. Samuelsson was forced to leave the team and the Olympics.

Meanwhile, the Russians handled Finland easily, 7–4, but the Canada–Czech game provided the tournament's greatest drama. Pavel Patera broke a scoreless game with a goal midway through the third period, and the Czech Republic, known at this time for their stifling defence, seemed prepared to win the game. But as had happened so often, Canada somehow created a late rally out of nothing. Trevor Linden tied the game with just 63 seconds left, sending the game to overtime. The Czechs, though, were happy to run down the clock and go to a shootout, a format they were more comfortable with than the drama of sudden-death overtime.

Canada's misery continued after losing the bronze-medal game to Finland, 3–2, the nation's top NHLers going home empty-handed despite being pre-tournament favourites.

The shootout featured Canada's Patrick Roy, playing his one-and-only international competition for Canada, against Dominik Hasek, the floppy, unpredictable, wildly unbeatable goalie in the Czech net. Robert Reichel, the first Czech shooter, scored when his shot bounced off the stick-side post and in, and then Hasek went to work. He had stopped Theo Fleury with the first shot, then stopped Ray Bourque and Joe Nieuwendyk.

Eric Lindros beat Hasek with a deke, but his backhand bounced off the crossbar and over the goal. Brendan Shanahan was Canada's last hope, but he, too, was stopped, sending the Czechs off the bench to mob the Dominator.

Canada then lost the bronze-medal game to Finland 3–2, and the Czechs rode Hasek to gold. Petr Svoboda's goal midway through the third period was all the Czechs needed. The goal came on a surprisingly unspectacular play. With a faceoff deep in the Russian end, Czech centre Pavel Patera won the draw from Sergei Fedorov. Martin Prochazka got the puck at the top of the circle and moved it farther back to Svoboda at the point, and his hard, quick shot beat goalie Mikhail Shtalenkov for the game's only goal.

Dominik Hasek celebrates his triumphant moment after fending off all five Canadian shooters in the semi-finals.

Amazingly, this was Svoboda's first appearance with the national team at the senior level, even though, at 32 years of age, he was the second-oldest player on the team. This was his only goal of the Olympics.

After the medal ceremony, Hasek said, "When I saw the flag go up, I saw my whole career flash before my eyes from the first time my parents took me to a hockey game until now." The team flew to Prague the next day for a celebratory parade, and estimates of more than a million people in the national capital speak to the win not just as a sporting moment of Czech history but also as a cultural one.

Perhaps, however, the single most important aspect about the win was the makeup of the team. The Czechs used only ten NHLers. The other players came from the Czech Extraliga.

The 1998 Olympics weren't the success many had thought they'd be for Canada and the United States – neither country won a medal – but for European fans and for those who wanted only the best players to participate in the Olympics the message was clear – this is the way of the future.

Teammates in another era in Edmonton, Canada's Wayne Gretzky (right) fights for puck possession with Finland's Jari Kurri.

MEN'S RESULTS

TOURNAMENT FORMAT

To allow for NHL participation, the tournament was divided into three distinct stages. The preliminary stage featured the eight lowest-ranking teams to qualify for the Olympics. These eight were divided into two groups of four teams each and played a round-robin series of games within each group. The top team from each then advanced to the main draw, which featured the "big six" of Canada, Russia, Czech Republic, Sweden, Finland, and United States. Again, the eight teams were put into two groups of four and played a round robin within each.

To ensure quality, this stage did not eliminate any teams. Instead, it allowed the players travelling halfway around the world from the NHL a chance to acclimatize to the time difference and play three games with new teammates. The positions of the teams then determined the quarter-finals matchups. The top team in one group played the fourth team in the other, and the second place played the third place in crossover games as well. This led to semi-finals and finals to determine medal winners.

BRONZE MEDAL GAME

February 21	Finland 3	Canada 2

GOLD MEDAL GAME

February 22	Czech Republic 1	Russia 0

The Americans shocked Canada not once but twice in 1998 en route to the first gold awarded for women's hockey at the Olympics.

SILVER
Canada

GOLD
United States

BRONZE
Finland

AMERICAN DREAM
(WOMEN'S TEAM)

It was a spectacular fall or a monumental victory, depending on the perspective. Heading into the Nagano Olympics, Canada's women were the clear favourites. There had been only four Women's World Championships before 1998, and Canada won all four convincingly over the United States: 5–2 in 1990, 8–0 in 1992, 6–3 in 1994, and 4–3 in overtime in 1997.

But in 1998, things were different. Six teams played a simple round robin, the top two advancing to the gold-medal game, the third and fourth teams to the bronze-medal game. There were no surprises when the two North Americans placed one-two, but the final day of the round robin produced one huge surprise when the Americans defeated Canada by a 7–4 score and the manner in which they achieved the victory.

The teams were tied 1–1 after the first and second period, but Canada came flying to start the final 20 minutes and built a huge 4–1 lead by the six-minute mark. All four goals came on the power play, and victory seemed imminent. But the United States was not to be so easily dissuaded, and the team did the unthinkable, roaring back to tie the game, taking the lead, and blowing the game wide open. Six goals in 12 minutes humbled the world's champions, giving the United States first place in the preliminary round.

Because the teams were clearly better than the others, they had only each other to play against as

Four-time World Champions but second-place Olympians,
Canadian women hang their head in bitter disappointment.

was their nemesis that won gold in the first Olympics tournament.

The win intensified the rivalry and set up a return engagement four years later, but it also helped catapult the game into the mind's eye of young North American girls as registration increased by hundreds of per cent after the Olympics.

But the 1998 Olympics were, in many ways, the end of a long journey as much as it was the start of one. The real story of Nagano began in 1975, when the Ontario Women's Hockey Association (OWHA) was established.

warmup leading to Nagano. Indeed, they played 13 exhibition games in the weeks before the Olympics (Canada winning seven), a series that intensified the rivalry more than the teams might have anticipated.

"A rivalry develops naturally when you have played a team so many times with such close results," American Sandra Whyte noted. "I think it's a healthy thing, but it's not a friendly rivalry."

Finland and China played for the bronze. The Finns trailed by a goal after the first period but scored three in the second en route to a 4–1 win and the first medal for women's hockey.

That set the stage for the final game. A scoreless first period gave way to a goal from Gretchen Ulion early in the second, and the Americans played perfect defence. They allowed Hayley Wickenheiser little room, and goalie Sarah Tueting was flawless.

Shelley Looney made it 2–0 midway through the final period, making Canada an even more desperate team, and Danielle Goyette finally scored at 15:59 to make it 2–1. But try as they might, the Canadians couldn't get the equalizer. The final goal, by Whyte, who also had two assists, came into the empty Canadian net. For all of Canada's success in the first seven years of women's hockey at the IIHF, it

Fran Rider, Maurice and Shirley Landry, Dave McMaster, and Bev Mallory were the people who got the process moving. Cookie Cartwright, a lawyer in Kingston, developed the first operational documents.

In 1987, six countries competed in a world champion tournament and another five sent delegates. Hazel McCallion was the honourary chairperson. The first and unofficial world championship took place in Toronto and was an unqualified success. But the word *success* cannot be quantified in attendance figures or gate receipts or TV ratings, all of which were minimal or close enough to zero to be ignored.

The first game featured Canada and the United States. International media covered the game, and the stands were full. Lina Baun Danielsen, a player on the Danish team, was the news anchor for TV 2 in Denmark, and the IIHF and Hockey Canada were watching. That December, the Swiss hosted the Ochsner Cup. It was an invitational event, and Czechoslovakia was there. This was a huge victory, given the influence that nation exerted on the international stage on the men's side.

In 1989, West Germany hosted the European Championship in Dusseldorf and Rattingen. Rider was invited as a guest of the IIHF and the West

American captain Cammi Granato played a key role in her team's 1998 Olympic gold.

German Federation, and again fans crowded the arenas to watch this new sport. It turned out to be the means to qualify for a 1990 World Championship in Ottawa, an official IIHF event for women's hockey.

There was one last major development. "At the 1992 Women's Worlds in Finland," Rider explained, "Gilbert Felli and Pirjo Hagman were sent by the IOC to Finland to see if this sport should be in the Olympics. The bronze-medal game went to a shootout, and Finland beat Sweden. It was one of the best hockey games I've ever seen. That game did a lot to seal our place in the Olympics."

Six years later, Canada and the United States played for gold in Nagano, the first Olympic event for women's hockey.

WOMEN'S RESULTS

TOURNAMENT FORMAT

All six teams were placed in one group and played a round-robin series of games. The top two teams played for the gold medal, and the next two teams (3rd and 4th place) played for the bronze medal.

STANDINGS

	GP	W	T	L	GF	GA	P
United States	5	5	0	0	35	7	10
Canada	5	4	0	1	28	12	8
Finland	5	3	0	2	27	10	6
China	5	2	0	3	10	15	4
Sweden	5	1	0	4	10	21	2
Japan	5	0	0	5	2	45	0

BRONZE MEDAL GAME

February 17   Finland 4   China 1

GOLD MEDAL GAME

February 17   United States 3   Canada 1

UNITED STATES
SALT LAKE CITY
2002
FEBRUARY 11–21

19TH OLYMPIC WINTER GAMES

SALT LAKE 2002

XIX OLYMPIC WINTER GAMES
FEBRUARY 8–24, 2002

XIXᵉˢ JEUX OLYMPIQUES D'HIVER
FEVRIER 8–24, 2002

SILVER
United States

GOLD
Canada

BRONZE
Russia

CANADA'S HALF-CENTURY WAIT OVER
(MEN'S TEAM)

Canada's double disappointments in Nagano turned into double victory in Salt Lake as the men's and women's team swept gold in hockey. For the men, it was the first victory since 1952, and for the women it was fitting payback for a devastating loss to the United States four years earlier at the inaugural event for women's hockey.

The decision to grant the hosting to the West Coast in the United States brought the Olympics to that part of the world for the first time since Squaw Valley hosted in 1960, and it was a significant impetus in the NHL's decision to go to Nagano. The league believed that 1998 was a good starting point for Salt Lake when NHL participation would be infinitely easier because of travel and jetlag, two issues that were a huge factor in Japan and virtually negligible in Utah.

As well, the history of international hockey has various

markers over the years to signify its evolution, and 2002 is one such important date. These Olympics were the first to include two major rules that were part of the international game but not the NHL and were being used for the first time at the Olympics – the elimination of centre ice for offsides, and hurry-up faceoffs. In the case of the former, allowing "stretch passes" opened the full rink to speed and offence as used first by the Swedish "torpedo" offence. In the case of the later, linesmen dropped the puck quickly and forbade delay-of-game techniques that players often used to catch their breath or to try to slow the game down. Both these rules had such an impressive impact with players and fans that the NHL was quick to adopt them for its league games the next season.

Curiously, while Canada and the United States had been favourites four years earlier, there was greater unease in making as bold a prediction for 2002 – yet these were the countries that met for gold on the final day. The Americans made Herb Brooks their coach, a decision so very "American," one might say because it was an appointment based on emotion more than logic.

After guiding the U.S. team to gold at the Miracle on Ice, Brooks experienced little success in the NHL or elsewhere, his most recent work being a dismal 11th-place showing with the national team of France at the 1998 Olympics and 58 games with the Pittsburgh Penguins in 1999–2000. Yet his stature within the hockey community in the United States was such that the move made sense – and was, of course, hugely successful.

Hockey Canada president Bob Nicholson also

Wayne Gretzky, Hockey Canada president Bob Nicholson, and captain Mario Lemieux celebrate Olympic gold in 2002.

made a calculated gamble of sorts when he appointed Wayne Gretzky as Canada's executive director. Gretzky had retired in 1999, and after a year off had indicated a desire to get back into hockey. His reputation on-ice, of course, was without compare, but he was lacking any and all experience as a general manager. Still, he surrounded himself with a team of advisers, assistants, and coaches such that he wouldn't be the lone selector of players anyway.

For all the attention the North Americans received, though, the Europeans entered the Olympics with rosters equally or more impressive. Consider Sweden, a team with more great players than at any other time in the nation's history – Mats Sundin, Nicklas Lidstrom, Daniel Alfredsson, Markus Naslund, Henrik Zetterberg, P-J Axelsson, to name but a few.

The Czechs still had Dominik Hasek in goal and teammates included Jaromir Jagr, Milan Hejduk, and Patrik Elias; and the Finns had Teemu Selanne, Raimo Helminen, and Teppo Numminen.

Jarome Iginla (far left) scores one of his two goals
in the gold-medal game which Canada won, 5–2.

Helminen was perhaps the most interesting story outside the standings. There may have been better players, players with a harder shot, players who could skate faster or score more often, but no player in hockey history represented his country more often than Finland's Raimo Helminen. From his debut with the senior team in 1984 to his last hurrah in 2003, Helminen played some 330 times, none more important than in Salt Lake City. He became the first hockey player – and only the sixth athlete all-time – to appear in six Winter Olympics.

Helminen won nine medals for his country, two of which in particular stand out. He played for Finland at the 1988 Olympics in Calgary, when his country won a silver medal, the first hockey medal for Finland going back to the country's debut appearance in 1952.

Then, in 1995, Helminen was on the gold-medal team at the World Championship in Sweden, again the first championship for Suomi. He also won four

silver medals – 1994, 1998, 1999, and 2001 World Championships – and three bronze – 1994 and 1998 Olympics and 2000 World Championships – during his 19 years with the national team. In fact, the only team in Finnish history to win a medal without Helminen up to the day he retired was the 1992 silver-medal team at the World Championship.

The first day of the final round robin in Utah was one of the monumental days in Olympics hockey history. Sweden played Canada in a game matching two of the powerhouses, but it also featured Canada's Toronto Maple Leafs goalie Curtis Joseph and coach Pat Quinn going against Tre Kronor's Leafs great Sundin. Rob Blake scored early for Canada, but that early excitement gave way to reality very quickly. Sundin tied the game three minutes later, the first of five straight Sweden goals over the course of the

first two periods. A late Canadian goal made it 5–2, but the opening game of 2002 was an unmitigated disaster for Canada. On the heels of Nagano, this best-on-best was in dire trouble.

Quinn immediately benched Joseph in favour of Martin Brodeur (the same tandem from the 1996 World Cup team where Joseph was the number-one goalie), and Canada managed a tenuous 3–2 win over qualifier Germany next time out. Mario Lemieux scored twice in a 3–3 tie against the Czech Republic to close out the round robin, after which Gretzky took the podium at the press conference and created a stir, focusing the attention on his criticism of world media, whom, he said, wanted Canada to lose, and away from his players, who were reeling from a weak performance in the first three games.

Canada beat the Finns 2–1 in a tense quarter-finals, but while the United States and Russia also won, it was the fourth quarter-finals that stunned the hockey world. Belarus and Sweden fought tooth and nail for some 57 minutes, and with the score tied 3–3, overtime seemed inevitable.

And then, the unthinkable happened. Belarus's Vladimir Kopat skated down the right wing. As

This on-ice portrait captures Canada's first Olympic gold in half a century.

soon as he crossed centre ice he fired a long shot at goalie Tommy Salo, content simply to get the puck deep. Salo, however, lost sight of the puck, and it hit him on the top of the helmet. He reacted but didn't know where the puck was. It fell behind him and dribbled over the goal line before he could find it. Kopat, in utter disbelief, slid along the ice toward his bench in celebration. The go-ahead goal came with just 2:24 remaining, and Belarus played perfect defence to preserve arguably the most remarkable upset in Olympic history after the "Miracle on Ice" win in 1980.

In the semi-finals, Canada beat Belarus easily, 7–1, while the United States and Russia played one of the most exciting games in recent Olympic history. The Americans jumped into a 3–0 lead after two periods, but a ferocious assault by the Russians in the third fell just short, the 3–2 result ending a tense and celebratory game for the home crowd.

It had been many decades since the two North Americans played for Olympic hockey gold, but

Belarus celebrates its unimaginable 4-3 win over Sweden in the quarter-finals in Salt Lake.

in many ways this was a 1996 World Cup rematch. Canada scored first on perhaps the most memorable (beautiful) goal of the Olympics. Chris Pronger played the puck inside the U.S. blue line, rifling a pass to the slot for Mario Lemieux. But the captain knew teammate Paul Kariya was in behind him, so Lemieux faked a quick shot and let the puck go to Kariya. Goalie Mike Richter positioned himself for Lemieux's shot, and Kariya simply redirected the puck into the empty side.

Jarome Iginla made it 2–0 a few minutes later, but the Americans scored twice to tie the game late in the second. Joe Sakic put Canada ahead at 18:19 of the middle period to restore the lead 3–2, setting up a final 20 minutes (or more) for gold. Canada got the only two goals of the third, winning gold for the first time since 1952. After the game Gretzky went out to centre ice and carved a one-dollar gold coin out from under centre ice, installed there by the Canadian ice crew, and the legend of the "lucky loonie" was born.

Canada's women got their revenge from Nagano, winning Olympic gold on American soil.

REVENGE, CANADA-STYLE
(WOMEN'S TEAM)

While there was little doubt the gold-medal game in 2002 would be another Canada–United States showdown, there was plenty to talk about in Salt Lake as the women played in their second Olympics.

In fact, Sweden was the story of the tournament outside the final game, notably because (a) the team was led by 15-year-old goalie sensation Kim Martin, (b) the Swedish Ice Hockey Association almost declined to send a team to Utah because it had performed so poorly in recent months, and (c) the Swedes won bronze, its first medal in women's hockey since the IIHF started a tournament, in 1990.

While gold had always gone to the North Americans, bronze was long the stronghold of Finland, which had placed third at every women's event except the 2001 Women's Worlds when Russia claimed the bronze. But at Salt Lake, the Swedes beat Finland 2–1 to win bronze, thanks to two early goals from Evelina Samuelsson and Martin, who stopped 32 of 33 Finnish shots.

It was the gold-medal game, however, that was the attention-getter. Not only did it preview by three days the men's final, but it also pitted two teams locked in a rivalry that got evermore bitter after Nagano. Canada won the world title in 1999, 2000,

Teenage goalie Kim Martin was the key reason Damkronor won bronze in 2002.

and 2001, but these meant nothing at the Olympics. The gold-medal game featured dramatic scoring, incredible drama, and controversy that nearly undid the quality of the game.

Caroline Ouellette scored early to stake Canada to a 1–0 lead, but the team couldn't add to the score after gaining two power plays in the middle part of the period. It was at this point that something amazing and bizarre started to occur – Canada was given one penalty after another and another.

If there had been both a significant positive development – and a significant weakness at this point in the women's history – it was that in 2002 virtually all of the best referees were also North American. The woman with the whistle for this final game was American Stacey Livingston, and it was her judgment of play that came under criticism. Canada took four penalties in the last half of the first

Canadian women point to centre ice where the "lucky loonie" was buried by the Canadian ice crew prior to the Olympics.

Jayna Hefford's goal with just one second left in the second period proved to be the gold-medal goal for Canada.

period but withstood the challenge and escaped with a 1–0 lead.

In the second, Canada was called for another penalty, and this time Katie King scored to tie the game. Hayley Wickenheiser reinstated the lead two minutes later, but Canada then was called for three more penalties. The Americans finally earned a minor and then offsetting minors were assessed, and while the teams played four-on-four Janya Hefford made it 3–1, jamming in a puck at 19:59 of the period.

Canada was then given four of the six minors in the final period, Karyn Bye scoring on the last of these at 16:27 to make it 3–2. The Americans couldn't tie the game, though, and Canada won the gold, sweet victory after an agonizing loss four years ago. But afterward the talk was about the penalties. The Americans had 15:51 of power-play time to Canada's 6:00 (eight penalties in a row at one stretch), yet the penalty killing saved the day.

WOMEN'S RESULTS

TOURNAMENT FORMAT

Eight teams were placed in two groups and played a round-robin series within each group. The top two teams from each advanced to a crossover semi-finals. Those winners played for the gold medal, and the semi-finals losers played for the bronze medal.

BRONZE MEDAL GAME

February 21   Sweden 2   Finland 1

GOLD MEDAL GAME

February 21   Canada 3   United States 2

ITALY

TURIN 2006

FEBRUARY 10–26

20TH OLYMPIC WINTER GAMES

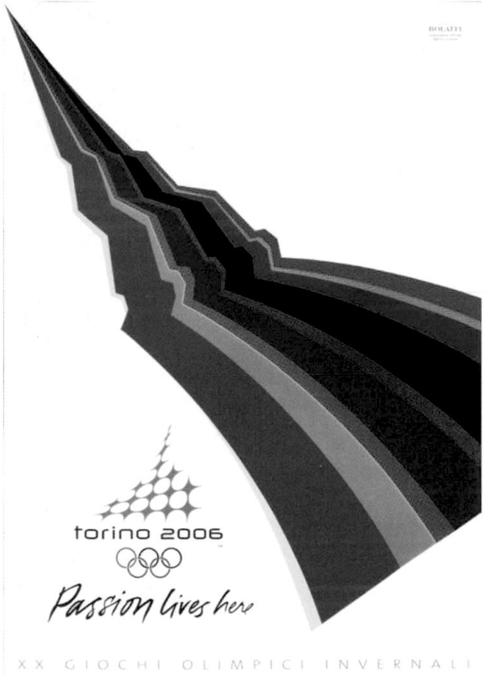
torino 2006
Passion lives here
XX GIOCHI OLIMPICI INVERNALI

SILVER Finland

GOLD Sweden

BRONZE Czech Republic

SWEDEN, SVERIGE, TRE KRONOR

(MEN'S TEAM)

Not only did Sweden's men's team start an historic double gold in 2006 (followed by the World Championship title a few weeks later) – a first – but the women's team made history by stunning the United States in a semi-finals shootout to advance to the gold-medal game, the first time in 16 years the finals was not a Canada–United States battle.

The men's win was accomplished by what was surely the best group of players ever assembled by the nation. Captain Mats Sundin fronted a roster that included Peter Forsberg, Nicklas Lindstrom, the Sedin twins, and goalie Henrik Lundqvist. Yet, in a season when the NHL shut down again for the time necessary to participate, all other top nations had their best players.

This year, Canada was surely the favourite. Having won gold with Gretzky and Quinn leading the way in Salt Lake, the pair had also teamed up in the same administrative capacity to lead Canada to victory at the 2004 World Cup. There seemed no reason, at first, to believe Canada wasn't fully able to win. That feeling, though, changed quickly. Gretzky was questioned

for selecting Todd Bertuzzi to the team, after Bertuzzi's vicious, career-ending attack on Steve Moore, while leaving 18-year-old Sidney Crosby off the team.

The Russians, meanwhile, had plenty of firepower with Alex Ovechkin, Yevgeni Malkin, Ilya Kovalchuk, and Pavel Datsyuk leading the way while the Slovaks, winners of the gold medal at the 2002 World Championship, were also a team to respect.

The preliminary round was surprisingly full of upsets and incredible results, notably the 2–0 victory by the Swiss over Canada. It was the first-ever defeat in Olympic competition, going back to 1924, and it was achieved when a transplanted Canadian, Paul DiPietro, a longtime player in Switzerland, scored both goals for La Suisse.

DiPietro, a fringe NHLer from the 20th century, had moved to Switzerland in 1999 to continue his

Sweden won gold for the second time in four Games by beating Finland 3–2 in the final showdown of 2006.

career and had enjoyed the hockey and country so much that he made this his permanent residence and became a Swiss national. He had played several times for the Swiss internationally but never against his homeland at such an important event. Yet, as fate would have it, he played the game of his life in Turin.

He scored late in the first period to give his adopted country a 1–0 lead, and amazingly Canada could do no right in this game. Rick Nash thought he tied the game in the second period, but goalie Martin Gerber made a sensational glove save right at the goal line.

Photographs later revealed the "save" had been made inside the net and Nash's shot should have counted as a goal, but it didn't, and DiPietro scored on a five-on-three a little later in the second to make it

Captain Mats Sundin begins the Olympic gold celebration at the end of the third period.

2–0. Gerber stoned the Canadians the rest of the way, stopping all 49 shots he faced to give his country its biggest win ever and its first win against Canada since the two nations started playing. The Swiss joined Canada in the quarter-finals, but the Canadians never recovered from that devastating defeat.

In the other pool, upsets were also the order of the day. The Americans won only one of five games while Slovakia was a perfect 5–0–0. The most controversial result, though, came on the final day when the Slovaks beat Sweden 3–0. Tre Kronor knew beforehand that if it won it would play Canada in the crossover quarter-finals, but a loss would mean a date with the far less intimidating Swiss. It may have been unethical, or the Slovaks may have won fair and square, but whatever the case the Swedes got their preferred opponent in the final eight.

The biggest game of the quarter-finals was the Russia–Canada game. After two tense, nervous, and thrilling periods, the game was still without a goal, but just 55 seconds into the final period Bertuzzi took an interference penalty and on the ensuing power play Ovechkin scored. Alexei Kovalev added an insurance goal in the final minute, and Canada left in seventh place, its worst showing ever in 86 years and a result no one could have imagined at the start of these Olympics.

The Nordic nations advanced to the finals to create the biggest Sweden–Finland game ever played. The teams lived up to the billing, though. Kimmo Timonen got the only goal of the first for Finland, but Sweden got two of the three goals in the second to make it 2–2 after 40 minutes.

A despairing Finnish captain Saku Koivu laments how close he came to realizing an Olympic dream.

Goalie Henrik Lundqvist rejoices in his team's Olympic victory.

The gold was decided right off the opening faceoff to start the final period. Mats Sundin and Saku Koivu faced off, but no sooner had referee Paul Devorski dropped the puck than Koivu's stick broke. He hustled to the bench for a new one, but Sweden had control of play. Sundin skated in over the blue line, dropped a pass for Lidstrom, and his wicked blast beat Antero Niittymaki over the glove.

That was all Sweden needed. As time expired, the players stormed off the bench to mob Lundqvist, celebrating their second gold since 1994. It was the last game of Sundin's international career and capped a Hall of Fame life in international hockey.

The Swedes went on to win gold at the World Championship in Riga, becoming the first nation to complete the double. Eight players were on both teams: Henrik Zetterberg, Jorgen Jonsson, Kenny Jonsson, Niklas Kronwall, Mika Hannula, Mikael Samuelsson, Ronnie Sundin, and backup goalie the late Stefan Liv.

Canada defended its Olympic championship by defeating Sweden – not the U.S., as everyone expected – in the gold-medal game.

SILVER Sweden

GOLD Canada

BRONZE United States

CANADIAN GOLD ... BUT DIFFERENT OPPONENT
(WOMEN'S TEAM)

Canada may have won gold for the second time with what history might show was the greatest women's Olympic team, but it was the Damkronor – Sweden's women's team – that stole the thunder in Turin. They defeated the United States 3–2 in a sensational shootout to create a Sweden–Canada game for gold, the first finals in 16 years *not* contested by the two North American powerhouses.

That game featured many changes of fortune and highlights. The Americans had a very expected 2–0 lead early in the second period and were humming along, having allowed only four shots on goal to that point. But at the six-minute mark of the second period the Swedes made it a bit closer when Maria Rooth beat Chanda Gunn with a shot from in close. Three and a half minutes later, the Swedes killing a penalty to Ann-Louise Edstrand, Rooth did the unthinkable, scoring short-handed and tying the game at 9:40. Later in the period the Americans had three more power plays, including 1:23 of five-on-three, but the Swedes would not concede a third goal.

After being outshot 27–9 through 40 minutes, the Swedes were in a 2–2 tie, and in the third they

Sweden celebrates victory in the shootout in the semi-finals.

played spectacular defence. Both teams had power-play chances, but the game ended in a tie, forcing overtime. The heart-wrenching ten minutes featured another U.S. power play after Danijela Rundqvist took at tripping penalty at 7:36, but again the Swedish penalty killers were impervious and a shootout was now required to decide the game.

Goalie Kim Martin was flawless, stifling the American shooters one after another. Pernilla Winberg scored on the third of five Swedish shots, and when Rooth scored with the fourth shot to make it 2–0, the game was over. The Damkronor poured off the bench to mob their goalie; the Americans stood in utter shock. They would play for bronze, not gold.

Canadians pour off the bench after winning their second consecutive Olympic gold.

The Swedes go crazy after Maria Rooth's goal advanced her team to the gold-medal game for the first time in women's hockey victory.

The Canadians got the job done by not taking the Swedes lightly. They built up a 4–0 lead through two periods, allowed one power-play goal in the third, and celebrated their gold medal after a perfect run of five straight wins during which they outscored their opponents by a 44–2 margin. The Americans closed out with a 4–0 win over Finland to take the bronze, and although this was the low point of the program it would, in a couple of years, pave the way for greater successes at the Women's World Championship.

WOMEN'S RESULTS

TOURNAMENT FORMAT

Eight teams were placed in two groups and played a round-robin series within each group. The top two teams from each advanced to a crossover semi-finals. Those winners played for the gold medal, and the semi-finals losers played for the bronze medal.

BRONZE MEDAL GAME

February 20 · United States 4 · Finland 0

GOLD MEDAL GAME

February 20 · Canada 4 · Sweden 1

vancouver 2010

WITH **GLOWING**HEARTS
DES**PLUS BRILLANTS**EXPLOITS

XXI OLYMPIC WINTER GAMES | FEBRUARY 12 TO 28, 2010
XXIes JEUX OLYMPIQUES D'HIVER | DU 12 AU 28 FÉVRIER 2010

SILVER
United States

GOLD
Canada

BRONZE
Finland

CANADA DOUBLES UP AGAIN
(MEN'S TEAM)

For the second time in eight years the Winter Olympics were held in North America, and for the second time both the men's and women's finals pitted Canada against the United States. And, yes, for the second time Canada won both gold medals, but in 2010 the achievement was nothing short of monumental, the pressure and expectations from the 33 million Canadians tremendous beyond what any athlete should have to endure.

For the men, the ending was perhaps the most breathtaking in Olympics history, and for the women a remarkable performance that was as special as the 2002 gold-medal victory. Canada was the favourites, but so, too, were the Russians, who, historically, played better in Canada than in their homeland or any other country.

The Canadians were now led by Steve Yzerman, who replaced Wayne Gretzky and who, like number 99 in 2002, had just recently retired. Yzerman selected a team that was big, but speed, skill, and experience were the overriding factors. Russia was a team laden with skill but perhaps short on goaltending, while the

The man with the golden stick, Sidney Crosby skates a large Canadian flag around the ice – with a gold medal around his neck.

Americans were the highly talented underdogs, to be ignored at one's peril.

The Czechs and Slovaks were strong, but not at the same level as previous years and not up to Canada and Russia, while Finland was always the country lurking in the shadows, not favoured to do anything incredible but capable of the same regardless.

While Sidney Crosby was a controversial non-participant in 2006, he was front and centre as the world's dominant player and the one everyone expected to lead Canada. Ditto for Alexander Ovechkin with Russia. Yet in the early going neither player was sensational. Canada began the Olympics with an easy win over Norway but then needed a shootout to beat the Swiss (Crosby getting the winner) and dropped a 5–3 decision to the Americans, who won in convincing fashion.

The Americans were a perfect 3–0–0–0 after the preliminary round while Canada was a lukewarm 1–1–0–1 and Russia 2–0–1–0. Sweden was also a perfect 3–0–0–0. The loss to the Americans meant that Canada had to play an extra game, in the qualification round, while the United States, Russia, and Sweden all received byes.

Canadian players later said this extra game was vital for giving the team a chance to develop chemistry, and given that the opposition was Germany, and the score an easy 8–2 win, one could see how this observation was relevant.

In an event like this, surprises were few and far between. Thus, the eight quarter-finals teams were the obvious seven plus Switzerland, and the Swiss

were eliminated by the Americans, 2–0, after putting up an impressive fight. Both goals came in the third period, the second into an empty net. Coincidentally, the Finns beat the Czechs in identical fashion, scoring midway through the third to go up 1–0 and adding an empty netter.

A surprise result saw Slovakia eliminate Sweden with a 4–3 win. The Slovaks led 2–0, but the Swedes came back to tie; the Slovaks went ahead 4–2, but a Swedish rally fell short and the defending Olympic champions were eliminated.

The game that had the greatest anticipation was the Canada–Russia quarter-finals, a repeat match from four years ago. This time, though, Canada came out "like gorillas from a cage," as goalie Yevgeni Nabokov described, building a 4–1 lead after the first period. The lead grew to 6–1 early in the second, and

Canada rolled to a 7–3 win in what might well have been the fastest, most skilled game ever played by Canada in the history of the sport.

The semi-finals could not have been more different. The Americans scored a remarkable six goals in the first 12:46 of play against Finland, chased starting goalie Miikka Kiprusoff from the net, and floated to a stunning 6–1 victory.

Canada, on the other hand, faced a dilemma. During the team's loss to the United States in the preliminary round, coach Mike Babcock replaced Martin Brodeur with Roberto Luongo, who also started the next two games. But Luongo was shaky at best, and he nearly cost the team a place in the finals against the Slovaks. Canada built a solid 3–0 lead through two periods, but Luongo let in two soft goals

in the third and the Slovaks nearly tied the game in the dying seconds.

The gold-medal game didn't start out as a classic. Again, Canada was dominant, building a solid 2–0 lead through the first half of the game. But Luongo muffed a long shot from Ryan Kesler later in the second and then, with Ryan Miller on the bench, the U.S. tied the game in the final minute when Luongo couldn't control a rebound. Sudden-death overtime.

Babcock decided during the intermission to play his best players and go for the win, and he got his wish when Jarome Iginla made a quick pass from the corner to Crosby. Number 87 took a low, quick shot before Miller could pokecheck him, and at 7:40 of the fourth period Crosby had scored the golden goal to give Canada victory in the final event of the 2010 Olympics.

What might have been an impressive but routine 2–0 victory in regulation instead turned out to be a classic and dramatic victory, Crosby's goal right alongside Paul Henderson's at the 1972 Summit Series and Mario Lemieux's at the 1987 Canada Cup.

Organizer John Furlong said it best when he enthused that Canadians would have traded in all their 13 other gold medals in Vancouver for the men's hockey gold. No amount of success in other sports could have replaced defeat in the premier event.

Finland rallied to beat Slovakia, 5–3, to win Olympic bronze.

MEN'S RESULTS

TOURNAMENT FORMAT

All 12 teams were placed in three groups of four teams each and played a round-robin series of games within each group. The teams were then placed in one standings, the top four teams receiving byes to the quarter-finals. Teams 5 through 12 played a qualification round, the winners also advancing to the quarter-finals, the losers being eliminated. The team ranked 5th played the team ranked 12th, the team ranked 8th played the team ranked fifth, and so on. Once the quarter-finals were set, the rest of the tournament was an elimination series of games until the semi-finals. Those winners played for the gold medal, and the losers played for bronze.

SEMI-FINALS

February 26	United States 6	Finland 1
February 26	Canada 3	Slovakia 2

BRONZE MEDAL GAME

February 27	Finland 5	Slovakia 3

GOLD MEDAL GAME

February 28	Canada 3	United States 2*

* Sidney Crosby 7:40 OT

Canada beat the United States, 2–0, in a thrilling finals to win its third straight Olympic gold.

SILVER
United States

GOLD
Canada

BRONZE
Finland

CANADA SCORES GOLDEN HAT TRICK
(WOMEN'S TEAM)

Although the imbalance between the North American countries continued – as did the second-tier imbalance between the Nordic nations and the other European nations – the Vancouver Games were the most successful event in women's hockey history. The main venue was sold out for every game, attracting nearly 17,000 fans, and the secondary venue was also sold out for every game.

In the end, there were no surprises in the preliminary round, and the medal games featured Sweden and Finland for bronze and Canada–United States for gold. The former game was decided in overtime, the winner coming on a fluky play when Karoliina Rantamaki's pass in front of the Swedish goal bounced off the skate of Erika Holst past goalie Sara Grahn.

That game, the morning of February 25, 2010, was only a preview to the one everyone had been waiting for – Canada and the United States for gold. Some 10 million Canadians watched the final game and could not have been more thrilled by what they saw. The backstory was radically different from Turin four years earlier. While Canada was dominant in winning the 2007 Women's Worlds, the Americans took over in 2008 and again in 2009. Canada's reign

Marie-Philip Poulin scores the first of her two goals in Canada's 2–0 win in the gold-medal game.

appeared in jeopardy, and for the first time it might be said that the Americans were favourites.

Of course, the preliminary round gave little indication if this were true or not. Canada outscored its three opponents 41–2 while the Americans were 31–1 against theirs. Both teams waltzed through the semifinals, giving no indication which team had the edge in the gold-medal game.

Perhaps the most stunning announcement prior to the game came from Canada's coach Mel Davidson, who decided to start goalie Shannon Szabados over the vastly more experienced Kim St. Pierre. Szabados had just two top-level games to her credit while St. Pierre had been with the national

team for years. Yet the decision was as brilliant as it was provocative, as Szabados was the difference in the game. She stopped all 28 U.S. shots, many high-quality, and this, paired with Marie-Philip Poulin's two goals, gave Canada a 2–0 win and its third straight Olympic gold.

"Team Canada's a great team," said American Hilary Knight. "It just shows their perseverance. We had tons of opportunities tonight and couldn't capitalize. Hats off to Szabados for doing a great job. The puck didn't bounce our way, but she did a great job."

Gracious in defeat, the Americans were teary-eyed
nonetheless by coming up one win short for Olympic gold.

The Americans had two five-on-three power plays
and many chances but couldn't beat the Canadian
goalie. "Szabados played great," said U.S. forward
Monique Lamoureux. "She stole the game from
us. We just couldn't bury the puck. They blocked a
lot of shots. We had rebounds to capitalize on and
she made some great saves. I tip my hat to her. She
played awesome."

"We trusted in ourselves," said Canadian Jennifer
Botterill. "[Men's general manager] Steve Yzerman
came and spoke to us before the game, and that was
one of his biggest pieces of advice: to trust yourself.
We were excited, but had confidence in all the preparation we did."

THE RECORD BOOK

OLYMPICS, MEN

ALL-TIME TEAM RECORDS

LONGEST WINNING STREAK

- 20 games CAN, April 24, 1920–February 8, 1936

LONGEST UNDEFEATED STREAK

- 24 games CAN, February 12, 1936–January 30, 1956

LONGEST LOSING STREAK

- 11 games HUN, February 8, 1936–present

LONGEST WINLESS STREAK

- 21 games NOR, February 12, 1980–February 16, 1992

GOAL-SCORING TEAM RECORDS

MOST GOALS, TEAM, GAME

EARLY ERA, 1920–1952

- 33 CAN 33–SUI 0, January 30, 1924

MODERN ERA, 1956–2010

- 23 CAN 23–AUT 0, January 27, 1956

MOST GOALS, TEAM, PERIOD

EARLY ERA, 1920–1952

- 15 USA, 1st half, April 24, 1920 vs. SUI

MODERN ERA, 1956–2010

- 11 CAN, 2nd period, January 27, 1956 vs. AUT

ALL-TIME INDIVIDUAL RECORDS

MOST OLYMPICS PLAYED

- 6 Raimo Helminen (FIN)

MOST GOLD MEDALS

- 3 Vitali Davydov (URS), Anatoli Firsov (URS),
  Andrei Khomutov (URS/RUS), Viktor Kuzkin (URS),
  Alexander Ragulin (URS), Vladislav Tretiak (URS)

MOST MEDALS

- 4 (3G, S) Vladislav Tretiak (URS)
- 4 (2G,S,B) Igor Kravchuk (RUS)
- 4 (2S, 2B) Jiri Holik (TCH)
- 4 (S, 3B) Jere Lehtinen (FIN)
- 4 (B, 3S) Saku Koivu (FIN), Andrei Khomutov (URS/
  RUS), Viktor Kuzkin (URS), Alexander Ragulin (URS)

MOST GAMES PLAYED

- 39 Raimo Helminen (FIN)

MOST POINTS, CAREER

- 37 Teemu Selanne (FIN) 20-17-37

MOST POINTS, ONE OLYMPICS

EARLY ERA, 1920–1952

- 36 Harry Watson (CAN, 1924) 36-0-36

MODERN ERA, 1956–2010

- 18 Bob Attersley (CAN, 1960) 6-12-18

MOST GOALS, CAREER

EARLY ERA, 1920–1952

- 36 Harry Watson (CAN, 1924)

MODERN ERA, 1956–2010

- 25 Sven "Tumba" Johansson (SWE)
- 24 Vladimir Zabrodsky (TCH)

MOST ASSISTS, CAREER

- 21 Valeri Kharlamov (URS)

MOST ASSISTS, ONE OLYMPICS

- 12 Bob Attersley (CAN, 1960)
- 12 Fred Etcher (CAN, 1960)

MOST POINTS, ONE GAME

MODERN ERA, 1956–2010

- 8 Vaclav Nedomansky (TCH), 6 goals, 2 assists, February 5, 1972 vs. POL
- 7 Paul Knox (CAN), 5 goals, 2 assists, January 27, 1956 vs. AUT
- 7 Ronald Pettersson (SWE), 3 goals, 4 assists, February 21, 1960 vs. JPN

MOST POINTS, ONE PERIOD

MODERN ERA, 1956–2010

- 4 Paul Knox (CAN), 3 goals, 1 assist, 1st period, January 27, 1956 vs. AUT
- 4 Ken Laufman (CAN), 1 goal, 3 assists, 2nd period, January 27, 1956 vs. AUT
- 4 John Mayasich (USA), 1 goal, 3 assists, 3rd period, February 4, 1956 vs. TCH
- 4 Carl-Goran Oberg (SWE), 2 goals, 2 assists, 1st period, February 21, 1960 vs. JPN
- 4 Yuri Lebedev (URS), 2 goals, 2 assists, 1st period, February 14, 1980 vs. NED
- 4 Alexander Maltsev (URS), 1 goals, 3 assists, 1st period, February 14, 1980 vs. NED

MOST GOALS, ONE GAME

EARLY ERA, 1920–1952

- 13 Harry Watson (CAN), January 30, 1924 vs. SUI

MODERN ERA, 1956–2010

- 6 Vaclav Nedomansky (TCH), February 5, 1972 vs. POL
- 5 Paul Knox (CAN), January 27, 1956 vs. AUT
- 5 Pavel Bure (RUS), February 20, 1998 vs. FIN

MOST GOALS, ONE PERIOD

EARLY ERA, 1920–1952

- 6 Harry Watson (CAN) 2nd period, January 28, 1924 vs. TCH

MODERN ERA, 1956–2010 — ALL HAT TRICKS)

- 3 Paul Knox (CAN), 1st period, January 27, 1956 vs. AUT
- 3 Dick Dougherty (USA), 3rd period, February 4, 1956 vs. TCH
- 3 Miroslav Vlach (TCH), 3rd period, February 20, 1960 vs. AUS
- 3 Raimo Kilpio (FIN), 1st period, February 22, 1960 vs. AUS
- 3 Juji Iwaoka (JPN), 3rd period, February 24, 1960 vs. AUS

- 3 Kalevi Numminen (FIN), 2nd period, February 25, 1960 vs. AUS
- 3 Jouni Seistamo (FIN), 3rd period, February 25, 1960 vs. AUS
- 3 Roger Christian (USA), 3rd period, February 28, 1960 vs. TCH
- 3 Josef Horesovsky (TCH), 1st period, February 12, 1968 vs. GDR
- 3 Vaclav Nedomansky (TCH), 3rd period, February 5, 1972 vs. POL
- 3 Arto Sirvio (FIN), 3rd period, February 9, 1984 vs. NOR
- 3 Peter Gradin (SWE), 2nd period, February 13, 1984 vs. POL
- 3 Erich Kuhnhackl (FRG), 2nd period, February 17, 1984 vs. FIN
- 3 Franck Pajonkowski (FRA), 2nd period, February 23, 1988 vs. NOR
- 3 Petr Rosol (TCH), 2nd period, February 8, 1992 vs. NOR

MOST ASSISTS, ONE GAME

- 5 Valeri Kharlamov (URS), February 13, 1980 vs. JPN

MOST ASSISTS, ONE PERIOD

- 3 Ken Laufman (CAN), 2nd period, January 27, 1956 vs. AUT
- 3 John Mayasich (USA), 3rd period, February 4, 1956 vs. TCH
- 3 Yrjo Hakala (FIN), 2nd period, February 25, 1960 vs. AUS
- 3 Bob Attersley (CAN), 1st period, February 28, 1960 vs. URS
- 3 Anatoli Firsov (URS), 3rd period, February 1, 1964 vs. SUI
- 3 Eduard Pana (ROM), 3rd period, February 9, 1976 vs. AUT
- 3 Erich Kuhnhackl (FRG), 3rd period, February 14, 1976 vs. USA
- 3 Alexander Maltsev (URS), 1st period, February 14, 1980 vs. NED
- 3 Viktor Zhluktov (URS), 1st period, February 16, 1980 vs. POL

GOALTENDER RECORDS

MOST GOLD MEDALS
- 3 Vladislav Tretiak (URS)
- 2 Martin Brodeur (CAN)

MOST MEDALS
- 4 (3 gold, silver) Vladislav Tretiak (URS)
- 3 (silver, 2 bronze) Vladimir Dzurilla (TCH), Jarmo Myllys (FIN)

MOST OLYMPICS PARTICIPATED IN
- 4 Dominik Hasek (CZE)
- 4 Jim Marthinsen (NOR)
- 4 Vladislav Tretiak (URS)

MOST GAMES PLAYED, CAREER
- 19 Vladislav Tretiak (URS)

MOST MINUTES PLAYED, CAREER
- 1,059:41 Vladislav Tretiak (URS)

MOST WINS, CAREER
- 17 Vladislav Tretiak (URS)

MOST SHUTOUTS, CAREER
- 5 Murray Dowey (CAN)
- 5 Tom Moone (USA)

MOST SHUTOUTS, ONE OLYMPICS
- 5 Murray Dowey, 1948 (CAN)
- 5 Tom Moone, 1936 (USA)

LONGEST SHUTOUT SEQUENCE (IN MINUTES), TEAM
- 245:00 USA, January 28–February 3, 1924

LONGEST SHUTOUT SEQUENCE (IN MINUTES), GOALIE
- 225:25 Murray Dowey (CAN), January 30–February 3, 1948

SPEED RECORDS

FASTEST GOAL FROM START OF GAME
- 8 seconds Miroslav Vlach (TCH), February 28, 1960 vs. USA
- 8 seconds Albin Felc (YUG), February 7, 1968 vs. JPN

FASTEST GOAL FROM START OF PERIOD
- 6 seconds Jorma Peltonen (FIN), 2nd period, January 30, 1964 vs. SUI
- 6 seconds Vladimir Petrov (URS), 2nd period, February 13, 1980 vs. JPN

FASTEST TWO GOALS, TEAM
- 5 seconds Vsevolod Bobrov (URS, 15:40) & Valentin Kuzin (URS, 15:45), 3rd period, February 3, 1956 vs. USA

FASTEST THREE GOALS, INDIVIDUAL
- 4:28 Vladimir Golikov, URS (14:59, 19:00, 19:27, 1st period), February 13, 1980 vs. JPN

FASTEST THREE GOALS, TEAM
- 36 seconds SWE, February 21, 1960 vs. JPN, 1st period (Carl-Goran Oberg 7:15 & 7:23, Anders Andersson 7:51)

FASTEST THREE GOALS, BOTH TEAMS
- 31 seconds February 10, 1976, 3rd period (Matti Murto FIN 14:16, Bob Dobek USA 14:35, Matti Hagman FIN 14:47)

FASTEST FOUR GOALS, TEAM
- 1:18 CAN, January 27, 1956 vs. AUT, 2nd period (Jack MacKenzie 12:52, Ken Laufman 13:13, Gerry Theberge 14:00, George Scholes 14:10)

OLYMPICS, WOMEN

ALL-TIME TEAM RECORDS

LONGEST WINNING & UNDEFEATED STREAK
- 15 games CAN, February 11, 2002–present

MOST GOALS, TEAM, GAME
- 18 February 13, 2010 Canada 18–Slovakia 0

ALL-TIME INDIVIDUAL RECORDS

MOST OLYMPICS
- 4 CAN Jennifer Botterill, Jayna Hefford,
  Becky Kellar, Hayley Wickenheiser
- 4 FIN Emma Laaksonen, Karoliina Rantamaki
- 4 SWE Gunilla Andersson, Erika Holst, Maria Rooth
- 4 USA Jenny Potter (-Schmidgall), Angela Ruggiero

MOST GOLD MEDALS
- 3 Jennifer Botterill (CAN), Jayna Hefford (CAN),
  Becky Kellar (CAN), Hayley Wickenheiser (CAN)

MOST MEDALS
- 4 (3G, 1S) Jennifer Botterill (CAN)
- 4 (3G, 1S) Jayna Hefford (CAN)
- 4 (3G, 1S) Becky Kellar (CAN)
- 4 (3G, 1S) Hayley Wickenheiser (CAN)
- 4 (1G, 2S, 1B) Jenny Potter (-Schmidgall) (USA)
- 4 (1G, 2S, 1B) Angela Ruggiero (USA)

MOST GAMES PLAYED
- 21 CAN Jennifer Botterill, Jayna Hefford,
  Becky Kellar, Hayley Wickenheiser
- 21 FIN Karoliina Rantamaki
- 21 USA Jenny Potter (-Schmidgall), Angela Ruggiero

MOST POINTS, CAREER
- 46 Hayley Wickenheiser (CAN)

MOST POINTS, ONE OLYMPICS
- 17 Hayley Wickenheiser (CAN), 2006

MOST GOALS, CAREER
- 16 Hayley Wickenheiser (CAN)

MOST GOALS, TEAM, PERIOD
- 7 CAN, 2nd period, February 17, 2010 vs. SWE
- 7 CAN, 1st period, February 13, 2010 vs. SWE
- 7 CAN, 1st period, February 12, 2006 vs. RUS
- 7 CAN, 3rd period, February 11, 2006 vs. ITA

MOST GOALS, ONE OLYMPICS
- 9 Meghan Agosta (CAN), 2010

MOST ASSISTS, CAREER
- 30 Hayley Wickenheiser (CAN)

MOST ASSISTS, ONE OLYMPICS
- 12 Hayley Wickenheiser (CAN), 2006

MOST GOALS, GAME
- 4 Stephanie Marty (SUI), February 20, 2010 vs. CHN
- 4 Pernilla Winberg (SWE), February 15, 2010 vs. SVK

MOST GOALS, PERIOD
- 3 Larisa Mishina (RUS), 2nd period,
  February 17, 2006 vs. SUI
- 3 Caroline Ouellette (CAN), 1st period,
  February 11, 2006 vs. ITA

MOST POINTS, GAME
- 6 Jayna Hefford (CAN), February 13,
  2010 vs. SVK (3 goals, 3 assists)
- 6 Cherie Piper (CAN), February 11,
  2006 vs. ITA (1 goal, 5 assists)

MOST POINTS, PERIOD
- 4 Larisa Mishina (RUS), 2nd period, February 17,
  2006 vs. SUI (3 goals, 1 assist)

MOST ASSISTS, GAME
- 5 Cherie Piper (CAN), February 11, 2006 vs. ITA

MOST ASSISTS, PERIOD
- 3 Hilary Knight (USA), 1st period,
  February 16, 2010 vs. RUS

GOALTENDER RECORDS

MOST TOURNAMENTS
- 3 Kim St. Pierre (CAN), Irina Gashennikova (RUS), Kim Martin (SWE)

MOST GAMES PLAYED, CAREER
- 14 Irina Gashennikova (RUS)

MOST MINUTES PLAYED, CAREER
- 816:25 Irina Gashennikova (RUS)

MOST WINS, CAREER
- 8 Kim St. Pierre (CAN)

MOST LOSSES, CAREER
- 7 Irina Gashennikova (RUS)

MOST SHUTOUTS, CAREER
- 4 Kim St. Pierre (CAN)

MOST SHUTOUTS, ONE OLYMPICS
- 2 Shannon Szabados (CAN), 2010
- 2 Jesse Vetter (USA), 2010
- 2 Charline Labonte (CAN), 2006
- 2 Sara Decosta (USA), 2002
- 2 Kim St. Pierre (CAN), 2002

SPEED RECORDS

FASTEST GOAL FROM START OF GAME
- 13 seconds Mari Pehkonen (FIN), February 14, 2006 vs. USA

FASTEST GOAL FROM START OF PERIOD
- 19 seconds Janka Culikova (SVK), 3rd period, February 17, 2010 vs. SUI

FASTEST TWO GOALS, TEAM
- 6 seconds CAN, February 19, 2002 vs. FIN (Hayley Wickenheiser 3:19, Jayna Hefford 3:25, 3rd period)

FASTEST THREE GOALS, INDIVIDUAL
- 5:17 Caroline Ouellette (CAN), February 11, 2006 vs. ITA (1:36, 1:52, 6:53, 1st period)

FASTEST THREE GOALS, TEAM
- 59 seconds February 17, 2010 vs. SWE (Jayna Hefford 5:14, Hayley Wickenheiser 5:36, Gillian Apps 6:13, 2nd)

FASTEST FOUR GOALS, TEAM
- 2:43 USA, February 14, 2002 vs. CHN (Katie King 7:48, Laurie Baker 9:22, Julie Chu 9:57, Katie King 10:31, 2nd period)

ACKNOWLEDGEMENTS

The author would like to thank the many people who have provided enthusiastic assistance and support for an ambitious and hopefully worthy project. First, to Jordan Fenn, publisher of Fenn/M&S and to Kristin Cochrane, Executive Publisher of the M&S Doubleday Canada Publishing Group. To the entire editorial team at M&S, notably editors Liz Kribs and Michael Melgaard, as well as Janine Laporte, Carla Kean, Bhavna Chauhan, James Young, Ruta Liormonas, and those on the Random House sales force. To Andrew Roberts and Five Seventeen for amalgamating so many stories and images into an aesthetic and imaginative whole. To everyone at the IIHF for much work and friendship over the years, notably Szymon Szemberg, creator of the Triple Gold Club, and the most biased Habs fan to walk the planet. As well, to all at the Hockey Hall of Fame, especially Craig Campbell, Phil Pritchard, Steve Poirier, and Anthony Fusco. To my agent Dean Cooke for sorting out the business side of things in a lucid and cogent manner. And, lastly, to my own Olympians away from the rink – Liz, Ian, Zac (2024 OG, basketball), and Emily (2020 OG, volleyball), my mom, and my wife, Jane, who has already won several Olympic gold in too many sports to mention here.

PHOTO CREDITS

All photos provided by the IIHF and Hockey Hall of Fame, with the exception of images on pages 155, 157, and 159, which have been provided by the International Olympic Committee.